Early Birds and Boys in Blue
A century of Radnorshire aviation

Early Birds and Boys in Blue
A century of Radnorshire aviation

by

Phillip Jones

Logaston Press

LOGASTON PRESS
Little Logaston Woonton Almeley
Herefordshire HR3 6QH
logastonpress.co.uk

First published by Logaston Press 2017
Copyright text © Phillip Jones
Copyright illustrations © as per credits and acknowledgements

ISBN 978 1 9010839 17 1

Typeset by Logaston Press
and printed and bound in Poland by
www.lfbookservices.co.uk

To Mr John H. Lucas who was there at the start

CONTENTS

ACKNOWLEDGEMENTS

I would like to thank the staff of the following organisations for their unfailing help in answering questions and producing material: Radnorshire Museum, Royal Aero club, The Radnorshire Society, The RAF Historical Society, Powys County Archives, The National Archives, The Air Force Historical Research Agency at Maxwell airforce base in Alabama, 579 Llandrindod Wells ATC Squadron, Libraries and Archives of Canada, The Australian National Archive, The New Zealand Archive and Auckland War Memorial Museum.

I would also like to thank the following individuals and family members of those mentioned in the book who provided information and in instances also photographs: the Anthony Family Archive, the late Ms Joy Ashton, Mrs J. Becket, Mr T. Bishop, Mr F. Bright, the Bufton Family Archives, G/Capt C. Coombes OBE RAF, Mr Colin Cummings, Mr P. Davies, Mrs N. Davies, Mr E. Doylerush, Dr C. Downer, Mr D. Earl, Mrs P. Eckley, Mr John Englested, Mrs C.A. Evans, Mr M. Evans, Mr R. Evans, Mrs D. Fellowes-Freeman, Mrs C. Griffiths, Mr Guy Griffiths, Ms Jasmine Grassie, the Hanne family, Mr M.J. Hasinski-Adam, Mr K. Hazlewood, Mr Mike Hines, Miss P. Hodgkiss, Mr R.I. (Allen) Hudson, Mr M. Insall, Mr F. Instone, Mrs Penny Kennedy, Ms Cath Kidston, Mr Simon Kidston, Mr H. Lambert, Mr N. Livingston, Mr T. Mace, Mr W. Matusiak, Mr B. Maund, Ms Y. Norton, Mr M. Peirson Jones, Mrs M. Powell, Mr G. Price, Mr R. Pye, Mr M. Rowland, Mr Pete Sellars of Skegness RNLI, Mr R. Speake, Mr D. Thayer, Mr R. Thomas, Mr T. Thorne, Mr E. Turner, Mr W. Wallace, Mr H. Webbon, Mrs M. Williams, Mr P. Williams and Mrs R. Williams.

I must also thank Andy and Karen Johnson of Logaston Press for helping shape this book and making several suggestions concerning the text. Any mistakes that have passed all our eyes are of course my own.

Finally I wish to thank Mrs Amanda Jones without whom this book would not have been written.

Introduction

This tells the story of flight and flying in Radnorshire – both the aircraft that have landed in the county by design or accident and those that used the short-lived airport at Llandrindod Wells, and the men (for men it then was) who were born in Radnorshire or came to later live in the county who joined the Royal Flying Corps and the subsequent Royal Air Force up until the 1950s.

The story starts in 1912, when aviation was in its infancy and Denys Corbett Wilson in a Blériot aircraft landed in Radnorshire by accident on his way to becoming the first to fly cross the Irish Sea. The county was shortly afterwards to host visits by a number of early exhibition flyers – young men as glamorous and adored as any of today's sports stars, who led tangled lives and possibly felt divided loyalties due to the friendships that had been created across the Continent as war spread across Europe.

That war led to a number of Radnorshire men joining the Royal Flying Corps and their stories are full of fascinating details, often having a strong individualistic streak.

The First World war was followed by the playboy era of the 1920s and '30s – handsome young men setting ladies' hearts racing and enthusing men with a thirst for adventure. The pilots, as comparatively rich and famous as many of today's film stars, lived the Hollywood lifestyle of fast cars, wild parties and multiple affairs. Here will be found not only the daredevil and devil-may-care aviator but also the six times married but only three times divorced pilot who did a disappearing act with a sponsor's plane. Apart from providing a landing strip in Radnorshire for such men, the aerodrome at the Ddole near Rock Park took tourists not only to the coast but as far away as Birmingham and London in an air taxi service.

The outbreak of the Second World War saw another group of young Radnorshire men take to the air, including those who had been inspired by the antics they observed during the 1930s. Their stories are of trainees, fighter and bomber pilots, air crew and mechanics, who saw service over Europe, North Africa, the Middle East and Far East. It includes the story of a remarkable family in which four of five siblings were involved in the war effort, not just by flying for their country but by setting up one of the most famous bomber forces in the war and going on to be prominent in the history of the Royal Air Force. Reading their stories is like reading a history of the Second World War from a strangely Radnorshire perspective.

During the war Radnorshire was both bombed and played host to a surprising number of aircraft that crash-landed. Some of these latter accidents were of course tragic but there are also humorous tales of survival, and of young boys being apprehended as they made off with a machine gun and ammunition almost before the plane had fully come to rest.

After the war not only did there remain a strong connection to the Air Force but the county became an RAF low fly zone. This brought with it tragedy of a kind not expected in peacetime as four fatal accidents happened in the county.

1   The First Flyers

On 6 August 1913, not quite ten years after the Wright brothers had made the first powered flight, a young aviator by the name of Gustav Hamel came to Llandrindod Wells to give a flying display. Such displays were becoming popular at county shows in England and Hamel was one of the best known names in the field, being also handsome and the darling of the rich and famous. Just how Radnor district councillor Mr R.P. Culley persuaded Hamel to bring his machine to an unpromising, slightly uneven field in what must have seemed like the middle of nowhere is unfortunately lost to us.

Gustav Hamel was the son of a prominent London doctor who was sometimes listed as King Edward VII's physician. Although German in origin, the whole family had become British citizens in 1910. Where and how Gustav gained an interest in flying is not known. We do know that he attended Westminster School, was a graduate of Cambridge University and had learned to fly in France, gaining his aviator's certificate at the René Caudron flying school at Issy-les-Moulineaux in January 1911. On 14 February that same year he gained his Royal Aero Club Certificate in a Graham White 'Blériot' monoplane. Armed with RAeC certificate no.64, by March 1911 he had become the chief instructor at the Graham White flying school at Hendon. That same month he won the inaugural Hendon to London air race. In the summer he became the first person to land an aeroplane at Wrexham, when he touched down in his new Blériot monoplane (price £475), which could attain speeds of 65mph.

The year continued to be a busy one for Hamel. Between 9 and 26 September he became one of the first pilots to operate an aerial postal service when, to celebrate the coronation of King George V, he flew several times a day between Hendon and Windsor carrying a total of 25,000 letters and 90,000 postcards. The king had given permission for the grounds of Windsor Castle to be used as a temporary airfield, and letters and postcards poured into the Windsor sorting office. Harrods and Selfridges, together with other major London department stores, sold specially designed stationery and the letters could be posted in the store. Even if you didn't pay extra for the unique stationery your letter would still get the new 'airmail' postmark.

Over a period of some 18 months to two years Hamel crossed the English Channel 11 times, twice carrying a lady passenger, an activity which became something of a trademark for him.

By 1913 Gustav Hamel's name would have been as well known as that of any of today's film or sports stars. Llandrindod Wells, meanwhile, was losing the small amount of notoriety that it had gained as a Victorian holiday spa, the local papers often carrying reports of dwindling visitors and notices of 'sale by auction' of hotels and boarding houses. One can only imagine the ripple of excitement that must have been generated by a small article on page 8 of the 17 July edition of the *Radnor Express*, which simply told its readers that:

> Gustav Hamel the eminent airman is coming to Llandrindod Wells. The exhibition will take place on the Rock Park grounds on August the 6th. This is another instance of the enterprise of Mr R.P. Culley, the chairman of the U.D.C., who, however, has declined Mr. Hamel's invitation to accompany him in his aeroplane.

Gustav Hamel taking off from the Ddole airfield in 1913.
Note the Rock Park Hotel in the background. (© Radnorshire Museum)

Gustav Hamel with his mechanic and an unidentified man and woman, possibly his parents,
at the Ddole airfield in 1913. (© Radnorshire Museum)

The paper subsequently reported that crowds flocked to see the exhibition of flying, coming not just from Radnorshire but also from surrounding counties. The field chosen for the display (known locally as the Ddole) was adjacent to the Rock Park Hotel (now demolished) and had been used as a horseracing track and polo ground since Victorian times. It has been estimated that around 4,000 people paid to get onto the field, with another 1,000 paying to get into the Rock Park, from where it was said they still had excellent views. In addition people would have crowded onto every vantage point in the surrounding area. The novelty of the aircraft was also a cause for alarm, and one report mentioned a veritable stampede every time Hamel's aircraft swooped low over a given area.

In between his flights, and long after he had stopped flying for the day, hundreds of people queued for his autograph or merely to shake his hand, and the event proved an undoubted financial success. Indeed, the council may have had cause to regret that some months previously they had turned down an offer of a flying display (by which aviator is unknown).

A few days later Hamel again took to the air, this time in the small town of Llanwrtyd Wells where yet again thousands paid the entrance fee to the 'flight field' and hundreds paid an extra fee to inspect his aeroplane. Large numbers of visitors were reported in the town and Sunday school children were bussed in from as far away as Knighton.

Indeed, Gustav Hamel seems to have spent most of August in Radnorshire – he flew at Builth Show, where he landed several times on the Gro, the original agricultural show site alongside the river (it is now a car park). He made a flight from Llandrindod Wells to Builth Wells, gave another full display in Llandrindod Wells only two weeks after his first one and attended Knighton Show, to which people who had already watched him at one of the other venues travelled in order to watch him again. Many paid a shilling to be admitted to the 'flight field' and it was reported that Knighton Show's gate money was up by between £30 and £40 on the previous year.

Gustav Hamel at Knighton Show on 29 August 1913.
(Picture from the collection of Peter Lloyd and taken by William Henry Lloyd, Peter's great great grandfather, Knighton's first photographer in the 1850s. © www.oldukphotos.com)

His last display in Llandrindod Wells did, however, attract some criticism, with one anonymous person complaining of the quantity as opposed to the quality of his flying. It was noted that he did carry out all his advertised manoeuvres but flew to Builth in the middle of the display (in a breathtaking time of four and a half minutes). Some spectators assumed the flying was over once he was out of sight, and so started back to their hotels and homes. Hamel gave extended displays over many other parts of the town on his return from Builth, including the golf links, and so satisfied most critics.

Signed photos of Gustav Hamel may have remained treasured items on many a Radnorshire mantelpiece, and young and old would have looked forward to the next summer and another round of town fêtes and shows that would bring the daring young aviator back into their midst. In the meantime, the local paper printed tales of his exploits. In September 1913 it reported on his winning the Walsall air race. The *Birmingham Daily Post* had offered £500 in prize money and Hamel had been challenged by C.B. 'Benny' Hucks, another aviator on the show circuit. Hamel was flying a Morane-Saulnier aircraft, his trusty Blériot having suffered some damage while being used by another pilot a few days before. This aircraft was far harder to manage but slightly faster, so Hamel took along a passenger as a handicap. He still won the race, coming in about half a minute faster than Hucks.

In January 1914 he flew a Morane-Saulnier from Hendon Aerodrome, taking as his passenger his good friend and wealthy patron Miss Trehawke Davies on a flight in which she became the first woman in the world to loop the loop. Hamel apparently followed it up with a half roll for good measure. There was much gossip about their friendship, though she was a good deal older than Hamel. Miss Davies never took flying lessons herself, but had a great love of flying, and indeed paid many notable aviators of the day to take her aloft. Just over a fortnight later, Lady Victoria Perry, who had accompanied Hamel to Llandrindod Wells in 1913, gained the distinction of becoming the first titled lady to loop the loop when on 18 January, with Hamel in the pilot seat, she 'looped' five times over Hendon.

Then in May 1914, only ten months after it first announced that he would be flying in Radnorshire, the *Radnor Express* once more carried a few small lines on Gustav Hamel, this time to announce that he had been lost in the English Channel while bringing a new plane back from France. He was only 23 years of age. The paper ended its short article with the words: 'Mr Hamel gave some brilliant exhibitions of flying at Llandrindod and Builth last year.'

Gustav Hamel's importance to early aviation, both civilian and military, cannot be over-stated and Winston Churchill (whom he was teaching to fly) mobilised the Navy to search the Channel for him and instructed all boats and planes in the area to keep an eye out for wreckage. There were reports of a body being spotted off Boulogne just a few days after his death, but the body was never brought to shore.

Rumours that he was alive and faked his death abounded for many years. In part this was because he had been so often seen in the company of well-connected women of the day, quite a few of whom were married, and stories of possible affairs proliferated. Other stories circulated that he was flying for the Germans in France in 1915, a rumour fuelled by the fact of his German descent. The charismatic and handsome Hamel slipped into legend, even being cited in a divorce case eight years after his death.

Although Hamel had been the first aviator to give a programmed flying display in Radnorshire, he had not been the first to land an aircraft in the county. This honour went to Denys Corbett Wilson, even if his visit was unintentional.

Corbett Wilson was the son of a wealthy Knightsbridge barrister. He was born, an only child, at the family home in Thames Ditton, Surrey on 24 September 1882. Educated at Eton between 1896 and 1899, he did not distinguish himself academically, being more of a sporting type and preferring horses and boats to books. He was soon to embrace the motor car, relishing any opportunity to get the family car off their chauffeur and drive it himself. He lost his father at an early age and formed a very close bond with his mother. She was a native of Kilkenny in Ireland, and she and Denys often travelled to her home there.

On leaving Eton he served in the Boer War as a 2nd lieutenant in the Dorsetshire Regiment. It was during this conflict that he sustained a leg injury that would leave him with a permanent limp.

The winter of 1911-12 saw Denys at the Blériot school in Pau at the foot of the Pyrenees in France, where he learned to fly and gained his certificate on 18 January 1912. The Blériot school had been in existence much longer than the Royal Aero Club which trained pilots at Hendon, and on 20 February 1912, in contrast to certificate number 722 from the Blériot school issued to Denys Wilson a month earlier, the Royal Aero Club issued its certificate number 183 to Damar Leslie Allen, a friend of Denys. The Royal Aero Club honoured certificates granted by any of the Blériot schools, and an announcement in *Flight* magazine duly confirmed that Denys Corbett Wilson was indeed a qualified pilot. Denys and Damar Allen each kept their planes at Hendon. It was a time of 'firsts' and every aviator was on the lookout for the next 'prize'. Damar Allen proposed that they become the first to cross the Irish Sea.

In 1912 it was possible to get your aviator certificate with only two to three hours of flying under your belt, which could have been done in a matter of days in ten or fifteen minute bursts. The Irish Sea crossing would take an awful lot longer; neither man was exactly sure how long. Many might consider the need for a back up team and possibly a boat travelling the same route in case they got into trouble, but all this might take months to arrange. Corbett Wilson and Damar Allen came up with a different solution, which appeared to be not much more than 'let's take off together and see what happens'. It was probably more youthful high spirits and a sense of adventure that prompted this attitude, but the other more experienced pilots around Hendon aerodrome did not think it was a good idea. The pair nevertheless settled on a date in mid April for the crossing, meaning that when they set out Denys had been a qualified pilot for three months and Allen for eight weeks. Neither pilot had flown more than 30 miles in one flight. And they had no back up if they ditched in the sea.

Flying across the Irish Sea had been attempted the previous year by Robert Loraine, a star of silent film. Loraine was in sight of the Irish coast when his Maurice Farman biplane developed a serious fault. He was a strong swimmer who felt that ditching in the sea would be slightly safer than crashing on land, and scrambled from his plane to swim the last 300 yards to the Irish shore near Liffey. He was therefore – just – denied the title of the first to cross the Irish Sea.

Denys and Damar arranged to leave Hendon on the afternoon of 17 April 1912, intending to fly to Chester and then on to Holyhead, from where they would race across the sea. Both men had employed a mechanic to help them. Denys enlisted the services of 19-year-old Frenchman Gaston Vial; it was quite possible that the two men had met at the Blériot school. Gaston was a talented mechanic but could speak very little English. Both pilots dispatched their mechanics by rail to Chester to await their arrival. Denys having tucked into his coat his teddy bear, a small mascot that was always to fly with him, the two aviators set off.

Allen was soon out of sight, but Corbett Wilson's Blériot XI was seriously buffeted about, so much so that he lost his compass. He flew on for some time then decided to land in order to ascertain where exactly he was. His first stop was in a field at Newchurch farm near Almeley in Herefordshire. Mr A. Lewis Williams of Almeley Manor was called out to meet the airman and offered him assistance. As it was early evening it was decided a car would be arranged to take Corbett Wilson to Hereford for the night, from where he could telegram Gaston Vial to come and check out the aircraft. He could also buy a new compass in Hereford, and also took the opportunity to stock up on petrol and the castor oil that was used as a lubricant for the engine. Gaston Vial did not arrive until the middle of the next day and after he had checked over the aircraft, Corbett Wilson made ready to take off.

A large crowd gathered to see this event, excited by what for most of them would have been their first glimpse of a heavier than air flying machine. Corbett Wilson had no idea at this point where his friend had got to, but must have assumed he was waiting either in Chester or Holyhead to resume the race. At about 4pm he finally took off, but changed his mind about his next destination and set off for the Pembrokeshire coast, having dispatched Gaston Vial to await his arrival, this time hopefully in Fishguard.

He had only just taken off when the engine began to cough and stutter, and it soon became evident that he would have to make another forced landing. The view from the air was none too promising as the aircraft bounced and jerked out of Herefordshire's air space and into that of Radnorshire. Luckily Denys spotted another handy field, this one belonging to the Gittoes family who, it seems, were none too pleased at the mess the machine made when landing in their pasture.

However, Corbett Wilson was again met with wonder and before long quite a crowd had gathered. A telegram was once more sent to summon Gaston but nothing could be done that night, so the aircraft was secured and the aviator spent the night in the Sun Inn at Colva (now Colva Farm).

The next morning Mr A. Lewis Williams once more came to his aid and fetched the mechanic from Kington train station. However it was not until Gaston Vial arrived and discovered that the wrong grade of castor oil had been purchased that the problem was identified. The engine had to be stripped and cleaned before it would go anywhere. Gaston Vial stayed the night at the Gittoes' farm and Corbett Wilson stayed at Almeley Manor with Lewis Williams. The Gittoes family made the young Frenchman very welcome and overcame the language problem with a series of mimes. When attempting to ask Gaston what he wanted for breakfast the next morning, the Gittoes' chicken impression accompanied by Vial's holding up of three fingers was interpreted as meaning three eggs, with which

Two photographs of Corbett Wilson's Blériot XI in the field at Newchurch farm near Almeley. The lower of the two shows him standing alongside the aircraft with his mechanic, Gaston Vial, standing in the aircraft. (© J. Grassie)

the young lad seemed more than happy. Denys had no such trouble at the manor and his was a much simpler and quieter breakfast.

It was now Sunday morning and although he intended to take off between 5 and 6am, a large crowd had already gathered to see the action. Word had spread and people had even made their way from Kington. He took off at around 5.45am and circled the field twice before heading for Fishguard, where Gaston Vial had once more been dispatched by train.

Two photographs of Corbett Wilson's aeroplane at Colva on 20th April 1912
and the crowds who had gathered to watch him take off.
(Top photo by W.H. McKaig, © Radnorshire Museum; lower photo by W.H. McKaig, © J. Grassie)

Denys Corbett Wilson touched down in Fishguard at 7.15am and this time at least he had had an uneventful flight. It was here that he received the news that his friend Damar Allen had taken off from Holyhead as planned but had not been heard of since.

The loss of a friend, two forced landings and poor preparation would have put off many people, but undaunted, Corbett Wilson was determined to press on. So it was at 5.47am on Monday 22 April 1912 he took off in front of a cheering crowd of around 300 people, and left Fishguard for Ireland. The weather was good for most of the way; he ran into a storm just off the Irish coast, but fortunately was able to see land in a gap in the clouds. His landing was somewhat inauspicious, in a field in the Parish of Crane, County Wexford about three miles from Enniscorthy. The Blériot XI (along with most aircraft of the day) didn't have a very effective braking system and he was unable to stop before hitting a hedge. Although he was uninjured, the Blériot was very badly damaged.

Again the assistance of a local farmer was called upon, and he was driven from Crane to Enniscorthy where he was able to telegram his mother in Kilkenny and Gaston in Fishguard with news of his success. Meanwhile he enjoyed a hearty breakfast at a local hotel. His mother motored up from Kilkenny, but Gaston was not to arrive until the following Tuesday.

Whether by luck, judgment or skilful flying we will never know, but Denys Corbett Wilson became the first man to fly from mainland Britain to Ireland, as well as the first man to land a plane in Radnorshire. The flight over the sea had taken almost exactly 100 minutes, longer than either he or Damar Allen had ever flown before. Allen had not been seen since he took off from Holyhead and it was concluded that he had crashed into the sea. At the same time that Denys made his record breaking flight the *Titanic* had just sunk, and news of this event largely overshadowed his achievement in the press. *Flight* magazine did announce that he had managed the crossing, and also made mention of another flight across the Irish Sea by Vivian Hewitt, an exhibition pilot of the day. It is to Vivian Hewitt that our attention now turns, as he was to be the exhibition flyer in Radnorshire in the summer of 1914, following on from the death of Gustav Hamel.

Born on 11 March 1888, Vivian Vaughan Davies Hewitt was the heir to the Hewitt brothers' brewery in Grimsby. His family however, having educated him at Harrow, told him he was to receive no financial support until he had proved he could earn his own living.

His parents had moved to Warren House, Bodfari near Rhyl and it was here that his younger brother Billy was born. Although there was a ten-year age gap between the boys, they grew up close, with Vivian leading his younger sibling into all manner of mischief in the school holidays and passing on his passion of all things mechanical. In 1904 this passion led to Vivian starting work in the marine engineering department at Portsmouth Dock. From there he joined the LNWR railway works at Crewe and would frequently ride the footplate of the Crewe-Holyhead express as an extra fireman. He had his own car and two motorbikes, became an official driver for Singer motor cars, and even started a small secondhand car business, buying up vehicles then tweaking the engines to make them go faster.

After the success of Blériot's Channel crossing in 1909, Hewitt become obsessed with the idea of flight, and a benevolent uncle bought him an 'Antoinette' high winged monoplane with a 50hp engine that was capable of doing 44mph. The legal speed limit on Britain's roads at the time was 20mph.

Hewitt had been experimenting with homemade gliders in the Welsh hills for some time but his real passion was for engines and speed. In January 1910 he travelled to France to pick up a Blériot and also started the formal training for his French aero club certificate. He had already had quite a bit of flying experience and the training started well. However, the weather closed in and flying was stopped, so the ever impatient Hewitt decided to return to Wales without qualifying for his certificate. As it was not compulsory at this time for anyone to hold a certificate in order to be allowed to fly – it merely told other aviators that you had been judged proficient by the relevant club – it seems that Vivian took the view that as he felt he knew what he was doing, and there was no need to bother with a bit of paper. He did however have several flights around his rural north Wales home before showing his skills to the certificate-holding pilots around what was usually a car-racing circuit at Brooklands in Surrey. Eventually he became one of the pilots who would take his aeroplane up to thrill the crowds on car-racing days at Brooklands. In February 1911 he upgraded again, this time to the Blériot XI, which cost him well over £1,000 and necessitated another trip to the Pyrenees to fetch it. Henceforth his business cards and company notepaper would bear the legend 'Dealer in Second hand cars and airplanes. ... Repairs to Blériot monoplanes a speciality'.

When Hewitt's father died in 1910 he took the opportunity to move out of Warren House. Even though the Brooklands flying had started to become quite lucrative, he now headed back to Rhyl, where he took digs in the town. Rhyl was a thriving holiday destination but seemingly unknown on the flying exhibition circuit. He established a landing strip at Foryd Fawr on the west bank of the River Clwyd and christened the field 'Foryd Aerodrome'. Next he constructed a large shed on the site which became what *The Aeroplane* magazine described as one of the best equipped workshops in the country. Here Hewitt employed two members of staff – Arthur Brown, a joiner who had worked at Bodfari and had been called on by Hewitt to help in some of his early glider construction, and Sydney Wingfield. Sydney had first approached Hewitt at a motor race when he had some mechanical problems and was found to be an able but unemployed mechanic. The three of them spent the summer working at Foryd Fawr and preparing for Hewitt's forthcoming exhibition flying. Hewitt also had a keen eye for advertising and designed special souvenir cards which read 'Dropped by Vivian Hewitt from his monoplane at Rhyl'. Next he painted 'Vivian Hewitt' in large letters on the undersides of his wings.

Hewitt's first flight over Rhyl took place on Thursday 12 October 1911. The flights were to become so popular that the town council held a banquet in his honour in recognition of the extra crowds that flocked to the town even in the 'off season'.

Although he was popular on the flying circuit, he had yet to make a public name for himself. However, he harboured a secret ambition. Inspired by Robert Loraine's attempt to fly across the Irish Sea, he became determined to become the first to achieve the prize. So it was that at 5am on 23 April 1912 Hewitt left Rhyl on what would be a much longer flight than Corbett Wilson's from Fishguard. As the winds were very strong and there was a terrible sea mist, he diverted to Holyhead. At 10.30 on 26 April, after the sea mist and strong winds had abated, Hewitt took off again. He carried no compass and navigated only by the sun as it occasionally showed through the clouds. Eventually he saw coastline ahead and recognized the Wicklow Mountains; he was 15 miles off course, but it was a matter of minutes to follow the coastline down to Dublin, where he touched down near the Wellington monument in Phoenix Park.

When Hewitt heard about Denys Corbett Wilson's crossing four days earlier and the loss of Damar Allen is unclear. It seems that Hewitt and a large part of the press chose to ignore Corbett Wilson's feat, and to many Hewitt became known as the first man to cross the Irish Sea. He was to put 'First to cross the Irish Sea' on his business cards when he appeared in Llandrindod Wells in 1914, but at Enniscorthy Castle in Co. Wexford is a small plaque that states that Denys Corbett Wilson made the journey first, just after his rather hasty landing in Radnorshire. Perhaps the final word should go to the issue of *Flight* magazine for 27 April 1912. They announced that Damar Allen has been missing for well over a week, and stated that Corbett Wilson had made a successful crossing to Ireland and that Hewitt was planning a crossing as the magazine went to press.

At the time that Hewitt performed his flight he did not hold a Royal Aero Club (or French Aero Club) certificate, but the rules were becoming tighter and he gained his certificate on 1 October 1912. Interestingly, his certificate lists the place it was taken as his own Foryd Fawr Aerodrome. He was evidently either rich enough or well connected enough for a Royal Aero Club official to travel to Wales and perform his test.

He now went from strength to strength on the exhibition front, and flew above Rhyl almost daily, dropping specially printed signed and dated cards over the holidaymakers. He then decided to extend his flying to other parts of Wales and took over the agricultural show circuit in which the late Gustav Hamel had had so much success. As a result, early August 1914 found Vivian Hewitt listed as the star attraction at many of Radnorshire's shows, starting with that at Llandrindod Wells on 5 August.

Flying at these events often started late in the afternoon (the advertisement for the Llanwrtyd show states that flying would commence at 5.30pm) and Hewitt was due to start his flying at Llandrindod Wells at 3pm. The Rock Park Ddole landing strip, scene of Gustav Hamel's successful flights, was situated alongside a river on the floor of a shallow valley. Whilst the landing strip was a long flat field, the other side of the river was quite wooded.

Hewitt took off without a hitch but misjudged the height of the nearby trees. The plane's undercarriage became entangled in the branches, part of the propeller broke off and landed in the river, and the Blériot disappeared from view. Before the crowd could fully take in what had

FLYING.

Mr. VIVIAN HEWITT

The well-known Aviator will give Exhibitions of

Fancy . Flying

ON THE

Rock Park Hotel Grounds,

ON

Wednesday, August 5th, at 3 p.m.

Admission to the Ground or Rock Park, 1/-; Motor Cars 2/6 and 1/- each occupant. ℭ. The Exhibition can only be seen from the Grounds, and not from the road sides.

An advertisement for Vivian Hewitt's flying display at Llandrindod Wells in August 1914

Vivian Hewitt's aircraft after his lucky escape on the Ddole airfield, August 1914. (Photo courtesy of Thomas Roberts via the Radnorshire Museum)

happened, the dishevelled but unhurt figure of Vivian Hewitt appeared on the opposite bank smoking a cigarette. This added fuel to the romantic hero image, but unfortunately ended the flying displays that summer, not just for the Rock Park Ddole but for the rest of Radnorshire.

But it wasn't only aircraft that were dropping out of the skies into Radnorshire. While the Hamels and the Hewitts were racing around the skies at seemingly horrendous speeds, the Aero Club of France was still holding onto the idea that balloons were the only way to travel by air. Although there were many aviators, plane designers and builders throughout France, the spirit of Montgolfier still hung in the air.

In July 1914 the club organised a grand balloon race from Paris. Exact details of the race are now a bit sketchy, but other balloon races at the time focused on getting the balloon as far away from the start as possible in the shortest possible time. The aeronaut would telegraph his position on landing and a winner would be announced in due course. The good prize money and universal acclaim attracted many competitors.

Among the participants in the July event was Monsieur Georges Blanchet, one of France's best known long distance aeronauts, who had a M. Duval as his passenger. Also taking part were M. Henri Foucault and M. Jean Laurenceau, as well as M. Charles Dolfuss and his passenger M. Charles Combes, both of whom lived in Paris.

At 4pm on a Sunday afternoon all the balloons were inflated and ready for takeoff. The wind freshened almost immediately and some of the balloons were blown towards Holland, while many other were blown towards the Channel and eventually England.

Disaster struck almost immediately. M. Blanchet and M. Duval had kept their balloon very low on leaving the field, whether to conserve ballast or to gain some other advantage is not known. They hit trees on the edge of the field, causing some of the ropes holding the basket to the balloon to snap, whereupon a number of spectators rushed forward, grabbed the trailing guy ropes and tried to pull the balloon to safety, but failed. The balloon gained about another 30 yards in height before the rest of the ropes gave way, causing the basket

Charles Dolfuss's balloon laid out to dry at New Radnor.
(Photograph by W.H. McKaig, © the Radnorshire Museum)

to fall to the ground just outside the gates of the park on the Place De La Concorde and landing on a cart that was waiting besides the road. M. Duval was thrown from the basket and landed on his head; he died later that night in hospital. M. Blanchet was not seriously injured. The balloon, however, exploded.

Meanwhile, M. Dolfuss and M. Combes drifted on peacefully, crossed the Channel and recognised Oxford before it got too dark to see. Around midnight they passed over what they described as a very well lit up town, but were unable to identify it. As dawn rose they drifted low over a forested area, but were unsure exactly where they were. In fact the wooded area was known as the Warren, and lay close to Radnor Forest by Water-break-its-neck. The balloon's basket became tangled in some of the taller trees and they took the opportunity to make the balloon fast. They descended into a clearing without any difficulty and after about an hour made their way into New Radnor.

The arrival of the two balloonists caused quite a stir, especially when they asked for assistance in bringing the balloon down the mountain so it could be packed and put on the train. The Eagle Hotel became a hive of industry. Sergeant Hitchman of the local constabulary at once requested that the proprietor Mr J. Niblett get his dray ready and accompany the aeronauts to the site of the balloon.

The policeman, the publican and several locals were able to bring the balloon down and lay it out in a field next to the railway station to dry, prior to its being packed and loaded on the afternoon train. Many locals visited the station field to converse with the two Frenchmen, including Mr and Mrs H. Duff Gordon of Harpton Court, who had quite a lengthy conversation with the balloonists.

Throughout the rest of the day it seems that French balloons were dropping on all parts of Wales. Henry Foucault and Jean Laurenceau, having drifted over London, came to earth on the Epynt Mountains in Breconshire. They could see the St George's Channel in the distance and thinking it was the Atlantic Ocean made a supreme effort to land, but a little too hastily as it turned out. At around 6am, they alighted on high ground on Dysgwylfa farm about a mile and a half from Upper Chapel near Brecon. Unfortunately they were unable to secure the balloon properly and resorted to throwing out their belongings and the sandbags before making a jump for it. The balloon drifted on and was lost. Again they were helped by local residents and gave the local vicar, the Revd Trevor Williams, their French Aero Club badge with balloon no.7 on it.

Other balloons from the race landed at Aberangell near Machynlleth. One landed near Barmouth, three landed in the vicinity of Aberystwyth, another at Foryd station near Rhyl, while yet another touched down outside Towyn.

Who won the balloon race has been lost to time. Now only a faded black and white photograph of a deflated balloon, drying out in a Radnorshire field, reminds us of those once hotly contested balloon races.

Charles Dolfuss went on to become a balloon specialist in the French navy and retained a lifelong passion for ballooning. He became the first Frenchman to do a double crossing of the channel in the Graf Zeppelin. After the First World War he went to work at the Museum of Air in Paris with special responsibility for the ballooning section. In 1927 he became curator, a post he held for the rest of his working life. He was so devoted to the museum and its contents that he stayed with the collection throughout the Second World War to ensure that nothing was damaged. He took his last balloon flight in 1978 when he was 85, and passed away in 1980.

The other Frenchman in this tale, Gaston Vial, Corbett Wilson's mechanic on his flight across Radnorshire and the Irish Sea, returned to France in 1912 and joined the army, originally serving in an artillery unit. In 1913 he transferred to the French Air Force, gaining his pilot's brevet (badge) in 1915. He served with distinction throughout the war, becoming an ace after shooting down eight enemy planes. He was awarded the Legion D'Honnour, the Medaille Militaire and the Croix de Guerre. He survived the First World War.

As for the pilot whom he had helped, Denys Corbett Wilson had a few very close friends and was not a showman. He did not seem to promote his crossing of the Irish Sea, almost treating it as a personal achievement. For a time he remained in Ireland, where he made a number of flying displays in the south, and continued his run of crash landings. Having crash-landed at one display, but doing no great injury to himself or his plane, the display was rescheduled for the following weekend. At this second chance he really did hurt himself, and the Blériot had to be sent back to France for a rebuild. Undaunted, he borrowed the aircraft of Miss Trehawke Davies, a wealthy patron of early aviators who liked being taken aloft, but never learned to fly herself. Unable to accompany him, he instead taxied

SPECIAL NOTICE !

As Mr.

Vivian Hewitt

(who is giving an Exhibition of Flying to-day in the Rock Park Grounds)

Has   Volunteered

his Services to the

War Office

He will be UNABLE TO FULFIL HIS SECOND ENGAGEMENT to Fly at Llandrindod Wells in September.

A sign of the coming times

along the field with an *Irish Times* reporter on board, hit a hidden dip on the field and took the tips off his propeller blades.

Following his time in Ireland, he took a commission in the newly formed Royal Flying Corps. He followed the usual training program but with no war on the horizon he seems to have led a leisurely life in the Corps, finding time to set a few firsts in long distance flying. More than one of these flights was promoted by a desire to see a girlfriend – flying home to see Madeline or crossing the Pyrenees to see Nicole, or flying off one weekend at short notice to a lady he just called 'naughty'.

In May 1913 he became the toast of Europe when he crossed the Jura Alps flying from Buc to Dijon then, after a brief refuelling stop in Dijon, flying on to Lausanne, a distance of 270 miles.

In July that year he got into a spot of bother with the authorities. A letter arrived in Kilkenny on 3 July asking for an explanation in writing without delay of the following flying offences contrary to the Aerial Navigation Act: namely that on 14 June 1913 he had been seen at 05.40hrs flying over Chatham dockyard. Then on 26 June at 07.45hrs he had flown low over Bembridge and St Helen's before landing opposite the coast guard station in the prohibited area of Spithead and Culver cliff signal station. All of this flying had been in prohibited air space and he was asked to inform the Army Council if he was guilty of these offences. There is no record of Corbett Wilson's reply, but less than two months later he had resigned his Commission in the Royal Flying Corps, sold his Blériot and it seems turned his back on flying altogether. He and his mother left Ireland and settled on the shores of Lake Como in Italy, where he turned his hand to racing motorboats on the lake.

The pair returned to England just before the First World War and on 19 August 1914 he once more enlisted in the Royal Flying Corps. He was sent to France, arriving on 16 October 1914, and was confirmed in the rank of 2nd lieutenant on 5 November. Serving with 3 Squadron, he was billeted in a farmhouse just seven miles behind the frontline. Rations could be a bit sparse and Denys frequently wrote to his mother for food packages from Fortnum and Masons. One letter asked for stilton with the words 'there are quite a few of us so it won't have time to spoil'.

An observer in the same squadron was James McCudden who, in *Five years in the Royal Flying Corps*, recounts how on the clear spring evenings they could watch their aircraft trying to make it back through anti-aircraft fire along the German lines. It was not uncommon for pilots to act as observers, and Denys found himself teamed up with the actor Robert Loraine as his observer, whose failed Irish Sea crossing had led to his own attempt. Loraine was badly injured one night when their plane was badly shot up by flak. A few nights later Captain Conran and Lt Woodiwiss struggled back to the field. As Conran came into land, petrol could be seen streaming from the tank. Conran was badly wounded by shrapnel in his arm and several fragments had entered his side and come out by his spine. The aircraft, a Morane Parasol type, was riddled with shrapnel, but miraculously Lt Woodiwiss was uninjured. Captain Conran was sent back to Britain and the aircraft, serial no.1872, was sent to be mended. The flimsy stick and string aircraft were quite easily repaired and before long the plane was back in action. This was the aircraft assigned to Corbett Wilson in early May 1915 and he took James McCudden up for a flight, both of them impressed with its speed and rate of the climb.

On 10 May, Denys and Lt Isaac Newton Woodiwiss (who was named after the famous distant relative of his paternal grandmother) took off for a reconnaissance flight to try and photograph the German lines. They were never seen again.

The next evening a German aircraft appeared over the airfield and dropped a message. The message stated that a Morane Parasol type of aircraft had been shot down by their anti-aircraft battery. The two British airmen on board had both been killed and they had been buried in the churchyard in the town of Fournes. A simple cross had been erected with an inscription that translated as 'RIP. Here lie two British flying officers 10/5/15'.

Denys and Isaac lay in the grave at Fournes until 1923, when the commonwealth war graves commission re-buried them at the British cemetery in Caberet Rouge. They still share a grave. Mrs Corbett Wilson wrote to Isaac's mother and between them they decided that the grave marker should be a cross bearing the inscription *Floreat Etona* (May Eton Flourish) and the quote 'Underneath are the everlasting arms' from Deuteronomy 33:27.

On the outbreak of the First World War, Hewitt's Foryd Aerodrome (along with many others around the country) was closed and Hewitt became an acting lieutenant in the Royal Navy Volunteer Reserve. Hewitt's younger brother Billy joined the machine gun corps and was killed in 1914; their mother never really accepted he was dead and was often known to lay the table for Billy.

Hewitt spent the war as a test pilot both here and in America with the Royal Naval Air Service, a bad crash ending his flying career in 1918. Despite Hewitt's readiness to embrace a title that did not belong to him, he was not the flamboyant showman that he would appear. Shy and retiring, he returned to live in Rhyl after he had ceased flying. He was generous both with his wealth and influence; if he could help a local cause or advance a man's career he would. His generosity even stretched to the government. A letter dated 27 June 1940 addressed to the chancellor of the exchequer states that he wished to lend, interest free, the sum of £50,000 to the government for the duration of the war and extending to a period three months after the cessation of hostilities. But like all millionaires he was a bit eccentric. After ten years in Rhyl he bought a house on Anglesey. Cemlyn was originally a farmhouse and over the next few years he set about buying land and even another farmhouse adjacent to his land. Shortly after he moved in he began building a huge wall around his property. It later transpired that this was to house a bird sanctuary which would eventually be over 200 acres in size. He was a keen ornithologist and birds became his passion now he could no longer fly himself. His generosity extended to handsome tips to the workers building the wall, and during the depression of the 1930s he bought several commercial fishing boats the catches from which he distributed among the poor and needy of the surrounding area. But there was one bill he hated paying, that for Income Tax. It was this that probably eventually drove him out of the country to the Bahamas, though he cited ill health and the cold damp Welsh winters. He retained Cemlyn, and the walled garden and lagoon for wading birds he built are still a nature reserve; he also turned part of his 67-acre estate in the Bahamas into a bird sanctuary. He kept several parrots as pets, one of which, Choo Choo, was treated to a first class seat on train journeys.

Hewitt was probably one of the most long lived of the early aviators. Unmarried and wealthy, he died in Wales in 1965 when he was 77 years old.

2 The First World War

This chapter tells the stories of those from Radnorshire who flew in or helped maintain the Royal Flying Corps (RFC) and subsequent Royal Air Force (RAF) during the First World War. Some of the airmen or mechanics were born in Radnorshire, and others moved to Radnorshire at some point in their lives.

At the start of the war the RFC, which had been formed in 1912 as part of the army, had some 113 aircraft, about two-thirds the number of the French Aviation Service and less than half the number in the German Air Service. At the start of the war the risk of injury to crew was largely as a result of accidents, but as air-borne armament and anti-aircraft fire improved, the dangers to aircrew increased to a level equal to that for the infantryman in the trenches. In addition, for much of the war German aircraft were superior to those flown by the British.

In September 1914, the RFC had 48 aircraft in France; by September 1915, 161 aircraft; by July 1916, 421 aircraft with a further 216 in depots. By the end of the war, 1,200 aircraft were deployed in France with a further 600 in depots, and others providing home defence against Zeppelin raiders, and in bases in the Middle East, the Balkans and Italy. On 1 April 1918 the RFC combined with the Royal Naval Air Service to form the RAF. By the end of the war the RAF had 99 squadrons in France, 34 squadrons serving elsewhere overseas, and 55 squadrons in the UK as well as 199 training squadrons, with a total of some 22,000 aircraft.

One of those who joined the RFC when it was in desperate need of manpower as it sought to both expand and replace losses in 1915 was William Thomas Lloyd Allcock. William was born in Knighton in 1897 to John and Sarah Allcock, who had a thriving grocery and bakery business. The youngest of four children, his elder brother Charley assisted his parents in the business and his sister Ethel Sarah was a bookkeeper in Knighton; not much is known about his other sister Dorothy (Dollie).

His early education was at Whitton School, close to where he grew up, but later he was sent to the Methodist-run Bourne College in Birmingham. It has long since closed, having been bulldozed to make way for the M5.

He clearly became not only a well educated but a very independent young man, for on 9 April 1914, aged just 16, he arrived in eastern Canada in the company of two friends. Canada was a popular destination before the First World War for a those seeking a new life and newspapers of the time were full of adverts asking for workers of all kinds. The Trans-Canada railroad also offered very low rents at easy terms on farms and equipment – they just wanted people to come out and fill the vast empty wilderness that their railway had opened up.

Once in Canada, Allcock and his friends took a train west. He, at least, worked first on a farm in Calgary and then moved on to a ranch in British Columbia. In January 1915 he was to be found in Winnipeg, and then he decided it was time to come home and, as the papers of the day put it, 'do his bit'.

He resolved to join the RFC. At the time the War Office would only consider appli-cants who had already gained their Royal Aero Club certificate, or ticket, as it was known, privately; then they would be granted their Royal Flying Corps wings. Many of the early RFC pilots did all their training at the Central Flying School and would then nip over to Brooklands or up to Hendon in an RFC aircraft to be met by an official from the Royal Aero Club. They would be asked to do a series of flying manoeuvres while the official and possibly some other cadets looked on, and often after only about 15 minutes the pilot would land, be told whether he had passed or not, then get back to his base for a celebra-tion. The ticket would arrive a few days later and the 'pilot' would be granted his wings. In general at the beginning of the war, pilots recorded an average of 2½ hours flying before qualifying. It was then the job of the Central Flying School to teach them to fly for combat

W.T.L. Allcock at the Central Flying School, Hendon 21 May 1915.
(© Guy Griffiths)

or in order to conduct formation flying or bombing missions. Oxford was then the home of the school of Military Aeronautics as well as an observer training school, and pilots would also be sent here as part of their course. In those early days, apart from being taught to fly, pilots would be expected to know how to make small repairs to the engine or the aircraft itself, such as resplicing wires and unjamming their guns, as well as navigation and Morse code.

Allcock therefore set off, with his parents' help, for the Beatty School at Hendon Aerodrome with a view to gaining his aviator's certificate. Twelve weeks later, on 16 May 1915, he duly received his certificate, having flown a Beatty Wright biplane. His certificate was no.1241; less than four years earlier Gustav Hamel had earned certificate no.64.

On 22 September 1915, a few weeks before his 18th birthday, the now 2nd Lieutenant William Allcock arrived at 2 Squadron on the western front in France. His first few sorties were reconnaissance flights. The brass hats at the time firmly believed that a pilot's main duty was the spotting of troop movements, and these early aircraft were only lightly armed. Pilots and observers, however, would often fly with pistols and rifles and take pot shots at enemy aircraft. The main danger to an aircraft came from anti-aircraft fire, and the ground-based German guns that would prove deadly to many a young pilot were given the surprisingly friendly nickname of 'Archie'.

Allcock had been with the squadron for less than two weeks when his diary (which he kept for most of the time he was in France) records a nasty near miss. The entry for 5 October notes that William and his observer Lieutenant Arthur Whitton Brown were on an artillery observation flight in a Vickers FB5, an aircraft known as the 'Gun Bus', in which the observer sat in front of the pilot.

> While doing so we were hit at 8,000ft by shrapnel over Hulluch. My engine gone [*sic*] dud, I turned for our lines, when just crossing them the machine caught fire at 6,300 ft. I immediately put her nose down; the flames burst out and spread along the fuselage ... Brown threw the ammunition overboard and climbed along back nearly into my cockpit as the whole front of the machine was a blazing mess. In the meantime we were speeding to earth at 120mph. Brown was trying to keep the fire from burning his clothes while I kept my eye on the pitot [a device that measured air speed], the ground and the flames, pushing my joystick further forward until we were nearly nose diving. Every minute I thought would be the last for I expected the whole machine to collapse from the strain as a number of wires were broken. Eventually I saw ground not far below and found myself going straight at a village so I turned to the right and spying a ploughed field decided to land there, cutting through telephone wires and a tall hedge, missing a horse and plough by inches. A few feet from the ground I levelled out and the machine took the ground at 70mph. A perfect landing but the undercarriage being burnt the machine only ran for a few yards and collapsed, digging her nose into the plough, and turned over. I was thrown right out 10 yards ahead, putting my hands out saved me a bit but I lay dazed, in the meantime the tail came down and hit me on the head. Staggering around to find Brown I found him hunting for me. He had fallen under the engine and just managed to crawl out seconds before the bearers broke and the engine fell on the spot. Looking on the wreckage we saw a mass of flames with every few seconds shots going off from the revolvers.

He later adds how a tender from a nearby airfield arrived and a sergeant was put in charge to keep a crowd of onlookers at bay while Allcock and Brown were taken back to the aerodrome. Allcock returned to the site later that night and took the compass, the revolver and a piece of engine bed that had melted in the heat of the fire as a souvenir. It was his 13th sortie. Neither he nor Brown could have had any idea, as they walked away from the wreck, that four years later Arthur Brown would become world famous, for Brown was the navigator who on 14 June 1919 took off with pilot John Alcock (no relation to William Allcock) from Lester field in St John's, Newfoundland and made the first non-stop flight across the Atlantic.

Allcock's wartime diary further records that he had time for test flights, practising aerobatics and the occasional joy ride – he took his mechanic, Ashton, up and did a few loop the loops to, as he says, 'put the wind up' him.

But the character of the war in the air was changing. Gone was the time when airmen from both sides would wave to each other, or even send condolences across the lines if an 'enemy' pilot was killed. (Many of the early pilots from both sides had flown together or met at air shows before the war). The Germans in particular were developing faster, bigger and better armed planes at an alarming rate. Allcock was now not just observing troop movements but engaged in bombing missions. His diary began to carry much briefer descriptions of his day's work, often just remarking that he 'dropped his two bombs, got shot at by a Hun but made it back alright', or '... back of plane riddled by Hun bullets, if there had been an observer in there he would certainly have been killed'.

In February 1916 he was promoted to the rank of captain and on 21 March 1916 he became a flight commander. He still held the rank of captain but this designation showed that he was deemed the most experienced pilot in the flight and 'in charge' of any sortie; on 13 March, for example, he flew four sorties totalling nine hours flying. He was now flying with 16 Squadron; it was very foggy on the first sortie he led out and many of the pilots got lost. One pilot (Lieutenant Thayne) made it to Herne Bay in Kent and claimed he thought he was in Holland. Allcock himself made a heavy landing in a field near the squadron's base but was unhurt. A few days later, when the weather had again closed in and visibility was very poor, he hit a ditch on landing and was catapulted into a pool of cold dirty water, emerging unscathed but 'looking like a drowned rat'. He crashed twice more, due on these occasions to engine failure, in the following two weeks.

In May, Allcock returned to England to act as a flying instructor, but in October he was back in France with 46 Squadron. His diary now gives very little information about his flying, except to state simply that he flew 45 hours in 21 days.

On 13 November 1916 his plane was shot up by an enemy aircraft and crashed badly at the aerodrome on landing. A week later William was evacuated to England with leg injuries. After two months recuperating he returned to the central flying school as an instructor, and numbered among his pupils the Australian pilot Charles Kingsford Smith. Smith became the first pilot to cross the Pacific Ocean and the first pilot to circumnavigate the globe.

In May 1917 Captain William Allcock once more returned to France. This time he joined 40 Squadron Flying Nieuport 17s. There are no more diary entries. On 5 June 1917 he took off in his Nieuport 17 (serial number B1548) at 7.22pm as flight commander of a group of six aircraft. Two of the aircraft reported engine trouble while in the vicinity

Captain W.T.L. Allcock RFC.
(© Guy Griffiths)

of Vitry and turned back, while the remaining four continued on with the sortie. Lt William (Bill) Bond in Nieuport B1545 spotted four German Albatross D111 aircraft a few thousand feet below them; almost immediately another five were spotted several thousand feet higher and off to the east. Allcock and Bond dived on the formation of unsuspecting Albatrosses opening fire as they closed in. Allcock hit one of the German machines several times and it was seen to spin out of control and dive to the ground. Bond emptied the magazine of his Nieuport's Lewis gun into another of the aircraft and in the heat of the moment he got so close to the Albatross that he almost collided with it, before the plane was seen to sideslip before also crashing to the ground in the swamp around the River Scarpe at Fampoux. Bond slipped away from the fray to change the magazine in his Lewis gun before returning to help his comrades, who had now been jumped on by the rest of the Albatrosses. What happened next no one can say for sure. Bond was battling two Albatrosses when his Lewis gun jammed and he high-tailed it back to base with the two enemy planes chasing him as far as the British lines. The rest of the flight scattered. Two of the other Nieuports had also suffered damage but managed to get back to base. Allcock did not return. His Nieuport 17 was never found and he has no known grave. He was posted as missing in action, but perhaps in the hope that he was a prisoner of war his commanding officer did not inform his parents for another three months. He was then listed as killed in action. He was not highly decorated, but General Haig mentioned him in dispatches.

There is a possible final twist to the story. A letter was written to the British Air Ministry on 14 December 1918 by the Mayor of Douai, a town on the River Scarpe close to where Allcock was lost, asking for the name of a British pilot of a Nieuport, serial number 3470, who was believed to have crashed in the area on 8 June 1917, as he wished to contact the man's family. The Air Ministry wrote back saying that they had no record of the aircraft and were therefore unable to trace the pilot. It is highly possible that the number quoted by the mayor was in fact a factory number and would not have been recorded in the files.

William Allcock joined the RFC straight from civilian life, but many chose to join the RFC from other branches of the army. One such recruit was George Walter Thomas Lindsay. George was born in Llanishen, Glamorgan on 29 January 1891, the son of wealthy Lt Colonel Henry Edzell Morgan Lindsay, the grandson of the first Lord Tredegar. On his mother's (Ellen Katherine) side he was the great nephew of Thomas Thomas of Llanbradach and Pencerrig, and it was the latter which gave him his Radnorshire connection, for the Pencerrig estate lies on the road between Builth Wells and Llandrindod Wells. The Lindsay family had holidayed in the area and at Pencerrig for some years, and shortly before the outbreak of the First World War, Miss Thomas (an elderly aunt to Mrs Lindsay), who was the owner of the Pencerrig estate, passed away and left the house and grounds to her eldest great nephew, George Lindsay. George visited the house several times while on leave but in 1915 he turned it over to a small group of Belgian refugees.

George had three brothers – Claude (b.1894), Archibald (b.1897) and David (b.1910) – and two sisters, Nest and Ellen. George, Claude and Archibald, were all educated at Wellington College in Berkshire, a boarding school for boys from the age of ten upwards. The school, established in 1837 had strong links to the Duke of Wellington, whose family coat of arms still features in the school crest. The school had an excellent sporting reputation. George played cricket for the school and would be described later on by his commanding officer as an unusually good all round sportsman.

The school also placed great emphasis on turning out officer material, and the boys were taught drill and other rudiments of military life. It is probably not all that surprising that George, whose father was a lieutenant colonel and who was educated at a school that promoted service life, enrolled in the Royal Military Academy at Woolwich, which his father had also attended. Here again sport was a large part of George's life, and he added hockey to his many sporting achievements. He passed out of Woolwich in the summer of 1911 and joined the Royal Artillery as a junior officer.

With the declaration of war on 4 August 1914, George was in the first wave of soldiers deployed to France later that month; he and his battalion were in the first Division of the British Expeditionary Force. On 5 November he sustained a gunshot wound in the left shoulder, and was evacuated through Boulogne and back to Southampton and thence to St Thomas's hospital in London, where he under-went an operation. In December he was judged unfit for duty and given eight weeks leave. The following March he appeared before another medical board. His shoulder had healed but was still stiff and painful and he had also suffered from muscle loss in his left arm, so the doctor concluded that he was only fit for light duties at home. George, however, was keen to return to his unit and appeared before several more medical boards before one granted his wish. By September he was back in France commanding No.30 artillery battery, and from there he was posted to Salonika in Greece.

By early 1916, however, Captain George Lindsay was back in the UK, having transferred to the Royal Flying Corps. It is unclear whether his injury led him to transfer, or whether flying appealed to his sporting nature. After his initial training George was attached to 62 Squadron

Captain George Walter Thomas Lindsay.
(© The late Jennifer Lindsay
via D. Sellwood)

in Bristol, becoming a test pilot at the Filton Aircraft Works for nearly a year. On 26 June 1917 George, with his air mechanic C.E. Sharmen, was on a test flight in a BE2d when the aeroplane suddenly crashed and both men were killed instantly. George's body was returned home and buried in the family vault at the Holy Trinity Church in Ystrad Mynach.

George left no will and had not nominated his next of kin. This meant that his father had to undertake a lengthy correspondence with the military in order to get his son's personal belongings returned. These included golf clubs and ball, tennis and badminton rackets and lacrosse and hockey sticks. His mother requested the return of his camera and photographs. These were scrutinised by the authorities to check that they contained no images that could be of use to the Germans before all 24 photos were returned.

George's brothers, Claude and Archibald, had also joined the army. Claude was in the Royal Field Artillery and saw service at Mons and on the Somme. In 1915 he married Dorothy Forde of County Wexford, Ireland. He was mentioned in dispatches in 1917 for gallantry in action and devotion to duty. Archibald joined the Royal Engineers and arrived in France in 1915. He became a full lieutenant, and was killed by a sniper's bullet at Hebutemu on 26 March 1918. He was buried in Fonquevillers Military Cemetery. Just five days later, on 31 March, Claude was also killed, and he is buried in Hailles communal cemetery in France. Claude's wife Dorothy gave birth to a son, Claude, that November. The Pencerrig estate passed on to a cousin; the Lindsay family no longer holidayed in the area.

Another to join the RFC from the ranks of the army was John Leslie Payton. Mrs Laura Eveline Payton, originally from the Birmingham area, had moved on the death of her husband to Torquay. Her son John Leslie was born on 31 March 1897. At the tender age of 16 John had already left home, having joined a mercantile marine shipping company and serving as an apprentice on ships out of Middlesbrough. John left the mercantile marine before the outbreak of the First World War and did not, as one might surmise, join the navy, but the army. In the meantime, for reasons unknown, Mrs Payton had left Torquay and had found her way to the gently fading splendour of Llandrindod Wells, a mid Wales Spa town which found itself at the beginning of the war with very many large hotels and no guests. She took up residence at Trevaldwyn in Montpellier Park, a short walk from the grounds of Rock Park.

John enlisted in the Royal Field Artillery Wessex brigade and by December 1915 had gained his first class instructor's certificate in signalling. The sea had apparently not suited John and now it seems that the land was not going to suit him either. Early in 1916 he applied to join the Royal Flying Corps and on 12 August he was posted to a training school at Reading, followed by the No.9 Radio School at Hythe. He quickly became a proficient pilot capable of flying a number of aircraft. By 10 February 1917 he had risen to the rank of 2nd lieutenant and by the 22nd had become an assistant instructor. Then there is an anomaly on his service record. He had obviously been to see the medical officer and whilst no injury or accident is recorded, he was deemed unfit for flying for six weeks. Throughout 1917 there were further periods when he was deemed unfit; however, he was still being posted to different training squadrons. August saw him move again, this time to 19 Training Squadron, where he learned to fly yet another aircraft, the De Havilland 4. On

11 September he was posted to 74 Squadron, another training squadron where he learned to fly yet another aircraft – the Avro 504K. The notes on his medical card become even more intriguing, as he was deemed medically fit for service in a warm climate, but not to fly above 5,000 feet. His service file suggests he was suffering from some sort of respiratory condition such as asthma and that he would be sent to a warm climate 'when a vacancy occurs'. (Had he stayed with his old Wessex regiment this would indeed have happened, as the Wessex brigade headed for India shortly after John left.)

1918 saw John move again, first to 84 Squadron and then to 56 Training Squadron. On 26 June he was posted to No.2 Fighter School. By 23 July 1918 no warm climate vacancy seems to have occurred and John joined the British Expeditionary Force as the pilot of an SE5 (short for Scout Experimental model number 5) and headed for France. Having flown or instructed on the following aircraft – the Maurice Farman short Horn, the DH2, Fe 2B, the BE5, the RE8 (known affectionately as the Harry Tate), the DH4, the Avro 540k, the Sopwith pup, the SE5, SPAD and the DH5 – he started flying missions over the Western Front in the SE5 with 84 Squadron. On 16 August, less than a month after arriving in France, John took off at 8.30am. One other SE5 of 84 Squadron took off with him, flown by Lieutenant Falkenberg. They were patrolling over the enemy lines at around 1,500 feet not in the warm climate but at least under the 5,000 feet recommended by his doctor. They were joined by Sopwith Camels of 80 Squadron when at approximately 9.45 they spotted two enemy aircraft – lumbering LVG (Luftverkehrsgesellschaft) two-seater reconnaissance aircraft. They pursued them over the enemy lines and Falkenberg fired repeated bursts at one of the aircraft, which was seen to spin into the ground in flames. At least one occupant of the plane jumped out but he did not have a parachute. During the engagement a burst of fire took both wings off John's aircraft and he was seen to spin into the ground. He was listed briefly as wounded but on the same day this was changed to missing. Probably because he went down in enemy territory the authorities waited to see if he might have been taken prisoner before declaring him dead. In John's case they seem to have waited an extraordinary length of time: the war ended in November 1918, three months after he was lost, but he was not finally declared dead until 16 August 1919, a year after he was seen to crash.

His mother, having seen the war out in Llandrindod Wells, returned to Torquay and took up residence in the Grenville Hotel. It was from here in 1921 that she finally applied for her son's War and Victory medals.

Some of those who joined the RFC were never to see action. Gordon Ivor Wilson was born in Lincolnshire in 1897 to the Yorkshireman Alexander Mills Wilson and his wife Amy. Alexander is listed as a gentleman living off his own means; three years before Gordon was born he had invested some money in the established Yorkshire confectionery firm Samuel Balmforth of Doncaster, which manufactured 'Parkinson's Celebrated Royal Doncaster Butterscotch', the firm sometimes being credited with inventing the term butterscotch. They were also experimenting with a form of dried yeast.

Gordon was the eldest and only son, but he had two sisters, Helga (born in 1900) and Irene (born in 1902). Gordon was privately educated at Repton, the public school in Lincolnshire then run by Howard Carlyle Hayward. The pupil list for the time that

Gordon was there is quite small. He joined the home defence cadet corps while at the school. In the meantime the family moved to Somerset; the Radnorshire connection was still to come.

When war broke out Gordon joined the Yorkshire Dragoons Yeomanry (Queen's Own); this may have been his father's idea, to keep up a Yorkshire connection. The division that Gordon joined, the 2/1st, had been formed in 1914 and mainly consisted of those unable or unwilling to serve overseas. This may have been due to some prior commitment such as education, as at that time Gordon was barely 18. A little over a year after joining Gordon applied to join the Royal Flying Corps, with whom he commenced his training at Oxford on 9 September 1916. On 1 December he arrived at the Central Flying School at Upavon, Wiltshire, close to the army camp on Salisbury Plain, where he would have started his actual flying training.

While Gordon was busy learning to fly in the skies above Wiltshire, his family moved from Somerset and settled in The Moor, Presteigne. Why they moved is unknown, but Alexander could have slipped into the role of gentleman farmer. The family still had a large contingent of servants to look after them, even though Gordon was away with the RFC and the girls were at school. It would be nice to think that the whole family got together that Christmas and Gordon thrilled his sisters with tales of his daring flying and the excitement of his first month in the Royal Flying Corps.

New Year 1917 saw Gordon continuing his training at Upavon, where the course was expected to last four months. Gordon like all would-be flyers was now a 2nd lieutenant. On 1 February 1917 a note in his service file says he was appointed as Flying Officer. This is a slightly confusing reference, as the rank of flying officer did not officially come in until after the RFC became the Royal Air Force on 1 April 1918. The day after this appointment, 2nd Lt G.T. Brown of the Welsh Regiment arrived at Upavon. Brown was on secondment, as officers who felt they might like to try flying but didn't wish to permanently leave their original regiment could ask to be seconded or even try flying during a period of leave. As yet Gordon had not gained his aero club ticket but was sufficiently advanced to be flying solo. Brown had also reached the solo stage even though he had only just arrived at Upavon. That February was extremely cold over the whole of the United Kingdom, with severe frosts, though less snow or rain than could be expected for the time of the year. There were light easterly winds under dull cloudy skies. 12 February dawned dull, but visibility was good with no rain, and the instructors at Upavon prepared for another day's flying. Among the pupils to take off that day were Gordon Wilson flying a BE2Ce (serial number 7246) and the newly arrived Lt G.T. Brown flying an American-made Martinsyde G102A (serial number 3939). Whether they were practising formation flying or whether one or other of them lost concentration is now unknown to us, but the two pilots collided near the town of Wilton some 19 miles away from their base. Both were killed. Gordon's youngest sister learned to fly just before the Second World War, while their parents lived on in Presteigne for many years, their father dying in Knighton in 1953.

Another Radnorshire-born man to join the RFC was Ralph Llewelyn John Davies, the eldest and only son of Llewelyn and Winifred Davies from the village of Cwmdauddwr, near Rhayader. His parents were both schoolteachers, Winifred teaching the infants in a school in Rhayader, while Llewelyn was a headmaster, probably in the same town. They also had a daughter Winifred Mary Rowena Davies, born when Ralph was 11.

The Davieses entertained high hopes for their son, and it seems that they did not think a village school education good enough for him. In 1911, at the tender age of 12, they enrolled him in Llandovery College. The college, whose motto was 'There are no riches better than learning', provided boys from the age of 11 upwards with a liberal and classical education, which focused strongly on Welsh language and culture. All the boys were expected to learn to speak Welsh. It seems likely that Ralph boarded at the school as it was a considerable distance from his home. What his experiences were and if he enjoyed his time there we do not know. Ralph's parents may have hoped he would go on to further education, but the First World War had already broken out and on 27 June 1917, six days after his 18th birthday Ralph presented himself to the Royal Flying Corps. Had he not done so he could well have been conscripted into an army unit under the Military Service Act which had come into force the previous January.

Ralph started flying training almost immediately, (by this time the RFC were teaching men to fly, and they no longer had to have a Royal Aero Club certificate before being considered). His service record lists him as becoming proficient on several aircraft types in the course of the next few months, including the De-Havilland 6, an Avro and the Sopwith Scout and Camel. In November he was transferred to No.7 Training Depot at Feltwell in Norfolk and was given the temporary rank of 2nd lieutenant. The RFC had two stages of training: first they would teach you to fly, then you would be taught how to fly in combat or for bombing or reconnaissance duties with the hundred and one little tricks that went with it.

Ralph was next posted to 89 Squadron in December 1917, a training squadron that never became operational. He was confirmed in the rank of 2nd lieutenant on 5 April 1918, five days after the RFC became the Royal Air Force. Ralph's proficiency on several types of aircraft led to his appointment as a flying instructor and he was on a flight in a single seat Sopwith Camel (number D9544) on the morning of Sunday 5 May 1918 at about 10am. (Instructors were often only a short step ahead of their pupils and would spend many hours practising aerial manoeuvres, map reading and familiarising themselves with the local area.) The weather was misty with bad visibility, when, for some unknown reason the aircraft was seen to side slip, before crashing into the ground from a height of around 150 feet. Ralph was killed. (Side slipping is where one wing of the aircraft is tilted towards the ground, either to decrease one's turning area, or to increase the angle at which to head for the ground, or sometimes to help land on one part of the aircraft's undercarriage if the other part is damaged. The manoeuvre adds strain to the plane's flaps and rudder.)

The wording on Ralph Davies' grave.
(© Author's collection)

Investigators looked into the accident and concluded that the crash was the result of lack of judgment on the part of the pilot while practicing aerial manoeuvres. They therefore took the decision not to call in a court of inquiry. Ralph is buried in St Bride's churchyard in Cwmdauddwr.

His fate was not dissimilar to that of Thomas Thompson Pritchard, who was born in Knighton in October 1888 to Ann and Edward J. Pritchard. Thomas was the fourth child; the family would eventually number three boys and two girls. Their father was a farm bailiff at Bowdler Farm just outside the town, and though he had been born in Worcestershire, their mother had been born and brought up in Llanyre, a mile from Llandrindod Wells.

His elder brother Edward left Radnorshire and set up as a baker, founding the Imperial Bakery in Gilfach near Bargoed in south Wales. Their father died in about 1910, and the family moved into Edward's bakery. Thomas and his mother worked in the bakery and his sister Minnie became a confectioner. (There is still a bakery on this site although it has now changed its name.) Thomas joined a territorial regiment and initially saw service with the Royal Gloucester Hussars, an old and prestigious regiment that had been formed in 1795. Like most of the old yeomanry regiments it had been split into home and overseas divisions at the outbreak of the First World War. The regiment sailed to Egypt and then to Gallipoli in April 1915.

Thomas was part of the home defence force, and this may have been the reason that he decided to apply to the Royal Flying Corps. On 11 May 1917 he arrived at the School of Military Aeronautics in Oxford, where his training seems to have been pretty standard although at the age of 29 he was rather older than the average Royal Flying Corps pilot of the time. Just two months later, on 14 July, he was training to be an instructor. Thomas served time with a training squadron, then went to the central flying school at Upavon near Salisbury plain and yet by August 1917 he was to be found at Yatesbury in Wiltshire with 59 Training Squadron.

On 8 August, 65-year-old Ann Pritchard died and was buried in Llanyre churchyard where her daughter Bertha, who had died at the age of 4, was also buried. On 30 August, probationary 2nd lieutenant Thomas Pritchard of the Royal Flying Corps took off in BE2e serial number B170 and was killed at Yatesbury Aerodrome. All other details are sketchy; his service file simply lists his death as a result of an aeroplane accident. His next of kin is listed as M. Pritchard, at the Baskerville Arms, Herefordshire. No record of a marriage has come to light; the M could have stood for Minnie, his sister, who had been born near the Baskerville Arms, in Clyro, close to the Radnorshire / Herefordshire border. His family brought his body back to Radnorshire and he is buried in the same grave as his mother.

Most men did, however, manage to survive their training, and Cyril Evan Robinson was numbered in their ranks. Cyril was born in Chorley, Manchester on 8 August 1899, where his father was an assistant in an ironmonger's shop in the city. His mother and maternal aunt, Eliza Anne Griffiths, completed the household. Both women had been born in Llansantffraid near Rhayader and early in Cyril's childhood, the family upped sticks and returned to Radnorshire, where his father opened an ironmonger's shop in Hundred House, a few miles from Builth Wells. The family, now including Cyril's younger sister Phyllis, lived in Ithon Villa, Station Road in Llanelwedd, placing him firmly on the Radnorshire side of the river.

Cyril did not follow in his father's trade. Instead, in July 1915, just before his 16th birthday, he started work with the American Express Bank Company in Liverpool. He spent two years at the bank before enlisting in the Royal Flying Corps on 8 June 1917. He completed his pilot training at Winchester and Oxford, his service file noting that he could now fly the Maurice Farman 'short horn', the BE2e and a De-Havilland 6.

On 13 October 1917 he became a 2nd lieutenant on probation; a probationary period was quite common before a promotion was finally granted. He was then sent to 25 Training Squadron at Thetford in Norfolk. His rank was subsequently confirmed and on 13 July 1918 he was sent to France, where he joined 27 Squadron, whose motto was *Quam celerrime ad astra*, 'With all speed to the stars'. The squadron was based at Ruisseauville, flying the De-Havilland 9, a single-engined, two-seater bomber.

Cyril as pilot was teamed up with an observer from Newcastle-on-Tyne, William Houston Telfer. On 24 July Cyril and William were flying in DH9 serial number C6340 when the engine stalled. The aircraft was only about 600 feet up at the time and it spun into the ground so quickly there was no time for either man to take any action. They would not have been able to bail out in any event, as during the First World War it was decreed that no one in a 'heavier than air machine' was allowed to wear a parachute; only members of the Balloon Corps were issued with parachutes. Both men were killed instantly.

Their bodies were taken to the French hospital at Coulommiers, where there is a small cemetery in the hospital grounds containing only 32 graves (one of an unidentified airman). Cyril and William are buried next to each other. They were both 19 years of age. His family placed a memorial to him in Llanelwedd church.

Another to complete his training successfully was Reginald Percy Bufton, whose flying was to lead to some interesting exploits. Born in Knighton on 21 April 1891, he was the third son of James, a ladies' tailor, and Mary, a dressmaker; they were first cousins who had both been born in Llanbister. The Buftons had three sons: James (known as Jim), Vincent John born

Two images of Cyril Robinson: the posed portrait and the relaxed pilot, both taken in 1917.
(© Cathy Evans)

25 September 1889 (who went by the name of Jack) and Reginald, who preferred to be called by his middle name, Percy.

When Percy was born the family lived in Wylcwm Villas in the Brookside area of Knighton, but by 1901 they had moved to No.8 Nelson Street, Llandrindod Wells. In around 1907 the family moved to Caerhyn in Dyffryn Road. This red brick, villa-style semi had been built by James snr's friend, Mr Francis, who rented it to the Bufton family while he lived in the other villa of the pair, which he had called Ashleigh. James and Mary must have been quite prosperous in their trade as in 1915 they were able to purchase Caerhyn from Mr Francis.

Percy was a keen artist and soon began not only sketching the flora and fauna around him but also learning all he could about the native wildlife; he was to devote a large part of his life to studying the natural world.

His brother Jim was of a more practical nature. Percy always told the story of a crystal radio set Jim built for them. One night in 1912, when Jim should have been in bed, he was playing with his radio when he picked up faint voices and a ship's distress signal. He listened closely and could make out that the ship in trouble was the *Titanic*. Jim rushed to tell his father but was reprimanded for playing about and sent back to bed. The next morning the newspapers were full of the terrible shipping disaster. Percy was always very proud of his brother for picking up the signal from such a long way away on his home-made set.

In 1911 Percy became a clerk to Powell's, a large ironmonger's in Llandrindod Wells. He worked here for four years before joining the Montgomeryshire Yeomanry on 25 May 1915.

In 1908 Britain had established a home defence force to train young men to be ready in the event of an invasion. Each branch of the force was affiliated to a regular army unit. D Squadron of the Montgomeryshire Yeomanry was based in Llandrindod Wells but also drew men from Builth Wells and as far afield as Rhayader, Llanidloes, Hay on Wye and Knighton. Initially the home defence force was very much like today's Territorial Army units, with men training for service but also keeping their regular jobs. On the outbreak of war these 'territorials' were asked to volunteer for service overseas, and many who did so went overseas to Egypt or other parts of the British Empire, allowing the regular soldiers to be sent to France.

In June 1915 Percy's brigade was sent to Brecon for further training. They became affiliated to the 6 Reserve Cavalry Regiment. Percy's book-keeping skills were put to work in the stores and a year later in June 1916, when the brigade moved first to Gobowen and then to Park Hall Camp in Oswestry, Percy acted as quartermaster. By Christmas that year Percy had reached the rank of sergeant and had become the regimental quartermaster. By this stage in the war Percy must have seen many of his friends leave and see active service overseas while he was still stuck in Oswestry dishing out supplies and counting socks. This lack of action did not sit well with him and he began looking into the possibility of a transfer to the Royal Flying Corps. He first had to attend an officer cadet training unit and then in November 1916 heard that he was to be allowed to transfer. On 21 January 1917 he sent in a formal request to apply for a commission in the Royal Flying Corps, but it was not till March that he heard any positive news and it was only on 9 April 1917 that he reported to Denham Royal Flying Corps Cadet Training Flying School. A month later he moved to Oxford to attend the School of Military Aeronautics. On being accepted into the RFC Percy would have been granted a commission to the rank of acting 2nd lieutenant, an immediate step up from his sergeant's rank in the quartermaster's stores.

Percy took to flying like a duck to water and had soon learned to fly a Maurice Farman biplane, an Avro biplane, the Be2C and 2D, the RE 8 and the De-Havilland 4 and 6. All these planes were the heavier two-seat variety designed to be used for reconnaissance and bomber duties. He was then appointed to No.1 Flying Training School.

Percy's next posting was to 25 Squadron based at RAF Montrose in Scotland. This had been a fighter and reconnaissance squadron but they changed to bombers in early 1917. Members of 25 Squadron had been flying in France since 1916, but Percy was not to arrive in France till 17 April 1918, and in under a month had been transferred to 79 Squadron. This squadron flew a very different type of aircraft, the newly commissioned Sopwith Dolphin. This was a revolutionary aircraft with a unique staggered wing design, placing the bottom set of wings 13 inches in front of the top set and having the cockpit set so high that the nose of the aircraft was not visible from the cockpit. This made it difficult for some novices to keep the plane pointed at the horizon; it also presented problems with landings. That said, the Dolphin was popular because of the cooling pipes that ran from the engine along the inside of the cockpit on either side of the pilot, so keeping him rather warmer than in the average open cockpit plane of the time.

The first Dolphins arrived in France in February 1918 and were flown by 79 and 19 Squadrons. Their début was marred somewhat by incidents of British and Belgian fighters mistaking them for German aircraft and attacking them. One pilot was even shot at by an allied anti-aircraft gun. However there is no reference in Percy's log book to actually flying the Dolphin; instead he was engaged in bombing and photographic missions in the trusty old DH 4. On 21 May he was involved in a collision with another DH 4, but neither pilot was seriously injured. Percy eventually transferred back to 25 Squadron.

On 25 July Percy crash-landed again in a DH 4 with Lt Olley as his observer, just outside the tiny town of Senlecques in northern France. Anxious for his plane not to be of use to the Germans, he removed the propeller and slung it over his shoulder for the long walk back to safety. This propeller subsequently hung on the wall of every house he lived in. Percy saw plenty of action in France and although he had a few near misses and had to execute more than one forced landing, caused (as he put in his log book) by 'engine gone dud', he didn't seem to suffer the stress and fatigue experienced by some of the RFC pilots.

He kept up his naturalist studies and in 1918 he was elected a fellow of the Zoological Society in London. He also started to develop a keen interest in tropical fish. This hobby was very expensive, as the journey times and fluctuating temperature made transport of these delicate creatures problematic, with a half to two-thirds of any shipment dying en route. Percy therefore hatched a plan. By early 1919 he was a captain and flying back and forth with all manner of supplies to the British Army in Germany. Occasionally he would bring one of his beloved pets with him. (He was known to keep a monkey in his house in Llandrindod Wells.) Among the mechanics and engineers who were still in Europe hanging around waiting to get home, Percy found someone who could make him a fish tank that would fit over the engine of his biplane, was sealable against spills and would hopefully provide a foolproof way of transporting his precious tropical fish. The water would be kept

*Percy Bufton in front of a
DH 4 (above), and in the
cockpit of one (left).
Below: the results
of his collision with another
DH 4 on 21 May 1918.
(© Jan Beckett)*

warm and the speed would mean the journey time would be much shortened. On his first trial run, all went well and after a four hour flight Percy landed in Lincolnshire to find that just two of the hundred tropical fish he had placed in the tank had died on the journey. Percy was so pleased and excited by his achievement that he rushed to telephone a friend in London who made his living as a dealer in 'Living Fish'. Percy's friend implored him to share half the consignment and bring them to London to sell in his shop. Percy agreed, as his success rate had surprised even him and he was not too sure where he was going to keep all the fish. A few days later Percy wandered into the local newsagents to collect his tobacco and was greeted by a friendly proprietor who asked, 'Hey are you the bloke who brought the first living fish over by air?' and slapped a copy of the *Daily Mail* into his hand. His London friend had made a large window display of the fish and their unusual means of transport. Percy hastily went to the post office to send off a wire imploring him to take the display down. Percy was still a serving Royal Air Force officer and the fish had arrived by RAF plane. He did not get into too much trouble, but he refrained from transporting wildlife for a little while.

Date and Hour.	Wind Direction and Velocity.	Machine Type and No.	Passenger.	Time.	Height.	Course.	Remarks.
		France.					
6:5:18. 3.30–4.0 pm		DH4	-	30m	500'		Landings "Rolls engine"
8:5:18. 5.25–7.0 pm		do	Lt Walburne	95m	8,000'	St Omer, Calais, Boulogne	Landed at Beauvois
14:5:18. 6.45–7.20 pm		do	Lt Norris	35m	5,000'		
18:5:18. 7.5–10.20 m		do	Lt Boer	195m	16,000'		Raid Aulnoye 2 – 112lbs
19:5:18. 6.20–9.0 pm		do	Lt Elliott	160m	15,000'		" " 2 "
20:5:18. 8.0–10.40 m		do	do	160m	15,500'		" " 2 "
4.45–6.55 m		do	do	130m	15,000		" Marquain 10–25lb
4.25 – 20:5:18		do	do	—	—		Crashed – struck another DH4
21:5:18 11.0–1.10 am		do	Lt Grey	120m	15,000		Raid Varssennaere 8–25lb
10.55–1.15 am		do	do	140m	15,000		" Valenciennes 8–25lb
23:5:18 6.55–9.25		do	do	170m	15,000	Very cloudy – struck Coast & flying at 200 ft reached Fruges & landed in darkness	" Varssennaere 2–112lb
29:5:18 6.20–8.45		do	do	135m	15,500		" Valenciennes 10–25lb
30:5:18 6.50–9.5		do	do	135m	15,000		" Aulnoye 10–25lb
11.45–2.25		do	do	160m	15,000		" " 2–112 lb
21:5:18 5.0–7.45		do	do	165	16,000		" " 2–112 lb
1:6:18 5.45–12.0 am		do	do	195	15,500		" " 2–112 lb
2:6:18 8.40–11.0 m		do	do	140	15,000		" Ruoigny 2–112 lb
1.40–5.30 pm		do	Johnson	230	17,000		Photos – Aulnoye (lost in clouds 22 photos)
				2405 Mins			

Percy Bufton's log book for the period from 6 May to 2 June 1918, showing he flew on roughly two days out of three in that period. All the flights were in a DH 4, most lasted for between 2 and 3 hours, the majority were flown at 15,000 feet and involved a raid dropping bombs weighing a total of circa 250 lbs, as either two 112lb bombs or ten 25lb bombs. (© Jan Beckett)

By September 1919 Percy was back in the UK. He spent a month at 46 Training Depot, possibly waiting to see if he was going to be an instructor. By 5 November, however, Percy was back in Llandrindod, and he was demobbed on 19 November.

Another who joined the RFC relatively late in the war was Percy Badham Yates. Born in Kington in Herefordshire to William and Eliza Badham Yates on 15 September 1893, by 1911 he was working in Presteigne as a photographer, and that year he joined the First Battalion of the Hereford Regiment Territorial Force at Knighton. He attended week long training camps in 1911, 1912 and 1913 as well as regular drill nights and occasional weekend exercises. On the outbreak of the First World War Percy did not take the home defence option that would have allowed him to serve in the UK, but readily signed up for overseas service. As it was, the Herefords stayed in the UK for the rest of 1914 and early 1915, carrying out further training. Then in July 1915 the regiment was engaged in the Gallipoli campaign, which Percy survived, though he may have been wounded or have suffered from frostbite. He spent much of 1916 back in the UK, where he married Elizabeth Smith, and then, in the autumn he applied for and was accepted into the RFC. In early January 1917 he was with the Royal Flying Corps in Farnborough with the initial rank of air mechanic third class. In July he was promoted and posted to the No.9 Training Depot at Shawbury in Shropshire, where he spent nearly a year before embarking for France on 22 September 1918. In October he arrived at the headquarters of 80 Wing which was comprised of several highly successful squadrons. With the ending of the war, Percy elected to stay on and help with the clean up effort in France, only returning to the UK in March 1919. He then spent a year on the reserve list of what was now the Royal Air Force before leaving the RAF and returning to Radnorshire to resume his photography business. When war was looming again in 1939 Percy again enlisted in the RAF, and it seems that his photography skills were used in one of the many photo interpretation units.

As the case for Percy Badham Yates shows, not all those who joined the RFC became pilots, for the aircraft needed ground crews to maintain and service them. Another who joined the RFC from the ranks of the Hereford Regiment and worked on servicing and repairing aircraft was John William Roberts, who was born in Knighton on 18 May 1881 and preferred to be known as Will. Knighton was a prosperous and bustling town at the turn of the century and Will set up his own carpentry firm making all types of furniture including commodes. He also acted as an undertaker. In 1909 he married Fanny Louisa. A year later he was serving in the Knighton detachment of the first battalion Hereford Regiment, a Territorial force, one of the many such battalions that were being set up to train men in home defence. The territorial battalions offered much the same training as the regular army but allowed men to stay in their home area and more importantly carry on working or in Will's case running his own business. When war with Germany was declared in 1914, Will would have been given the option to serve in the home defence force and not be sent overseas, an option only open to men who had already served. Choosing to stay, he served in the Knighton territorial detachment of the First Battalion the Hereford Regiment until 1917, when he joined the Royal Flying Corps. Many members of the Hereford Regiment had already served overseas and as losses mounted and conscription was brought in, the option of staying at home was withdrawn. Given his age – he was now 35 – and the

The Knighton detachment of the 1st Battalion of the Hereford Regiment in 1910.
John Roberts is third from the left in the third row. (© Malcolm Evans)

Brothers in arms. John Roberts is seated,
in the middle is his brother and on the left
his brother-in-law. (© Malcolm Evans)

Taken with RFC colleagues at Farnborough in
Hampshire, John Roberts is on the right.
(© Malcolm Evans)

fact that he had a skill (most of the aircraft were them made of wood, so a skilled carpenter would have been invaluable), the move to the RFC may have been motivated by a desire to stay in the UK. Just before he left Knighton, Will took out an advert in the local paper announcing to all his customers that the business was still carrying on.

On 29 January 1917 he started his training in aircraft repair. His rank is listed as air mechanic second class and he was posted to No.5 Aircraft Repair Depot (ARD). The ARDs were somewhat misnamed. They didn't just repair aircraft, but salvaged parts and in many cases practically built the machines. They were also very innovative, working closely with pilots on modifications to aircraft. Will spent most of the rest of the war with either No.1 ARD based just south of Farnborough or No.5 ARD at Henlow in Bedfordshire, and it was January 1919 before he was discharged. This may have been simply because returning aircraft were all moved through the ARDs before being sent on to service as training aircraft or sold off as war surplus. He did eventually return to his business in Knighton, and enjoyed a quiet life and retirement in the town. He died in Knighton in June 1957, at the age of 76.

Another who worked on repairing aircraft was Arthur James Colcombe. It is known that he was born in the parish of Llanelwedd in about 1890, but the exact date is unclear – even his army service record does not carry his full date of birth.

Arthur and his elder brother Robert were born into a working class background, their father (William) having at one time been the gardener to the Revd George B. Sharpe, who lived with his sister in the vicarage next to

Arthur Colcombe, RFC.
(© Author's collection)

Robert Stedman Lewis was born at Nantgwyllt in the Elan Valley. He attended the Military College at Woolwich in 1915 and then joined the Royal Field Artillery. In the course of the First World War he was to spend three years with the Royal Flying Corps. It is not clear what sort of service he saw, or why in 1919 he transferred back to his old army unit. In 1922 he joined the Indian Army. He was appointed Director of Ordnance Services and granted the rank of temporary Major General. He remained in India throughout the Second World War, retiring in 1948, the year that India gained its independence. He was awarded an OBE and later a CB. In 1949 he and his wife moved back to Wales and lived in Y Neuadd, about a mile from Rhayader on the Elan Valley road. In 1951 he was appointed High Sheriff of Radnorshire. (From W.I. Scrapbooks held at Powys County Archives)

Llanelwedd church. By 1907 the family were living at Wellfield Lodge in Llanelwedd. Arthur was working as an apprentice at Tom Norton's bicycle works in Llandrindod Wells and had also joined the Brecknockshire branch of the South Wales Borderers Territorial force (Volunteers). The volunteers would have had to attend the garrison in Brecon for drill and exercises conducted much along the same lines as the regular troops. By 1911 Arthur had become a qualified chauffeur and his brother Robert was also working for Tom Norton as a bicycle repairer.

As a volunteer in the reservists, Arthur would almost certainly have been called up on the outbreak of the First World War. On 27 July 1916 he transferred to the Royal Flying Corps, where he is listed as a motor mechanic, but there is not much information in his service file. For every qualified pilot in the RFC there were around a dozen mechanics, riggers, engineers and other ground crew, and it is more than possible that his peacetime skills as a mechanic and driver made him an ideal choice for ground crew. Arthur was posted overseas to France on 27 September 1916 and remained there until 15 July 1919. He returned to the peace and quiet of Llanelwedd, where he married Gladys James in 1925. Arthur remained in Radnorshire for the rest of his life, and died in March 1959.

3   It runs in the Family

The Hamars

In some Radnorshire families the desire to join the RFC was not restricted to a single son; one such family were the Hamars, who had a thriving wholesale grocery business, supplying customers and village shops within a 30-mile radius of Knighton. It was a long established business and the Hamars were well known. William Hamar was also a keen sportsman, with a reputation of having the fastest horses in the town and a passion for speed which he seems to have passed on to his four sons, Arthur, Ernest, Alfred and Richard, who were known locally as the 'Mad Hamars' for, among other things, careering around the lanes of Radnorshire on a series of fast motorbikes. One young Radnorshire lady, who rather nervously agreed to be Alfred's pillion passenger, recalled being left 'sitting on air' as Alfred made a particularly fast getaway on his motorbike. Alfred also had a Model T Ford, in which he would shuttle between his three cinemas, situated in Knighton, Presteigne and Rhayader, so it seems he inherited his fathers' business head as well.

Alfred enlisted in the Royal Flying Corps on 2 December 1915 and by April 1917 was a lieutenant in 55 Squadron. This squadron is first mentioned in the record books on 1 May 1916 when, along with 34 Squadron, it came under the command of the 8th Wing. The squadron was based at Castle Bromwich and listed as having three serviceable British designed Blériot Experimental 2c planes, but no officers to fly them. Towards the end of June 1916 the squadron moved to Lilbourne near Rugby, by which time they had not only a squadron commander but a full complement of officers, including eight under instruction in aviation.

No.55 was primarily a bomber and training squadron, and the time at Lilbourne was spent training the pilots for bombing raids. The battle of the Somme was drawing to a close and so far the British flyers had maintained supremacy over the German airforce. However, it was becoming apparent that the Royal Flying Corps would have to send many more planes to France if this situation was to continue.

In January 1917 No.55 became the first squadron to receive the new De-Havilland 4 aircraft, a powerful two-seater machine with a 250hp Rolls Royce engine. It was to be used for bombing and reconnaissance duties. Both new and veteran pilots had to be trained to fly this new machine, so it was the middle of February before the squadron was ready to go overseas.

On Sunday 4 March 1917, with only the squadron's medical officer and his dog to see them depart, 55 Squadron left for France. They crossed to Boulogne the next day and eventually arrived at their destination of Fienvillers late on the night of 6 March. The aeroplanes had started to be flown over on 5 March, but weather severely hampered the crossing and it was not until 15 March that the first four planes were seen at Fienvillers. It must be remembered that there were no transport planes capable of carrying large numbers of passengers, so a squadron moved in much the same was as any other army unit.

Alfred's first three weeks in France were spent practising formation flying and learning the layout of the local countryside as seen from the air. A first patrol along the front line was carried out on 3 April 1917. On 5 April, seven De-Havilland 4s crossed the line into enemy territory, but Alfred was not on this raid. Six of the planes carried and dropped bombs (ten 20lb bombs from each plane) on enemy targets. Captain Davidson crashed on the return journey but was not badly hurt, Lieutenant Burd ran out of petrol and landed close by, whilst the seventh aircraft had engine trouble early on and returned safely to base. All in all 55's first day of active flying was reported as a success.

The following two days for the squadron were also deemed a success, with all bombs falling on or near their targets. An anti-aircraft battery went up in smoke and a railway was severely damaged, whilst useful reconnaissance information was brought back on every flight. It is more than probable that Alfred would have taken part in some of these raids.

On 8 April, Easter Day, six DH4s set out to bomb Valencionnes, whilst another four were sent to bomb a château at Hardenpont near Mons. (Many such châteaux were used as headquarters by the generals and minor princes who were in command of the German army.) Alfred was the pilot of one of the four aircraft on this second mission. The formation had only just crossed the line when one of their number turned back with engine trouble. The remaining three aircraft, including Alfred and his observer, 2nd Lieutenant John Adrian Myburgh (a South African pilot who had joined the RFC in 1916), dropped their bombs and were on the return journey when they were 'jumped on' by a large number of German aircraft, whilst an anti-aircraft battery also fired on the formation. The three aircraft were soon in trouble and Alfred, although injured, flew as fast as he could back to base, but crashed close to the aerodrome, sustaining further injuries.

He was carried from the wreckage and was able to impart valuable information, including details of a hitherto unknown enemy airfield, before being taken to the New Zealand Stationary Hospital. Lieutenant Hamar died at the hospital at 3.50pm that afternoon. His commanding officer Major Jack Baldwin later described the circumstances of his death as 'one of

2nd Lt Alfred Hamar, RFC.
(© Author's collection)

the finest acts of endurance I have heard of in this entire war'. Two days later Lieutenant Myburgh also died of his wounds. They were both buried at the St Pierre cemetery in Amiens, and Alfred is also remembered on his family's grave in Knighton cemetery.

Of the two other aircraft that Alfred had been flying with, one crewed by Lieutenant R.A. Logan and his observer 2nd Lieutenant F.R. Henry was shot down. They survived the subsequent crash but were taken prisoner. The fate of the other pilot, Lieutenant B. Evans and his observer 2nd Lieutenant B.W. White was never discovered. They were posted as missing in action, but no report of a crash was ever received. They were subsequently presumed dead.

Alfred was never to know that the aeroplanes he outran belonged to the infamous Jasta 11, better known to us now as 'Richthofen's Flying Circus' commanded by the Red Baron (so called because he painted his plane bright red) Manfred Von Richthofen.

Alfred's youngest brother, Richard was born on 23 November 1895. In 1913, at the age of 17, he emigrated to America. Settling in Detroit, his trade was initially listed as civil engineering, but by May 1916 he gave his occupation as a bond salesman and trustee of the Bonbright Trustee Security Company. On 17 November 1917, two weeks before his

22nd birthday, he joined the Royal Flying Corps CW (Canadian Wing) in Toronto (which is why his obituary probably suggested he had emigrated to Canada rather than the US). He was posted almost immediately to the Beamsville School of air gunnery. Richard was initially an Air Mechanic 3rd class, but was soon selected for observer training.

The RFC became part of the RAF on 1 April 1918. A few days later, on 3 June, Richard was taking part in gunnery practice. For this particular exercise he was in the back seat of the aeroplane. He and the pilot, Lieutenant W.E. Lambert took off on what was supposed to be a routine training flight, but for reasons unknown, during the manoeuvres the plane nose-dived into the ground. Both men were badly injured, Richard dying of his injuries the next day, whilst Lt W.E Lambert survived. Richard Hamar was buried in the Mount Osbourne Cemetery in Beamsville, with full military honours, in a ceremony which over 1,000 people were estimated to have attended. He is also remembered on the family grave in Knighton.

*Richard Hamar, RAF.
(Courtesy Brecon & Radnor
Express via the Radnorshire
Museum)*

The Millichamps

The Millichamps, were a large family who lived in Presteigne, and three of the sons – Frederick Oakley, Bertram Harley and Sydney Walter Ian – saw service in the air during the First World War.

Frederick was born on 13 January 1897. When he left school he worked as a motor mechanic in his family's garage, G. Millichamp Motor Works, in Presteigne. He also became a stationary engine operator for the Great Western Railway. Fred loved tinkering around with engines and would take motorbikes to pieces and conduct experiments with radio and even electricity. His father was a gunsmith, watchmaker and inventor, and Fred seems to have inherited his passion for mechanical things.

On 2 May 1914 Frederick decided to join the army. Although there was tension in Europe there was as yet no inkling of the war that was to come. The details of Fred's army career are now lost to us, but on 14 August 1916 he transferred to the Royal Flying Corps where he became a gunnery and weapons instructor. Shortly afterwards, Fred and his father, Charles, took out a patent on a new type of loader for loading ammunition into a machine gun, their design apparently knocking a minute and a half off the time taken to load the gun. They sent the design off to the War Department but heard nothing. For almost two years Charles continued to send off letters and drawings but received no response, and eventually he went with Fred to the War Department only to be told that the boffins had indeed seen the design ages ago, and had sent a reply saying that the design would not be taken up.

In the meantime Fred, now a sergeant, had settled down to his instructor's job. It seems likely that he had had a similar role in the army, as there is mention in his service record of a refresher course at a gunnery school where he underwent training on the Lewis gun, a common weapon fixed to aircraft. He was to spend the rest of the war in this role, moving between various gunnery schools in the United Kingdom. Towards the end of the war it seems that Fred decided to continue with the newly formed RAF and he learned to fly, receiving his pilot's licence at the Military Flying School, Colney, London on 1 November 1918. The war was about to end and up to this point Fred seems to have survived it unscathed, but 23 days after he learned to fly he appeared before a war pension committee to be assessed for the award of a silver war badge. This was only given to people whose discharge was of a medical nature and had been caused when on active service. Though the process took some time, Fred was sure he would be pensioned out and decided to go home for Christmas, leaving his base at 11am on 21 December 1918 and returning on 30 December to discover that he had been posted Absent Without Leave. He was docked ten days pay. Just two days later his medical discharge came through and by 11 January 1919 Fred left the Royal Air Force with a weekly pension of 26 shillings. The nature of Fred's disability is not known, but he returned to Radnorshire where he and his father continued inventing things. In 1921 they patented a new weapon for shooting down airships, but they were told flatly that the days of airships were over. He later became an electrician in Leatherhead in Surrey and in 1927 he married Renée Pickthorn. The couple had two sons Billy and Jack. Fred

A photograph of Frederick Millichamp taken for his pilot's licence on 1 November 1918.
(© ancestry.com)

re-enlisted in the Second World War, but although he wore his wings he did not fly again and was pensioned out in 1942. He died in Surrey in 1973.

The second of Charles's sons, Bertram, was born on 2 January 1899 and joined the Civil Service on leaving school. In 1917 he joined the Royal Naval Air Service (RNAS) and trained to become a radio operator on a seaplane. The RNAS had started experimenting with seaplanes as early as 1913 at their base in Felixstowe under the command of Captain C.E. Risk, and it was indeed a risky business.

Bertram was interviewed in the 1970s and told some hair-raising tales of his time with the RNAS. On one patrol on the morning of 24 April 1917 while U-boat spotting in a H.12 flying boat, they had been airborne for about 50 minutes when one of their two engines simply cut out. The pilot, Lieutenant Galpin, had to make a hasty and bumpy forced landing in the sea. Bertram recalls that the plane was put down so sharply and with so little warning that he hit his head on the hull. The flying boat bobbed about uselessly for half an hour or so before a British destroyer spotted them and came alongside and took Bertram and two other crew members on board. The pilot remained behind as the flying boat was taken in tow. Bertram had just settled down to a hearty breakfast of ham and eggs in the petty officers mess when a call was put out for him to return to the aircraft. The transfer back was made at what Bertram described as dangerous speed, due to the fact that the destroyer captain did not like hanging about hove to in open sea during wartime.

Once on board he found a frantic Lt Galpin, who was not only trying to steer the boat but also bailing out a considerable amount of water. Bertram's wireless equipment included an aerial which could be let down through a length of copper tubing in the base of the hull and trailed along behind the aircraft. This 2 inch diameter pipe would normally be covered with a cap when the aerial was retracted, but it seemed that the cap had been torn off the pipe. The destroyer had been pulling the flying boat through the water at a considerable rate of knots and seawater was being forced up through the tube at an alarming rate. As the destroyer got underway once more, Bertram crouched over the hole and pressed down hard first with one hand then the other. It stopped the water but the pressure involved meant his arms were soon becoming too tired to carry on. He tried pressing his foot over the pipe, awkward as it was in the cramped corner under his equipment. There was not enough give in his military boots to stop the flow of water, however, so his next ploy was to remove his boots and stick his stockinged foot over the hole. This worked a treat, but he now had to keep the water out for the two hours it took to get the flying boat towed back to Felixstowe.

At 8am on 10 May 1917 Bertram and crew set off once again on a submarine-spotting patrol over the North Sea. The entire crew were mystified to see what looked like a ship's funnel protruding from the waves belching smoke, the funnel appearing to be proceeding along at quite a pace. After a short conference they decided it must be a new type of steam-driven submarine. To the best of their knowledge this was not something the Royal Navy had, but they decided to send it a signal anyway. When the mystery vessel failed to respond they decided to bomb it.

Their flying boat (serial number 8667) was equipped with four bombs which the second pilot now released. Three dropped and one got stuck in the rack, but his aim had been poor and the crew could not even claim a near miss. The mystery vessel carried on unperturbed, not altering its course or speed. Shortly afterwards, they came across four British warships going full speed towards the Belgian coast. One of the ships sent up a Morse code message by searchlight: 'Can you see the enemy?' Bertram signalled back 'No, but just bombed a submarine'. The four warships carried on their way and a little further on Bertram and his crew saw that the British warships were chasing 11 German destroyers, one of which dropped a decoy smoke canister over the side. These canisters were designed to fool the Royal Navy into thinking they were looking at a ship's funnel on the horizon. The canister bore a remarkable resemblance to their steam-powered submarine, and the mystery was solved. A minute later Bertram happened to glance out of the rear window and saw to his horror a German plane right on their tail; it was a small fighter plane and easily capable of out-manoeuvring the heavy and ponderous flying boat. Bertram's heart skipped a beat as it was the first time he had seen the crosses that marked the German aircraft so close up. Bertram as wireless operator and the flight engineer both doubled as air gunners and if they were attacked it was part of their job to climb out on the wings of the aircraft and man the two Lewis machine guns that were strung between the wing struts. The only safeguard to stop them being blown off was a wire attached to their belts. Keeping one eye on the German fighter, they had started to get themselves ready to crawl out when they realised that they were not wearing belts to which they could attach the safety wires. It was with great relief that they saw the fighter turn away and head straight for the Belgian coast. Bertram further recalled that not only was there danger in crawling out on to the wing but that more than one unlucky air gunner had shot up the tail of his own plane as they swung the guns wildly around in a dog fight.

At noon on 29 May 1917, Bertram and his crew once more set off on patrol. After two hours of flying in worsening weather they decided to call it a day and were turning for home when Lieutenant Gordon, the second pilot, called back to him, 'Here wireless, take a look below.' Looking out of the main hatch Bertram saw almost immediately below them the broken float of a seaplane with two figures on it. One was lying still but the other was trying to wave. Gordon then said to all of the crew, 'Well, what about it? Are you prepared to have a go?' Bertram said 'Yes' immediately. Hodgeson the pilot and Anderson the flight engineer both agreed, so Bertram quickly radioed their intention back to Felixstowe. The plane was only designed to take off and land in the calm waters of the harbour, but seeing fellow airmen in trouble had spurred them on to action without thinking clearly about the danger. Down they went and hit the sea with an almighty wallop and taxied straight for the float. One of the men managed to jump almost onto the nose of the flying boat and was quickly pulled in by Gordon. The other much weaker man attempted the same jump but missed and was left clinging to a wire that ran from the nose to the wing-tip, suspended a couple of yards from the hull, Bertram climbed out on to a bulge just below the main hatch and at full stretch managed to grab the man's arm. Bertram then not only managed to steady himself sufficiently to pull the rescued airman through the water towards the boat, but was then able to lift the man straight onto the bulge and push him through the hatch in almost one go, a feat he later said should have been physically impossible even given the fact that he was an extremely fit 18-year-old. As the crew rushed to get the two

'Almost a Resurrection' by C.R. Fleming-Williams
gives an impression of the actual rescue.
(© Imperial War Museum, ref 1221)

rescued airmen some brandy, Bertram was in for another surprise, as one of the men calmly said 'Well, hullo Milli, fancy meeting you!' He had rescued a friend, G.L Wright, with whom he had trained at the Cranwell radio school. Wright and his companion Flight Sub-Lieutenant H.M. Morris had been sitting on the float for five days. Six days earlier they had crash-landed on the sea but their plane had gradually broken up overnight and they had been left with only the float as a sort of metal raft. The only supplies they had were a tin of Horlicks tablets and they had eaten one each in the morning and one at night. As for drinking, they had drunk sea water. Bertram expressed astonishment at this as they had been told time and again during training that if you drank sea water you would go mad. Wright replied, 'I think we did go a little mad. After three days we threw the pistol overboard or we would have been tempted to end it all.' The flying boat was still bobbing about in the water as the two rescued airmen were made comfortable ready for the journey home. Morris had slipped into a deep sleep but Wright muttered how bumpy the flying was that day. Bertram hadn't the heart to tell him that the bumping was actually the waves, that they had not taken off yet, and were not likely to do so any time soon.

As they had landed in the wreckage-strewn sea something had knocked a hole in the hull and they were taking on water rapidly. Bertram and Anderson set about frantically bailing, using a toolbox from which they had hastily torn the lid, Bertram scooping up the water then passing the box to Anderson, who emptied it over the side. Not only was their effort insufficient, but Anderson was getting very seasick with the bobbing up and down. He clambered forward and consulted with Gordon, who was at the controls. They concluded that it would be near impossible to get off a sea this rough, but Bertram pointed out that if they didn't they would sink – so they decided to 'have a smack at it', or at least try and go hell for leather towards the shipping lanes and contact a friendly vessel. Gordon set off at full throttle and they bounced along the waves ever faster, with spray and bits of aircraft flying in all directions, but with no lift for what seemed like a lifetime – then all of a sudden they were airborne. Cheers broke out among the crew only to be silenced almost instantly as they smacked down on the water once more, smashing a float and their tail plane. There was now no chance of flying, but they felt that if the engine would keep going they could stay afloat and reach the shipping lanes. A fine mist started to descend and at almost the same time Bertram noticed a sinister shape in the water. They were passing through a mined area. Suddenly their spirits soared as they saw funnels of three ships on the horizon, and when the plane was near enough for the crew to see that they belonged to British ships, Bertram fired a green distress flare. The ships all turned away, obviously thinking it was a ruse from an enemy submarine. The crew valiantly tried to keep the plane afloat, and then all of a sudden they saw a tramp steamer heading straight for them. The *Orient* was coming to investigate, and sure enough she hove to alongside and threw them a rope. Bertram was so anxious to be rescued that instead of waiting for the sailor to haul in the rope and get a better throw he hopped straight out and ran along the curved wet hull – another one of the strange and almost impossible things that happened that day. Morris and Wright were almost unconscious as they were winched aboard the *Orient*. The flying boat crew helped the sailors tie a tow rope on the plane and then scrambled up a ladder and on to the deck. Later that day Bertram and his crew transferred to the *White Lilac*, a steam drifter (a type of fishing boat), which got them back to Felixstowe at around 10pm that night.

For their action Bertram, Hodgeson, Anderson and Gordon were all awarded the Sea Gallantry Medal for saving life at sea. The award had been instituted in 1855 and had three degrees of award – gold, silver and bronze – depending on the severity of risk to life. There is no record of a gold medal ever having been issued, and Bertram and the crew each received the silver medal.

Bertram Millichamp, his mother and future wife collecting his Sea Gallantry Medal. (© R. Millichamp via R. Pye)

The summer of 1917 saw Bertram make many more sorties out over the North Sea in all kinds of weather. Some were uneventful, some a little more hair-raising, like the time they fought a headwind all the way back to the English coast and landed near an anchored navy ship near Deal just as the engines spluttered and died as they ran out of petrol. As the sailors were passing across a steady stream of two gallon tins of petrol to refill their flying boat, one of them casually asked the pilot 'So how many did you get then?' 'How many what?' was his bemused reply. 'Jerry planes, of course' came back the sailor, who went on to tell them that 17 German fighters had passed overhead just minutes before the plane had landed. The crew were pretty glad they hadn't seen them, as the seaplane would not have been able to manoeuvre much with its dwindling petrol supply.

Under normal circumstances the flying boats wouldn't have been out on 23 October 1917 as it was a foul day, but despite the weather two H12 flying boats were dispatched to try and find a reported submarine that had been picked up by a radio direction finding station. Bertram was not flying with the crew who had rescued the airmen back in May, but instead had Gooch and Perham as pilots and Sivyer as engineer. The flying boat got off to a very bumpy start and the whole crew were bounced around for about two hours, then the whole boat began to vibrate alarmingly and swing around to starboard. It soon became apparent that the starboard engine was malfunctioning and the boat was becoming unflyable. The pilot took the decision to ditch in the sea, which it hit with a tremendous crash and with the help of the engines immediately bounced back up about 200 feet into the air. The pilot shouted to Bertram to 'pull the rope', a Heath Robinson affair that was designed to counteract the plane spinning if an engine was out. It consisted of two ropes running from each side of the rudder along one side of the fuselage, and in theory it would allow a crew member to exert extra pressure on the rudder used to steer an aircraft and hopefully keep it from spinning. The ropes were badly tangled and Bertram took a guess and hauled with all his might. Unfortunately he picked the wrong rope and the plane nosedived straight back into the sea. The plane went down so fast that it trapped air in the hull and so fortunately it bobbed back up again just as quickly, although in the process it had dislodged or broken almost everything inside the hull; a Lewis gun dislodged from its mounting clipped Second Pilot Gooch, cutting his face as it went. He was not badly hurt but they were all very shaken. Bertram tried to inflate his life jacket and found that it had been used and the air cylinder had not been replaced, so it was useless. The Aldiss signalling lamp and the radio were likewise useless, as they had been thrown around and bits were now floating around in the waterlogged hull. The pilot called over to Bertram 'Well, wireless, what do we do now?' As it was the third time he had ditched, he was considered the expert among the crew.

There were no rubber dinghies aboard the planes in those days so the crew set about bailing out the hull and had to hope it would stay afloat until they were rescued. The pilot meanwhile sent off one of the two carrier pigeons they had on board with the message 'Crashed 8 miles off the North Hinder lightship'. The sea was very rough and the useless starboard engine had been torn off as they ditched, which meant that the now unbalanced plane was in danger of tipping over, and Bertram and engineer Sivyer had to crawl out on to the wing to act as a counterweight while the two pilots bailed. An hour later the pilot decided to send the other pigeon with the same message, though Bertram tried to dissuade him as this would be their last hope of communication and, as he put it, he wanted to save the pigeon for a possible farewell message. Bertram attempted to rig up an aerial outside the hull but the pilot thought this was a waste of time and Bertram returned to acting as a counterweight; he and Sivyer took to lying full length across the wing to avoid being washed off. As darkness fell Perham suggested that Bertram try and fix the Aldiss lamp. Bertram had mentioned it earlier but the pilot, maybe hoping that they would not have to spend the night at sea, had made everybody concentrate on bailing. In the now near pitch darkness of the partly submerged hull he felt he had been given an almost impossible task. He groped around with freezing fingers and thanked God that some foresighted engineer had deeply engraved the positive and negative terminals on the batteries and he could still feel them with his numb fingers. The mended light cheered them up but they did not catch sight of any boat to signal. The long night passed in the heavy sea – they were all bitterly cold and saturated and there was little chance of sleep as they were either bailing out or lying on the wing to keep the shattered plane afloat. In the early hours Bertram climbed back into the hull to get out of the wind for a bit and as he was dog tired, hungry and miserable he settled down on his shattered seat and pretended to be asleep. Before long Perham asked him to go back outside and Bertram pretended not to hear. Gooch then piped up, 'Let the boy alone; do you know he's only 18 and he's lucky to be asleep out of this worry.' Bertram sent up a silent prayer and was to say afterwards that although they were all very British and didn't admit they were frightened, he would bet that they all prayed at times that night.

The next morning, stationed back out on the wing, Bertram noticed a dark shape in the distance whenever their boat bobbed up on a wave. He watched it for several minutes until he was sure that the shape didn't move and then, in the accepted naval manner, cried out 'Land Ahoy'. Sivyer, Gooch and Perham all took turns standing on the wing straining their eyes while Bertram tried to convince them he was right. Finally all four agreed they were heading for land. The tide was gradually taking them towards the land, but Bertram remembered that he had heard a story of two airmen who, when they thought they were safe, had been swept back out to sea, so a decision was made to try and start the remaining engine to propel them faster towards land. The effort was wasted, however, as they couldn't keep the boat straight, so they cut it off and trusted to the tide. A town was now becoming visible and they decided to send up distress flares. The Very pistol was retrieved, and Bertram and Sivyer found the driest spare cartridges they could and tried the pistol. By a miracle it worked, although they had to use green flares, not the regular red for distress. Fortunately it wasn't long until a torpedo boat came bobbing towards them. Not knowing where they were or which nationality might be coming to their rescue, Perham quickly threw the four Lewis guns and ammo over the side while Bertram put his radio and code books in a weighted box and threw them over too; they hoped that they might be taken for shipwrecked sailors and not be subject to internment. The torpedo boat that pulled up beside them proved to be a Dutch vessel with a Javanese captain, who was pleasant and started to help them on board and instructed his sailors to tie up the plane ready for a tow. Perham was having none of this, and he and Bertram kicked holes in the fragile hull before leaving. The flying boat didn't stay afloat long enough for it to be tied and the Javanese captain turned around and headed back towards land. It turned out that they were in the estuary of the River Scheldt.

The four of them were taken to Flushing where their plea to be treated as shipwrecked mariners was heard but not surprisingly rejected and they were interned. They were incredibly lucky to be prisoners of the Dutch. They were housed in hotels in the Hague and allowed considerable freedom – except the freedom to leave and rejoin the war. Queen Wilhelmina would often promenade in the parks accompanied by her footman, and it was known that if a group of men passed by and doffed their hats she would acknowledge them with a royal bow. Spotting her majesty one morning, Bertram decided to hang back from the crowd and stroll slowly along an almost deserted stretch of pavement. He drew level with the queen on the empty spot and got a royal bow all to himself. He would also see General Snijders, commander of the Dutch army and naval forces, riding around on a push-bike with his sword clipped to the side of the front forks.

It was in this way that Bertram passed the rest of the war. He was not to learn for many years that Flight Lieutenant Morris, whom Bertram had helped rescue the previous May, flew seven sorties over the North Sea to try to find them when their sea plane had been reported missing. In November 1918, when Bertram returned home to England, he was finally able to visit London, where King Edward VII presented him with his silver Sea Gallantry Medal.

After the war Bertram married Jane Ann Graham, a ballerina who went by the stage name Jennie Winifred Graham. He joined the Civil Service and went to work in the Colonial Office in whose service he was sent to Africa, but on the outbreak of the Second World War he returned to Britain and settled in Ludlow, Shropshire, not far from his Presteigne birthplace, where he became the manager of the local National Insurance office. Bertram and Jane had no children and Bertram died on 21 September 1979.

The youngest of the three brothers, Sydney, was born in Presteigne on 5 June 1900 and on leaving school he joined the Civil Service as a junior clerk. In September 1917 he too joined the RNAS but as he was still under 18 he was still considered a boy. Sydney trained to be a wireless operator in the same radio school at Cranwell where his brother Bertram

Sydney Millichamp,
(© R. Millichamp via R. Pye)

had also trained. On 1 April 1918 Sydney transferred to the Royal Air Force, as his other brother, Frederick, had done, but just 23 days later he fell ill, to be subsequently diagnosed with Filmid Phthisis, a form of non-viral tuberculosis. Sydney was released from active service on 25 May 1918 and returned home with a silver war badge and a pension, the badge denoting that the authorities concluded that he had contracted the TB while in the service of his country. It was 11 days before his 18th birthday.

Sydney married Lillian Victoria Bunker in 1922 and they moved to Aberystwyth, where they had two sons. In 1937 the Millichamps moved to London, where Sydney acted as the Air Raid Precaution officer for the Ministry of Supply. At the end of the war in 1946 the family moved back to Aberystwyth where Sydney, like his brother Bertram, became manager of the local National Insurance office. He retired in 1965 and died in 1982.

The Insall Brothers

The Insall brothers did not hail from Radnorshire, but Jack was to retire to the county, and died there in 1972.

Algernon John Insall, known to his family as Jack, was living in France just before the First World War broke out. His father had a thriving dentistry practice in Paris where Jack, his elder brother Gilbert, younger brother Cecil and sister Esme, had all been born. The family had seen first-hand the storm clouds gather over Europe and Dr Insall would discuss world events over dinner with his sons. In 1911, when the Germans sent the gun-boat *Panther* to Agadir in Morocco as a protest at France's rule of the country, Dr Insall was fully on the side of the future British Prime Minister David Lloyd George, who gave a strongly worded speech denouncing the move. Dr Insall watched closely as first one then another act of aggression was perpetrated by Germany against France. The boys would also talk with their fellow French students – Jack and Gilbert were at university, and Cecil was still at school – and loudly voiced the opinion that Britain would come to France's aid if Germany did declare war. The Bosnian Serb student Gavrilo Prinzip shot the heir to the Austrian throne, the Archduke Franz Ferdinand, and his wife on 28 June 1914. On 2 August 1914 German troops entered the Duchy of Luxembourg and also crossed into French territory shooting at the border guards.

The Insall family initially decided to stay in Paris, and Jack along with his father and his elder brother Gilbert joined a small group of British subjects who marched up and down the grand boulevards waving huge Union Jacks. However it soon became obvious that the German army had every intention of fully occupying France and Jack's mother reluctantly got out the dust sheets and started to shut up their Paris apartment. They handed back the keys to a tearful concierge and headed for the coast. It was far harder than they had imagined getting a boat out of France. Not just British nationals but also many French citizens with relatives in Britain were trying to flee the advancing Germans; there were also several wealthy Americans who were willing to pay well over the odds to get a boat to Britain and then home to America and safety. The French border guards were painstaking in their scrutiny of documents and Jack and his family endured endless hours of sitting on hard wooden benches while every document was checked and rechecked, but eventually they were allowed aboard the *Maid of Kent* heading towards Britain. The family intended to stay with relatives in Surrey, their father repeatedly assuring everybody that this was a temporary arrangement, Dr Insall being firmly in the 'this will be over by Christmas' camp. He was already discussing with his wife plans for reopening his practice and the boys resuming their studies before they got off the boat. In the dawn light Jack and Gilbert watched one of the ship's officers come on deck with a large blackboard. It bore a short message stating that Britain and Germany had been at war since 11pm the previous night.

In the years that the Insall family had lived in Paris, Jack and Gilbert had spent many a happy hour cycling out to the airfield at Issy-Les-Moulineaux close to their home in Auteuil. It was on this ground that Blériot prepared for his famous crossing of the English Channel and the boys had the opportunity more than once to peer excitedly into his cockpit. It was also on that field that the Farman brothers built and flew their experimental biplanes, and before long both Gilbert and Jack had managed to secure a joyride. Gilbert actually flew twice with Maurice Farman. Nevertheless, when the call for volunteers came the Insall brothers set about enlisting in the university and public schools brigade of the Royal Fusiliers, using their Sorbonne connections. They put their names down and two days later found themselves in Hyde Park. Next it was back to Surrey and training establishments at Epsom, then Ashstead and Leatherhead. For the next six months they marched around, did drill and learned to bayonet straw dummies. Then one fine spring morning in

1915 they listened as one of the officers read out an urgent appeal for volunteers to join the Royal Flying Corps and be trained as pilots. Neither Jack nor Gilbert took all that much notice of the announcement, but that night in the mess they regaled their fellow soldiers with tales of flying and this led to the sort of nudging and whispering common in groups of people who wish to draw attention away from themselves and on to a mate if they think it will get them out of a sticky situation. Noticing the rumpus their platoon commander came over to see what the fuss was about, and on learning that the boys had flying experience he immediately pounced on them, waving more War Office communiqués and telling them this would be right up their street. As far as the boys could see they were the only potential candidates among the several hundred men on parade that morning and Jack was doing some very fast thinking when Gilbert piped up, 'Well, what about it?', and before realising it Jack had replied, 'Why not?'

That evening on their way back to their billets they were met by the adjutant, who gave them the necessary forms to fill in for the transfer to the Royal Flying Corps. On the forms they both put 'ascents' in the previous experience column whereas in reality Jack had only been up once and Gilbert had had two ten-minute flights. Their application was accepted and three weeks later they were told to hand in their uniforms and equipment and report to the commanding officer of the Royal Flying Corps station at Brooklands just outside Weybridge in Surrey. They also had an immediate promotion; they were no longer mere privates but acting 2nd lieutenants in the Royal Flying Corps (RFC). In their excitement Jack and Gilbert had neglected to mention their change of occupation to their parents and although there was never any remonstration from either of them, Jack was to learn later that his mother particularly had not been able to understand why they had chosen a course that would put them in even greater danger than being in the regular army.

In the early days of the Royal Flying Corps a mish-mash of army equipment and clothing were used. Just before the outbreak of the war the War Department had designed a new uniform for the RFC. It was still made of the same khaki material as the army uniforms, and featured a high-necked collar with the front of the uniform crossing over the wearer's chest to be fastened by a row of concealed buttons down the right-hand side. A wide brown leather belt similar to the army belt was used at the waist. The concealed buttons and crossover design were to stop anything catching in the many wires and braces that the airman had to negotiate in order to get into or out of an aircraft. The uniform resembled a certain ladies' fashion and became known as the maternity jacket. Jack and Gilbert and their fellow officers would have been issued with the tunic along with a pair of breeches and a belt and would have also been given an allowance of £70 in order to purchase anything else they might need. Pilots would often use this money for a leather flying helmet, large gauntlets and even fur coats to help keep them warm in the draughty open cockpits. The German pilot Manfred Von Richthofen (known as the Red Baron) was often seen wearing his mother's full-length fur coat while flying.

RFC men and machines had gone over to France with the British expeditionary force in 1914, leaving only a handful of men and machines in Britain. Although they had been provisionally accepted into the RFC, Jack and Gilbert would still have to gain their Royal Aero Club Certificate or 'Ticket', before they would be accepted onto the flying course.

Jack highly commended his two instructors (Sgt Porter and Sgt Wyatt) who took their life in their hands during every flight, as it had been known for a pupil pilot to go 'bonkers' and freeze on the controls, leaving the poor instructor to try and wrestle back control as the aircraft plummeted towards the ground. Jack's training was almost laughably brief. Firstly Sergeant Wyatt took him for a spin round the aerodrome explaining what the various levers did, then at around 500 feet above the ground, when all Jack could think of was how ridiculously small the oval of grass they had to land on was, Wyatt bellowed those chilling words, 'Why don't you take over?' The machine veered off course almost immediately but Jack soon had it back under control. After a few minutes Wyatt took back the controls but Jack, heart pounding, was almost frozen with terror. Later that night in the cosy bar of the Blue Anchor where the airmen were billeted, Jack took a more relaxed view of his trip. Two days later he was back in the plane, this time in the front seat, with Sgt Porter telling him to start the engine. Then the instruction came to 'Go ahead' and Jack pulled the throttle lever right over. The machine let out an incredible roar but over the noise Sgt Porter managed to scream, 'What the bloody hell are you doing? You'll tear the engine out of the bleeping machine.' For one dreadful moment Jack thought he was going to be failed then and there, but clenching his teeth until they hurt he eased the stick back, waved away the chocks and soon felt the soft bump and wallow that told him he was airborne. The rest of the flight was uneventful, with Sgt Porter only having to make a slight course correction. Three more short flights with Sgt Porter and a 40-minute jaunt with Sgt Wyatt and it was decided that Jack was ready to take his Ticket. Jack did not readily agree with this decision, for the test was to be his first solo flight; until then he had always been conscious of a ready and steady pair of hands that could take over if something went wrong. (It must be remembered that the RFC were dangerously short of pilots, so it was not only Jack who underwent such brief training.) On 15 March 1915 Jack arrived at the Brooklands airfield to find his station commander Major Beck and a Royal Aero Club official waiting for him. The test comprised of being asked to fly up to 500 feet and describe two figures of eight, then land. Next he was to climb to 450 feet, switch off his engine and glide down to land on an adjacent tennis court. Jack had never glided before and over-estimated his switching off point. He also had no experience of mending a glide by making sweeping 'S' turns, so he just pushed the nose down and tried to shorten his glide. This method was frowned on by the establishment and his efforts led to a very heavy landing accompanied by splintering sounds as one of the undercarriage struts did its best to give way. Neither his commanding officer nor the Royal Aero Club official regarded this as any great disadvantage, apparently, and Jack was informed that he would receive his Ticket in due course. His elder brother Gilbert had gained his certificate the day before.

After receiving their Tickets, their training continued at Brooklands. This followed the same path as that of every other pilot, and as they had the enthusiasm typical of young men everywhere it was all an adventure. One morning just as they were finishing breakfast the pilot sitting next to Jack got up and announced he had a date with a Blériot. They heard the engine start and Jack, having finished his coffee, took out his pipe and strolled towards the door to watch the flight. Jack heard a commotion and the sound of a truck starting up and as he got to the door the station sergeant major staggered in white as a sheet, muttering 'Oh my God!' Jack caught his arm as he seemed likely to fall. The adjutant then appeared demanding to know what had happened. The sergeant major replied, 'He didn't have a chance, sir. He side slipped in and the windscreen caught him', he held his hand horizontally across his forehead, 'took the top of his head off like a boiled egg, sir. Bloody Blériots!'

Jack and his friends stood around shocked. Their breakfast companion was the first loss from their group. Sergeants Wyatt and Porter were not going to let panic and fear grip the group, however, and everyone was ordered up for extra flying all that day.

Soon it was time for the brothers to leave the Blue Anchor and Brooklands, to be posted to the training establishment where they would learn to fly the planes that they would be taking to France. They were sent to the RFC training base at Netheravon in Wiltshire and billeted close to a large contingent of army personnel who were getting ready to go overseas. The rumour was strong in the camp that they too would be in France by the summer. A captain who had served time in France and who was now an instructor on the Henri Farman biplane was charged with getting them ready for action. This officer had an extremely loud voice and a barrack room vocabulary and took great delight in tearing a strip off a pupil in earshot of those waiting to go aloft. Quite often the pupils would be busy at study in one of the many sheds on the edge of the aerodrome, engaged in learning Morse or navigation or some other vital part of their training, when they would hear their name called from a nearby hangar. The drill was for that pupil to immediately drop whatever he was doing and get into his flying helmet, coat and gloves, often while running full pelt towards the hangar. If he hadn't made it by the time the engine was turning over, the captain was quite likely to take off without him and he would go to the back of the queue and have to wait days for another chance to fly. Jack took to keeping his coat on during lessons, especially if he thought he was close to being called. He felt he was progressing as well as any other pilot on the squadron, but he did learn quite a lot about his mental capacity and parentage from the captain that he had hitherto not known. Other instructors at Netheravon were calmer and gentler and would endeavour to win a pilot over with patience and kindness, but Jack recalled that both types of instructor had their merits.

Whilst Jack and Gilbert shared a bedroom at Netheravon, it was generally considered not to be a good policy to have blood relations serving too close to each other, so the brothers were on separate flying courses. Jack was in B flight learning to master the Henri Farman while Gilbert in C flight was getting to grips with the Vickers fighter. Gilbert judged that he was more advanced than Jack and likely to get his wings quicker as the Vickers were the planes that they would be flying in France. A few days before Jack was to be switched on to the Vickers he followed the familiar circuit from Netheravon and around Sidbury Hill and back, now so at home in the Henri Farman that he was able to admire the view and comment to himself on various aspects of the army manoeuvres going on below. He had then done a few practice take offs and landings and was once more heading for the field when he realised he had come in 'short', that is, he had landed further over to the edge of the field than he had anticipated. He taxied forward but the edge of the field was rutted with old cart tracks and the next thing Jack knew, he was being catapulted through the air, with the Henri Farman plane following close behind. Jack was knocked briefly unconscious and when he came to he found his commanding officer Lt Col T.I. Webb Brown standing over him. Webb Brown had been standing on the tarmac watching various pilots when he had witnessed the accident and had come running over. He helped Jack to his feet and examined a nasty gash on his knee that was bleeding freely through his torn breeches. He offered a few kindly words and told Jack to go and find the medical officer while he took care of this lot. Jack limped off slightly dazed and was almost knocked over again by a group of mechanics and fellow learners who were rushing to the scene.

Jack was grounded for ten days and spent his time trying to increase his Morse speed and master the finger-slicing intricacies of wire-splicing. All the while he tried to put memories of his recent somersault behind him.

At the end of ten days' rest Jack found himself once more soaring over the rolling green hills of Netheravon, accompanied by the kind and patient Captain C.C. Darley.

Gilbert S.M. Insall.
(© Imperial War Museum, ref 1221)

With Darley uttering reassuring noises from the back seat Jack was once more at ease – until Captain Darley suggested they had had enough for one day and should land. Jack throttled back and began to feel butterflies in his stomach. As the ground got closer he felt physically sick and had to hand over control to Captain Darley. Without making a fuss Darley took off again and let Jack take the controls until he felt settled, but the same thing happened. After three abortive attempts at landing they decided to stop for the day and Darley suggested that Jack had another 48 hours rest. Two days later Capt Darley was waiting for him, nothing was said about the earlier attempts, and kind and patient as ever, he proceeded to get Jack to try and land the plane without panicking. Seven attempts later and Captain Darley landed the plane for him. The accident had clearly left Jack with a serious phobia. It also came at a time when the squadron was almost ready to leave for France. Jack therefore suggested that he should become an observer rather than a pilot. At this stage of the war, aeroplanes were largely two-seaters used for spotting troop movements, with a pilot flying the aircraft and an observer taking down the relevant compass bearings and details. Quite often the observer was also a trained pilot, though with less experience. Instructors who had seen active service were beginning to see the value of trained observers who could not only observe and keep a look out for the enemy but also act as machine gun operators (as warfare moved to the skies) and navigators, as well as being on hand to restart the engine if a pilot landed away

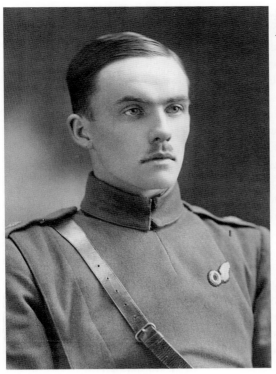

Algernon John (Jack) Insall.
(© M. Insall)

from help. His suggestion was accepted. Jack was far happier now that a pilot had the responsibility of landing the plane and settled down to learning all the other duties of an observer.

25 July 1915 was officially the day that 11 Squadron reached France, but some personnel such as their flight commander Captain L.W.B. Rees had already arrived and were making their new quarters ready. No.11 was to share an aerodrome with 4 Squadron at Vert Galand before No.4 moved on to new digs at Baizieux near Albert.

In theory a week or two should have seen the squadron up and operational, however the reality of life meant that No.11 was only really fully up to strength almost six months later. This did not mean they were not in action, far from it, but the 157 personnel, 32 motor vehicles and six motorbikes with riders ready to relay messages night or day that the War Department had decreed was the right and full complement for a new squadron took a little time to organise.

Jack started patrolling straight away and all the airmen got first-hand views of the increasing trench lines that were beginning to criss-cross the French countryside. Jack and Gilbert were already able to identify scenes of childhood ramblings that had been decimated by digging and shell fire. They also saw the lines of exhausted miners who would return each night from wherever the latest trench digging had been taking place.

Jack's first few months in France were relatively quiet. He experienced a few forced landings, although as he was not the pilot they did not affect him so much. Indeed, he even went to the expense of buying a luxury pigskin cigarette case to house the double row of Adulla no.11 (his favourite brand of Turkish cigarettes) to smoke while he and his pilot lit a fire and waited for rescue if the plane could not be restarted.

In the autumn of 1915 Jack and H.A. Cooper, an expert Maori pilot with whom Jack was always keen to fly, were preparing to make a forced landing on a promising-looking field along the road to Amiens. Jack was keeping a keen eye for obstacles such as tree stumps or wire, and seeing none they decided to land. One thing that was not clear from above however was that the lush looking field was in fact a bog. Immediately the wheels touched the surface they sank almost up to their axles, the sudden stopping of the front half of the plane leading to the back of the machine rising up in the air and flipping the whole aircraft over on its back. The whole head-over-heels manoeuvre happened so quickly that neither

Jack nor Cooper had time to do anything about it. Cooper, being much the taller of the two men, smacked his head on the grass, while Jack, imprisoned in his cockpit with his head between his knees, could only watch as his Lewis gun described a perfect arc and dug itself into the mud in front of him. Cooper was first out of the plane and tried to pull Jack out, and was still struggling when a breathless contingent of soldiers who had spotted the accident arrived from their billet a few fields away. The soldiers gathered about the machine and started to lift it off the slightly dazed Jack. He was a little dismayed to see that they had medics and two stretchers with them and was loudly telling them that these items would not be needed when the roar of another Vickers engine drowned out all communication. To their horror Jack and H.A. Cooper realised that a fellow airman was going to land and help. The two of them ran up the field trying to let the pilot know that it was too dangerous to land, but to no avail. The machine came to rest with a sickening and deafening crunch. This time the medics and stretchers were needed for both occupants. Neither man was killed, but they had to be evacuated immediately to the nearest casualty clearing station.

Gilbert meanwhile had endured many the same troubles as his brother in terms of forced landings and engine troubles, but was seeing far more action, having taken part in many more sorties over the German lines. On 7 November 1915, near the town of Achitet-Le-Grand, Gilbert was on patrol in his Vickers FB5 Gun Bus (serial number 5074) with T.H. Donald, air mechanic first class, when they engaged a German two-seater Aviatik aircraft. Gilbert kept at close quarters to the aircraft while Donald did his best to shoot it down, eventually damaging it sufficiently so that it was forced to make a bumpy landing in a field. Gilbert followed the plane down in case, as sometimes happened, it was faking a landing and would swoop up and chase them immediately they turned away. This time it was not a feint and the plane crashed. The crew, however, immediately jumped out and attempted to fire back at Gilbert and Donald using both the machine gun and the pilot's side arm. Gilbert took his aircraft down to around 500ft and Donald opened fire. One of the German airmen appeared to have been hit in the leg as the two men fled into the trees, one limping and the other helping him on his way. Donald dropped an incendiary bomb onto the downed German aircraft and turned for home. The Vickers had been hit in the petrol tank so Gilbert had to fly low and fast back over the German trenches. As soon as they were sure they had crossed back into British territory, Gilbert landed the stricken plane and he and Donald set about repairing the damage in order to get back to their base. However, they had only landed about 500 yards inside the British lines and as the night fell a bombardment started. Around 150 shells landed close to them as they attempted to repair their plane by shaded torchlight. Eventually Gilbert felt ready to try to take off. They made it and got back to base in the early dawn in time for breakfast. Jack had been told that his brother had not returned but he had wisely waited until the morning before he sent any message to his parents.

Almost a month later Gilbert was involved in a far more serious incident. As Jack landed after an uneventful trip he was told that his brother had again not returned from an early morning sortie. A few weeks earlier the rest of the Insall family had returned to Paris and as the days went by with no news of Gilbert, Jack was sent to Paris to tell his parents personally that their eldest son was missing. The next day the news appeared in the *London Gazette* and Gilbert and Donald were listed as missing.

Then just before Christmas Jack received one of the plain buff postcards which contained almost no information but just the bare facts. The facts were that Gilbert had been shot down and been taken prisoner. Having been injured, he was being looked after in a German hospital, and the Red Cross had been to see him. This welcome news came the day before Jack was to leave for London in order to marry his fiancée. While Jack was sitting in the St Ermin's Hotel on the morning of his wedding, 14 December 1915, he read in the paper that Gilbert had been awarded the Victoria Cross and that Donald would receive the Distinguished Conduct Medal. His joy was not marred by the fact that Gilbert was a prisoner and would not be able to receive his award in person. The full details of Gilbert's capture were not to come to light until much later. Gilbert had been shot down on 14 December 1915 after a very brief skirmish with Hauptmann Martin Zander and his air gunner. The action only took a few minutes and in that time both planes had strayed several miles into German territory. Donald, Gilbert's observer/gunner, had managed to get several shots into Zander's machine despite the latter twisting and turning frantically. Just as the German machine began to lose height one of its last shots went straight through the engine of Gilbert's machine and hit Donald in the leg. With faint hope Gilbert attempted to put the machine into a shallow dive and turned back towards the British lines in the hope that the machine would glide to safety. Moments later a German anti-aircraft gun opened up and a shell exploded just below the plane. Shrapnel peppered the underside of the machine; some of it lodged itself in Gilbert's spine and he briefly lost consciousness. Donald shouted to revive him and he came to, but had to put the plane down as soon as possible. They landed safely in the vicinity of Achiet, on the German side of the lines. Even with his injured leg, Donald managed to kick one of the incendiary bombs back towards Gilbert, who was trying to ignite it when a group of German troops, who had been watching the plane's descent, arrived through the trees. Both men scrambled from the machine as best they could in their injured state, and Gilbert threw the bomb into the cockpit in the hope that it would explode and destroy the plane. Realising they were injured the German officer summoned a medical party. One of the stretcher bearers seemed to recognise Gilbert, and it transpired that he and Gilbert had played university hockey against each other barely two years before, when the Sorbonne university team on which both Jack and Gilbert played had visited Hanover for a match.

Meanwhile, although still engaged on his observer duties, Jack was spending quite a lot of time in the squadron office. University educated and also careful and meticulous, he was trusted with quite a lot of the paperwork, including secret correspondence from HQ. Many of his fellow pupils from the Netheravon days had been killed, injured or sent back to the UK for rest and instructing duties, but Jack remained with 11 Squadron seeing men come and go, including pilots like Albert Ball who served briefly with 11 Squadron before becoming one of Britain's most famous First World War aces. Eventually, in May 1916, his commanding officer Major T. O'B. Hubbard (known in the squadron as Mother) raised the matter of his future. He asked if Jack had thought of returning to the UK and re-learning to fly, but Jack still felt that he lacked confidence in his ability to land. Hubbard seemed pleased by this reply for he immediately told him that a post of wing adjutant had arisen and that his name had been put forward. Jack decided to take the job and by way of celebration that afternoon he and Mother decided to take a kite up for a patrol of the lines. All the time they were airborne they never saw so much as a hostile speck in the distance. Jack would have had no idea that this was to be his last ascent in an aeroplane.

He reached his new posting two days later at Bertangles on the Somme. Here he was met by the rather austere adjutant who announced he was leaving in two days time but not to worry as they could do the hand over in a morning, so why didn't they nip of for a spot of tea? Almost immediately Jack noticed a difference in the way that the 'flying types' treated the office staff, and Jack had a nostalgic pang for all the high jinks that the airmen had got up to in his former billet, and the free and easy chats that accompanied their meals in the mess as the latest gramophone records filled any gaps in conversation with their tinny strains.

Jack was soon to be grateful however for his mainly administrative role at Bertangles, as shortly after his arrival one of the bloodiest battles of the war was to begin. Although Jack readily acknowledged that the airmen were shielded from the excesses of filth, death and deprivation that many of the soldiers faced, nobody in France in July 1916 would forget the battle of the Somme.

During this time Jack was getting sporadic mail from his brother Gilbert, who was still recuperating in the German hospital. All mail would be censored but over the course of several letters Gilbert was obviously outlining his intention of escaping before he was transferred to a prison camp. Jack's response to this was to use his influence as adjutant to get some of the military maps that had been put together by the reconnaissance teams and have them reduced to about the size of a birth certificate and printed on tissue paper; it was however some months before he was able to send them to Gilbert.

In the meantime the rest of the family were trying to carry on in their Paris apartment. Cecil, their younger brother, was still just under age to join up so he volunteered for Red Cross duties. The Red Cross had found his brother and managed to get communications to

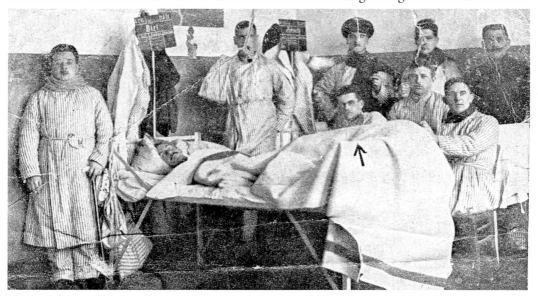

A photograph from a newspaper cutting showing Lt Gilbert Insall (indicated by the arrow) while in hospital and captivity in Cologne. (Courtesy of P. Kennedy)

OUR PRISONERS IN GERMANY.

A V.C. CRUELLY CONFINED.

TO THE EDITOR OF THE TIMES.

Sir,—Your readers will have noticed that a Commission is sitting in Holland, at The Hague, to deal with the different delicate questions concerning the treatment of prisoners of war. I am afraid they are not aware, however, of the scandalous treatment meted out to many of our officers and men in Germany.

It seems to me that it suffices for a German officer to write home making the slightest complaint on his treatment in England, for the German authorities to immediately seize the opportunity as a pretext to inflict what they are pleased to term "reprisals" on those of our own officers and men whom they hold as prisoners.

The eldest of my three sons, Lieutenant G. S. M. Insall, V.C., R.F.C., who has been a prisoner in Germany since December, 1915, wrote me from Crefeld on April 28 last, to say that he had just been removed to a cell, approximately 6ft. by 9ft. in size, with a small window fitted with an apparatus to shut out all light, but which at the time he wrote had not been brought into use. One hour's walk a day in a small yard shut in on all sides was the only exercise allowed him. He was sentenced to solitary confinement for 20 days with the door of the cell unlocked, to be followed by five months with the door kept locked. Seven other British officers were undergoing the same sentence, and my son had been instructed to tell me that this was a "reprisal" for supposed similar treatment to German officers in England. His letter reached me on May 29.

The German authorities were well aware that no protest could possibly be made before these officers had undergone a considerable part of their sentence.

This is the sort of thing our Minister in Holland has to contend with, when instructed to inquire into and protest against the measures adopted by the Germans towards some of our sons who have had the misfortune to fall into their hands. Without the slightest doubt his task would be materially facilitated were he strongly backed up by public opinion. The case of my son and his seven comrades is not an isolated one.

Will not the relatives of other prisoners having cognizance of similar so-called "reprisals," join in strengthening the hands of those in charge of the interests of our officers and men in Germany, by letting it be clearly felt that the British public is whole-heartedly with them in whatever measures they may decide upon, and uninfluenced by the vapourings of those who, not having felt the sting of the war, object to reprisals?

Yours faithfully,
GILBERT J. INSALL.
1, rue Blanche, square de la Trinité, Paris, June 28.

Letter to The Times by Gilbert J. Insall concerning the treatment of his son held by the Germans. (Courtesy of M. Insall)

the family, and now young Cecil, still referred to as the infant by his siblings, scoured the hospitals and aid stations using his fluent French to deal with both official and civilian personnel in order to find missing soldiers. His official role as Red Cross Searcher cannot be underestimated; the hospitals and aid stations were filled with badly injured servicemen, many suffering from shell shock, blindness, deafness or an inability to communicate. Often all he had to go on was a letter from a loved one simply saying that they had not heard from a son, father, husband or brother and asking the Red Cross if they knew what had happened to them. All too often 17-year-old Cecil would have to sit down after a long day interviewing soldiers and medical staff to compose a telegram to the family telling them the worst.

Meanwhile Gilbert was getting better and stronger, and had been promoted to full lieutenant while still in captivity. He had also attempted to escape.[1] Gilbert had written to Jack outlining his intention of increasing the distance of his morning walks ever further. This was the first of Gilbert's coded messages. Unfortunately he was sent from the hospital to a prison camp before he could put his plan into action. In camp Gilbert continued to send coded messages home asking for items and help, not just for his own but also for other prisoners' escape attempts. Gilbert learned that the Germans had discovered that the prisoners

Painting of a Vickers Gun Bus in action against an Aviatik by Jack Insall. (© P. Kennedy)

were manufacturing a sort of invisible ink that would be reactivated if the letter was heated, but he also observed that the officer in charge of censoring the letters would take each letter out of its envelope and hold it in front of the fire to see if any writing appeared but neglected to subject the envelope to the same treatment. Gilbert simply steamed open the envelopes, wrote his letter in the invisible ink on the insides, refolded and sealed the envelope and sent his innocent letter. Several communications were received by Jack and his father before Gilbert was able to send a coded message indicating that the envelopes should be heated. Luckily Gilbert's methodical mother had kept all his letters safe and had even asked Jack to send on any letters after he had read them.

While Jack travelled to and from Paris on adjutant duties he heard about a mysterious Captain K who was helping French and British soldiers escape from German camps. Through a long-drawn-out series of meetings and denials he eventually managed to meet Captain K and was surprised to learn that the captain not only knew all about two failed escape attempts by Gilbert but also that he was planning another one that was quite far advanced.

Jack returned to his parents' apartment with the news of Gilbert's new escape attempt and came up with a plan with Cecil and Esme, who were also living in the apartment, to

Painting of a Vickers Gun Bus by Jack Insall. (© P. Kennedy)

prepare a parcel of items that would aid the attempt. Cecil, who was particularly good at woodwork, came up with the idea of hollowing out some wooden dominoes. Dominoes in those days tended to be made of ebony or rosewood with a layer of ivory on top secured with a brass rivet. The idea was to take off the ivory, hollow out the wood, then reattach the ivory, thus providing a way of passing messages around the camp, and Jack devised a code to tell Gilbert about them. However the letter with the code never reached him. Gilbert was to tell them afterwards that he had scrutinised the dominoes but came to the conclusion that they had been sent as a cover for other items in the parcel and they were never used. Towards the end of August, Jack and his family received word that Gilbert had made it out of his prison camp near Hanover, but it was an anxious time for his mother, particularly as they heard nothing more for nine days. Later they heard that Gilbert and two companions had walked 150 miles into Holland and safety. Gilbert made it back to London for debriefing before returning to his family's Paris apartment late in September 1917, almost two years after his capture. Jack obtained a few days' leave and was able to take Gilbert to visit Captain K, who had helped him gain his freedom. Two weeks later Gilbert was summoned to Buckingham Palace to finally receive his Victoria Cross from the king; he was subsequently awarded a Military Cross for his successful escape. Gilbert returned to active duty in January 1918, when he was given the rank of captain and put in command of 50 Squadron.

Gilbert would make the air force his life. He was eventually promoted to the rank of squadron leader and was mentioned in despatches for action in Iraq in 1927/28. He served until 30 July 1945 and retired with the rank of group captain. He died on 17 February 1972 of bronchial pneumonia at the RAF hospital in Lincolnshire and is buried in Nocton churchyard in that county.

Cecil joined his brothers in the Royal Flying Corps just before it became the Royal Air Force on 1 April 1918 and became an airship pilot. Esme and his mother continued their Red Cross work helping the misplaced persons who flooded into Paris at the end of the war. Dr Insall kept his dentistry practice until his retirement.

Jack joined the reserve list of the RAF in 1923 and was finally pensioned out of the RAF on 24 October 1927, retaining his final rank of flying officer. This however was not the end of his association with aircraft, although he did not fly again. He flew a desk through most of the Second World War and became one of the founder members of the Imperial War Museum with special responsibility for its aircraft exhibits; he also became a noted aircraft historian. Jack spent his retirement at Church House in Llandegley. He died in December 1972 and is buried in the churchyard at Llandegley, Radnorshire.

Cecil Insall.
(© P. Kennedy)

4   Exhibition Flyers between the Wars

Autumn 1918 saw rumours that this year the war would indeed be finally over by Christmas. As October drew to a close the air was heavy with the talk of armistice and finally, on the morning of 11 November, word went up and down the lines that the war would stop at 11 o'clock that day. The morning air was heavy with shell fire as both sides seemed determined not to finish the war with any explosives left. Whistles were heard on both sides of the front signalling 11am and gradually the noise stopped. Tension filled the air as the men in the trenches struggled to come to terms with the silence. Many broke out hoarded rations, some got drunk and celebrated, others sat in silence unable to comprehend that it was over. Pilots and observers initially stood about aimlessly, but as the weather was good for flying some pilots suggested they went aloft for a look at what was happening. However, all flights had been grounded in case they were misconstrued as a breach of the truce.

During the course of the war the Royal Flying Corps had grown from a small band of men largely dismissed as a gimmick by many of the top brass into an elite and valuable force of war. Even the most stuck in the mud general was now able to recognise the value of an aerial force in wartime. By Christmas 1918, however, with the war over, mumblings were once more being heard as to the usefulness or otherwise of what was now the Royal Air Force. Soldiers, who could be put to work helping to rebuild Europe, were still expected to parade and show the uniform, be visible on the streets. But the air types were a different matter. Many members of RAF ground crew had gained highly useful transferable skills that would stand them in good stead in all manner of light industry after the war, but pilots and observers often found themselves first in the demob queue. This presented them with two problems. Firstly, there was next to no civilian aviation industry for them to join, and secondly, no job in Civvy Street was going to live up to the thrill and excitement of flying. For some the answer was obvious: scrape up some cash and buy an aeroplane. Whilst there were many surplus military planes now in existence, however, it would be another matter to find someone to pay them to fly. The British public were still by and large uneasy when it came to air travel, and there were also severe limitations to the number of passengers that could be taken up at one time. All this led to a not very promising career path for the ex-RAF pilot or observer.

A few brave pioneers were set on doing their best to change this situation and to that end the inter war years would become the age of exhibition flyers – men dedicated to

Letterhead for The Llandrindod Wells Air Port. (© Powys County Archives)

making air travel as common as getting on a bus. Radnorshire was not left out of this trend. Before the war the county had played host to some of the most famous names in aviation (as recounted in Chapter 1) and plans were afoot to revive flying in Llandrindod Wells. The Rock Park Hotel was again the scene of the action and the Ddole airfield was given the grand title of The Llandrindod Wells Air Port. Mr R.G. Sissons, an events organiser, acted as a liaison between the Northamptonshire Aero Club, for one, and the local council in matters pertaining to air displays in the county town, writing letters on notepaper headed 'The Llandrindod Wells Air Port'. The Northamptonshire Aero Club had established several links with the area, and many of their planes would soon hop back and forth between the two counties, followed by a series of private individuals who would use the landing ground.

One local man whose flying exploits at this time took him much further afield was George Pearson Glen Kidston. A small grave in the churchyard of St Peter's at Glasbury-on-Wye, adorned with a sundial and the words 'Time and tide wait for no man', marks the resting place of a truly remarkable man. Born on 23 July 1899 into a wealthy family, he was one of five siblings, having a brother and three sisters. Glen Kidston (he dropped his first two names early on) seems to have craved adventure from an early age. In 1909 he was the first Boy Scout to enrol in the newly formed first Glasbury scout troop. At just 11 years old he enrolled in the Royal Naval College at Dartmouth. A bright lad, he passed all his exams easily and was soon a midshipman on *HMS Hogue*. His first taste of action came when the *Hogue* was torpedoed on 22 September 1914. The cruiser and two of her sister ships were on patrol, but were temporarily without a destroyer escort. Glen recounts how he was taking a photograph of *HMS Aboukir*, one of the other ships which was rapidly sinking and which at that point was thought to have hit a mine, when the *Hogue* was hit. He recalled how three great spouts of water rose next to the ship and showered the decks in large splinters of wood torn from the decking. The *Hogue* began to list dangerously and soon the order to 'save yourselves' was shouted. Glen tore off his coat and shoes and jumped into the sea. As soon as the *Aboukir* had been torpedoed, the *Hogue* had launched her boats to go to the rescue; these now turned around to help their own survivors. The first boat Glen swam to was full of sick and injured sailors so he struck out towards another 'vessel', which turned out to be a floating target that had been used by the Navy for shooting practice. He joined the other 24 men who were clinging to the buoy. The *Cressy*, the third cruiser, meanwhile tried to ram a submarine which had come to the surface due to the weight loss of firing two torpedoes at the *Hogue*, but failed and was herself torpedoed and sunk. The action took place not far from the Dutch shore and soon Dutch boats came to the rescue, followed by British trawlers and then destroyers. Glen was rescued by the Dutch steamer *Flora* and informed that he would be taken to Holland and would have to remain a prisoner for the rest of the war. All told, the *Flora* rescued 287 men and 25 officers, some of whom were badly hurt, one officer having been pulled from the water with two broken legs.

When it was discovered that Glen was only aged 15, he and a small band of other juvenile midshipmen were sent back to the UK. On his return he was granted a ten day furlough. Glen's father had died in 1913, so his mother took the car to London to fetch her son. Although there was little time for preparation, a welcome home was arranged for the young man. He was driven through the streets of Hay-on-Wye to loud cheering and when he got to Glasbury the scouts acted as a guard of honour. Many of the village residents lined the road to Gwernyfed Park, his three sisters were waiting for him dressed in red, white and blue, and some of the employees on the estate had stretched a German flag across the driveway. There was much loud cheering from the scouts as the car raced forward and tore through the flag. After barely a week's leave Glen was back on active service.

His next ship was the dreadnought *HMS Orion* on which the then 16-year-old Glen ran gunnery orders along an open deck directly under enemy fire during the battle of Jutland in 1916.

That same year his mother remarried. Her second husband was 38-year-old Sir Walter George Windham, a man straight out of the *Boy's Own Paper*. Before he was 20 years old he had circumnavigated the globe four times in sailing ships. He drove a car in the first ever London to Brighton rally in 1896. In 1908 he sponsored a gold cup to be presented to the first person to fly a heavier than air machine across the English Channel, a cup won the following year by Louis Blériot. Just two weeks later his friend Hubert Latham flew a letter from England to France, believed to be the first 'airmail' letter, which inspired Windham to look into the idea of an aerial postal service. In December 1910 he made the first passenger flight in Asia and February 1911 saw him fly the first airmail across the River Ganges. In September that year he oversaw the first aerial postal service in the UK when Gustav Hamel and three other pilots ferried mail back and forth between Windsor and Hendon for a week to celebrate the king's jubilee. During the First World War he served with the Indian Navy.

At the end of the First World War, Glen Kidston's experience of being torpedoed led to an interest in submarines. He seemed to slip easily into the role of a submariner and during trials in the North Sea he was involved in the notorious X1 incident, where a newly built experimental British submarine simply nose-dived into the mud due, it was subsequently found, to faulty gauges. The crew were rescued in the nick of time.

He married in 1925 and in 1926 gained command of his own submarine, the H24, a 171 foot long, 22 man vessel that had been commissioned just at the end of the First World War. He was also developing an interest in the field of naval aviation. In his spare time he began to pursue a career in motorcycle and car racing and owned several of the leading sports cars of the day.

On 18 April 1928 Glen took his civilian flying licence with the Hampshire Aero Club, and there is some evidence that he had been flying for some time previously. He soon became a well known figure in Llandrindod Wells, buying aviation spirit at the rate of twenty tins at a time and specially ordered spark plugs at ten shillings each from Tom

The burning wreckage of the Luft Hansa flight from Croydon to Amsterdam in which Glen Kidston was badly burnt. (© Simon Kidston)

Norton at the Automobile Palace in the town. There are tales of him taking off from the Royal Welsh show ground at Builth Wells and racing his sisters in their Bentley back to Gwernyfed near Glasbury.

Glen decided that motorcycle racing had become boring when he 'won all the time', so concentrated his attention on the car racing circuit. He became one of the Bentley Boys, a group of young racing drivers sponsored by the Bentley car company to bring their cars to victory in countless European races. The Bentley Boys raced fast and played hard. There were tales of all day and night parties at Glen's London home, which was also called Gwernyfed Park.

In November 1929 he suffered a serious and harrowing air crash. Twenty-one minutes after taking off from Croydon on a flight to Amsterdam in a Luft Hansa airliner on which Prince Eugen von Schaumburg-Lippe was the second pilot, he sensed the plane was in trouble and instructed his fellow passengers to assume crash positions. The aircraft burst into flames on impact and Glen had to kick his way out with his clothes on fire. He rolled in wet grass to douse the flames and immediately re-entered the aircraft and dragged the prince out. He was unable to re-enter a second time as the flames were too intense. Glen made the prince comfortable and staggered through almost a mile of woodland at night seeking help, eventually flagging down a motorist. The motorist later reported that some of Glen's clothes were still smouldering. Glen then phoned the details of the crash through to Croydon. A rescue team arrived, but the prince had died of his injuries. On his return

Glen Kidston (centre) with Owen Cathcart-Jones (right) and mechanic in May 1931.
(© Simon Kidston)

to Croydon airport Glen immediately took a short flight to rebuild his nerve before being admitted to hospital with extensive burns.

He was soon up and about again. In 1930 he entered the Monte Carlo Rally. Then during the Lands End to John O'Groats car race he slid on ice just outside Glasgow and, as he wrote to a friend, 'seriously bent the Bentley'. Later that year he and Woolf Barnato (the millionaire who had stepped in to save the Bentley Company from folding) raced at Le Mans. They won, and Bentley retired from the race circuit.

Glen then concentrated once more on aviation, soon setting a commercial record by flying from Croydon to Le Bourget in France in a Lockheed D1-1 Special Vega, with three passengers, in 1 hour 20 minutes. In March 1931 he teamed up with Owen Cathcart-Jones, who he had known for several years, to attempt another record.

Owen Cathcart-Jones had been born in London on 5 June 1900, to Cathcart Wight Jones and Alice Sophia Jones (née Vinnells). Owen was originally given 'Cathcart' as his second name, but as he grew up he decided to hyphenate it with his surname. The family, which included an elder sister, lived at No.39 Penywern Road, Earls Court in London, a quite prosperous area, and his father was the manager of an insurance company. Alice died in about 1902 and the children were brought up by a nanny. Owen joined the Royal Marines just after his 18th birthday, but deciding they were not adventurous enough he

Owen Cathcart-Jones.
(© Mr Dave Thayer)

Glen Kidston.
(© Simon Kidston)

began looking into the possibility of becoming a pilot. In January 1925 he enrolled at Netheravon and in August gained his wings as a fully fledged pilot, whereupon he was transferred to RAF Leuchars as a member of the Fleet Air Arm, the flying wing of the Royal Navy. In 1926/27 he served in the China seas flying off *HMS Hermes* with 403 flight, later transferring to 404 flight on *HMS Courageous.*

He soon earned a reputation as a daring and seemingly fearless pilot, but also for being a bit troublesome. Once, during a Fleet Air Arm exercise, he took it upon himself to deliver a load of 'Service Brown' (toilet paper) to the battleship *HMS Revenge.* Cathcart-Jones' own story was that the commander leading the exercise had inverted the line of ships, leading him to drop his load on the deck of *HMS Queen Elizabeth* which was acting as the flagship and loaded with dignitaries. Unfortunately the plane he was flying (a Fairey Flycatcher) had the number 7 emblazoned underneath in large letters, making it easily identifiable when enquiries were made into the name of the pilot. Cathcart-Jones was summoned before the admiral; he escaped serious punishment but had to be on his best behaviour for quite some time afterwards.

His exploits did not all end in reprimands and in 1929 he became the first pilot to land an aeroplane on an aircraft carrier at night. His private life, however, was getting a bit tangled. During his time in the China seas, the ship had docked at Hong Kong, where the pilots had been entertained by members of the Colonial Office and their wives. Cathcart-Jones got on rather well with Audrey Bloxham, the wife of Captain Hugh Bloxham. Audrey and Hugh had been married in 1925, and in May 1928 Hugh sued for divorce, citing Cathcart-Jones. Neither party contested it, and Owen and Audrey got married in Malta later that year. They had two children, Imogen and Anthony.

Soon afterwards Cathcart-Jones became restless with service life and although he had a family to support he decided to take extended leave from the service and go on half pay for six months from 17 February 1930. His intention was to try out civil aviation and he joined a firm called National Flying Services, but commercial flying was still a bit hit and miss and the company was financially precarious. Then he had a call from his old friend and fellow aviator Glen Kidston, who needed a co-pilot for his next record-breaking flight. Cathcart-Jones took the bait and left the Fleet Air Arm.

Glen's plan was to beat the current world record for flying between England and South Africa, and the pair set out in a Lockheed Special Vega from Netheravon military airfield in Wiltshire. After a stopover in Cairo to change Marconi wireless operators they headed on for Capetown, where they arrived six days after leaving England. With a total flying time of 57 hours and 10 minutes they had indeed set a new world record for the 7,500 mile journey.

While they were planning the return journey Glen borrowed a De-Havilland Puss Moth, an aircraft he was familiar with, and he took a friend (Captain Gladstone) with him for a spot of sightseeing over the Drakensberg Mountains in the Natal. 5 May 1931 dawned bright and clear and it should have been perfect sightseeing weather, but as they reached the mountains a dust storm blew in, the aircraft broke up and both occupants were killed. (After eight similar accidents with the Puss Moth it was ascertained that the wings were not strong enough to withstand the pressures exerted in such conditions.)

Sundial erected at St Peter's church
Glasbury-on-Wye in memory of Glen Kidston.
(© Author's collection)

Commander Glen Kidston's remains were brought back to his family home in Glasbury and buried in St Peter's churchyard. Sir Walter Windham and Glen's mother had moved from Gwernyfed Park to Tyrcelyn in Aberedw shortly before Glen's death. Windham died here in 1942 and was buried in the churchyard at Aberedw.

The loss of his friend hit Cathcart-Jones hard and although Glen may not have been the most steadying influence, after his death Cathcart-Jones seems to have gone even more off the rails. His Navy flying days had been littered with reprimands but now he was to get into even more hot water. The start of his troubles were small routine things like being summonsed for driving a car without a valid road licence, escalating to another summons for buzzing a military airfield. In Argentina he was banned from operating an aircraft as a result of dangerous flying near a naval air base.

He moved out of the family home and took up residence in the Military and Naval

Two views of Mr James's plane crumpled against Rhyddllandu farmhouse having overshot the Ddole landing strip on 27 August 1932. The young boy in shorts nearest the camera is Peter Davies (see page 181). (© Powys County Archives)

Club in Piccadilly. After less than four years of marriage he was subject to another divorce case, having lured another man's wife away; he was eventually to marry six times. When she tried to divorce him, his third wife, an American lady, was to discover that he had not actually divorced his first wife, but only had a separation agreement. When the courts finally pursued him for maintenance he declared himself bankrupt and didn't bother to turn up for the hearings. Somehow he managed to escape a possible sentence for bigamy.

All the time he was still breaking world records and gaining the sponsorship and friendship of the rich and famous, and he would yet have a further connection with Radnorshire, but in the meantime other airmen were making their impressions on the county.

On 27 August 1932, Mr James of the Northamptonshire club was seen to pass over the Ddole airfield in his De-Havilland Moth (serial number G-AAIE). He overshot the airfield by several hundred yards, ran out of fuel and crashed into the front of Rhyddllandu farmhouse, causing some damage but fortunately no injuries. A year later, on 2 September 1933, another De-Havilland Moth (serial number G-AAJN) also crashed in the vicinity of the Ddole airfield. The owner was Mr Leslie Horne of London-based Horne Brothers outfitters. Nobody was reported hurt in the crash and it is not clear if Mr Horne was involved in the incident. Universal Air Services had started running a regular taxi service from the Ddole air field only a month before this second crash.

In an effort to aid aerial navigation around the British Isles many towns and cities had taken to painting their names on prominent landmarks. Newspapers of the day proclaimed that these letters could be seen from a height of 5,000 feet. Llandrindod Wells Town Council saw this as a way of putting the town on the map and approaches were made to the manager of the local gas works to have the town's name emblazoned across the top of the gasometer. Although a series of letters went back and forth and everybody was seemingly

The site of the Ddole landing strip. (© Author's collection)

in agreement, the large white letters proclaiming Llandrindod Wells never appeared.

Nevertheless, the Ddole Airfield was set to become the venue for more flying displays, this time the aerial circus led by Alan Cobham.

In 1904, at the age of ten, Alan Cobham's father took him to the Crystal Palace to see an airship flight. He reacted so enthusiastically that one of the aviators suggested he take Alan up for a flight, but his father vetoed the suggestion with the words 'When you are older and have more sense, you will see it is safer to stay on the ground.' The experience nevertheless encouraged Alan to make a series of ever bigger and better kites, inspired as he was by Samuel Cody, pioneer of the man-carrying kite and credited as the first man to fly a heavier than air machine in Great Britain.

In his teenage years Alan, along with his good friend Laurie Stocks, would career around the lanes on Laurie's motor bike, and both were keen on aeroplanes. When they discovered that a flying meet was to take place at Brooklands aerodrome near to where they lived, they determined to sneak in and see the machines close up. Clad in overalls, they stashed the bike behind a handy wall and were soon strolling around getting a good close up view of all the aircraft. Alan recalled being particularly impressed by the sight of Gustav Hamel using an out-sized spring balance fixed between a stake in the ground and the back of the aircraft in order to test the thrust of his engine.

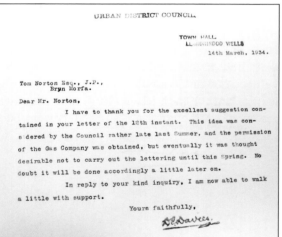

Letters from Tom Norton suggesting the painting of the gasometer at Llandrindod Wells with the town's name in order to help promote the town, and the response from the Urban District Council suggesting it would be undertaken, but it never was.
(© Powys County Archives)

Early machines had very few instruments and certainly they did not have a rev counter, so individual airmen improvised as best they could.

When the news that a large prize was being offered for the best 'aviette' (a man-powered aircraft) the two boys set about coming up with a design, determined to win the prize. Their machine was to be a kind of bicycle with wings. The project completely terrified both of their

Alan Cobham.
(© Royal Aero Club)

parents who had visions of them crashing to earth from a great height. They need not have worried, for the design failed, a failure that Alan blamed on Laurie. Laurie was the better mathematician, and Alan firmly believed him when he claimed that Alan would be able to pedal fast enough to make the three and half horse power needed to take off.

Still thinking about flight but also needing to do something constructive with his life, Alan, who had always held a great love for the rural idyll, took up the offer from one of his father's cousins to work on his farm in Herefordshire. His parents were disappointed. Alan had been working in a drapery warehouse and at the age of 18 was responsible for his own department. His parents couldn't understand why he would give up a job in 'the City' to go messing about on a farm, especially as his father had already explained that they would in no way be able to set him up in a farm of his own. So Alan left Streatham for the farm at Brockbury Hall near the Malverns. He had a natural aptitude for working with horses and seemed set to take up farming as his career.

At Christmas 1913 he returned to Streatham for the holidays and found his father in serious business trouble. Deeply saddened, he decided to give up his dreams of farming and return home so he could be of help, once again entering the drapery trade but this time with the firm of Hicks and Smith who specialized in lingerie. After a bad start he settled down to the trade and even entertained ideas of going into business with his father. In June 1914 his manager suggested he should become their West End representative. His parents were delighted at his prospects, but on the outbreak of war just weeks later Alan joined up immediately. Armed with his knowledge of horses gained on the farm, he tried first for the cavalry. This came to nothing so he then tried for the Honourable Artillery Company. Again he was not accepted, but a chance conversation with a recruiting officer made his direction clear. The Army Veterinary Corps were chronically shorthanded and Alan was 'Specially enlisted' at the rate of four shillings a day – quite a talking point when ordinary privates were only paid a shilling a day.

Alan rose quickly in the corps and was soon a sergeant. By November 1917 he had been in France for three years and had only had five days' leave. He was able to get home and all the way he brooded over what his future might be. Much as he loved his horses and his work, every car that passed him on the road home reminded him that horses were not the future. He also felt he lacked the educational standard needed to become a vet in civilian life. He had not lost his taste for adventure and having seen the progress of aircraft first-hand in France, he was beginning to wonder if he could join the Royal Flying Corps and learn to fly at the government's expense. A neighbour, Mr Grouse, a retired civil servant, had been drafted back into the War Office and Alan's mother suggested he go and have a word. Exactly what influence Mr Grouse had is hard to say, but when Alan got back to France his colonel was most put out by the high level communiqué announcing that Alan would transfer to the Royal Flying Corps with immediate effect.

Alan made his first solo flight on 1 June 1918 after six hours of instruction at Manston flying school in a DH6. Manston was a new flying school and Alan's Canadian instructor, Lt Holly, who had only just qualified as an instructor, seemed determined to be the first to get a pupil to go solo. From that day, Alan knew without a doubt that aviation was somehow or other going to be his lifelong career. First though he had to finish his training, and this he did on 17 August 1918 after 138 minutes flying. In the time he was at Manston Alan gained a reputation for being cool-headed and patient, which may be why instead of being posted to an operational squadron, he was asked to stay at Manston and become an instructor. Alan accepted, and his first pupils consisted of pilots who had suffered accidents and needed refresher courses to rebuild their nerve. Early in September the flying school was relocated to Narborough near Kings Lynn in Norfolk. The bags and baggage went by road and Alan, Lt Holly and the rest of the instructors were to lead groups of pupils across country in formation.

Not only was this further than any of the instructors had flown before, but at that time aircraft compasses were inaccurate, with the needles prone to spinning around rather than sticking to pointing north. Alan therefore obtained some road maps and identified a series of landmarks to help navigation, before obtaining permission from various RAF bases to land and refuel. He also enlisted the help of one of the mechanics, who agreed to fly with him and bring along his tool kit and a load of spares, so that if anyone did get into trouble they could land and repair the aircraft while the rest of the pupils circled close by and then all set off again. Alan tied a white streamer to his aircraft so that there could be no doubt about who they were following. With hope and enthusiasm the flying school took to the air. Holly and Alan had a little private bet on who would get there first.

Soon the various instructors had scattered, taking their pupils on what they thought was the best route. Alan's first refuelling stop was reached, everybody landed safely, and they even had time for lunch before they set off again. Shortly afterwards, Alan's engine simply cut out and with little time to plan what to do he spied a flat but closed-in field on which to land. Seeing their leader down, his pupils panicked and instead of circling until he was once more airborne they all descended one by one on to the cramped field. The engine was soon fixed but now Alan had the problem of getting all his pupils out of the tree-lined field. One by one the six men, all flying Avro 504 Ks, staggered up and over the tree line. Alan's plane was much heavier, however, as he had an extra man and all the tools and spares, but he scraped over the trees and once more they were on their way. Next they hit a patch of bad weather; rain and mist made visibility rather tricky and the open cockpits offered almost no protection. Alan flew low, navigating largely by railway lines, and they were all extremely relieved when the hangars of Narborough aerodrome came into view. They landed safely and found they were the first group to arrive. As night fell it became obvious that Alan and his six pupils were the only ones to make it. Holly had crashed; he was not badly injured but his pupils had landed with him and milled about unsure what to do. Some of the other instructors had got lost in the bad weather and had landed anywhere they could. One or two pupils turned back. Members of the ground crew were sent to round up all the missing airmen and it was just over a week before they were all in Norfolk. Alan and his six pupils meanwhile had all the facilities to themselves for a few days' uninterrupted flying.

As the Armistice approached Alan began to worry that there were far more qualified and experienced pilots than he who would have trouble staying in a smaller post-war RAF, and he began looking into the civilian side of instructing. He managed to stay at Narborough until the beginning of 1919 but in early February he finally got his demob orders. The RAF wasn't unsympathetic to his situation, but a kindly demob advisor pointed out that they had estimated that for every civilian flying job available there would be 1,000 demobbed airmen, so perhaps he should consider returning to the lingerie business. Alan hated the very thought.

As the government was selling off surplus stocks of aeroplanes, many of them almost new, Alan considered buying one and setting up in business for himself but although he had managed to save some of his pay, it was not enough to purchase an aircraft. He therefore took a job with the Aerial Transport Company, identifying fields in which aeroplanes could land to give pleasure flights, but the company folded after a month. Then Alan answered an advert in the *Aerial Register and Gazette*. Two brothers, Fred and Jack Holmes, were very much in the same boat as Alan. Jack had been an RFC pilot who had been shot down in the war and had got very much out of practice while recuperating, whilst Fred was a first-class mechanic and rigger. The three men decided to pool their resources, buy one of the government surplus planes, and set up in business giving pleasure flights.

The newly formed Berkshire Aviation Company spent the summer of 1919 giving pleasure flights the length and breadth of Britain. It would be easy to think that Alan was now set on the road that would make him the world famous Sir Alan Cobham, but 1920 saw things go somewhat downhill. Many of his friends and business associates encouraged them to expand and get more planes and pilots, promising financial backing – but when it came to the nitty gritty they had sudden changes of heart. Then to make matters worse the weather closed in for three weeks around Easter and all their flying displays had to be cancelled. Rent and wages still had to be paid but there was no money coming in. Alan sold his plane to pay back money he had borrowed from his uncle and joined an engineering firm which went bust a month later. He tried the film industry for a few weeks but the lack of organization didn't appeal to him. He was also now in love and felt he should be settling down, so he went back to the rag trade, selling gowns. He stuck at this for almost a year until one lunchtime he met an old friend in a pub who was involved with an aerial photography firm that had just sacked one of its pilots.

Two days later Alan had the job and was back in an aeroplane flying slowly and steadily over Manchester with a photographer in the back taking aerial survey photographs. Other jobs came his way, such as flying a policeman above the traffic jams on Derby day so that the police could clear the roads quickly, or ferrying newspapers to outlying areas so they could get the news at the same time as London. Next he flew newsreels around the country, the first one being of the 1922 Derby, the idea being that people could watch the Derby in cinemas around the country on the evening of the day that the race had taken place. All went well as they dropped the hastily developed newsreels attached to parachutes at prearranged landing points around the country, until Alan's tired assistant neglected to use enough force to jettison one package as they were over Aberdeen. They both watched as it dangled from the tail plane where it had snagged before dropping off without its chute.

Alan landed in a fit of depression: at best the film was lost, at worse it might have killed someone. However, on landing he learned that the film canister had landed in the back yard of the very cinema in which it was to be shown.

He had now proposed to Gladys, his fiancée, and wanted more out of life than this ad hoc flying offered. It was the era of breaking aviation records and Alan started to set his sights on a round the world flight. He was now working for the De-Havilland aircraft company as a hire pilot, a sort of aerial taxi driver. One day a wealthy American, Mr Sharpe, breezed into the office and asked to hire an aircraft for a European tour. This was the beginning of an association that was to last several years. Sharpe was passionate about travel and quizzed Alan about the times taken to reach various destinations. For the next two years Alan and Sharpe travelled not just across Europe but throughout the Middle East and Africa as well. Although technically Alan still worked for De-Havilland, Mr Sharpe's influence meant that at the drop of a hat he and Sharpe could be setting off to visit a vineyard in Greece, hear a concert in Seville or attend some lavish Moorish feast. All these flights gave Alan the experience he needed for his next big adventure. Mr Sharpe had pooh-poohed the idea of a round the world flight when Alan had asked him for sponsorship, but in 1924 Alan had a breakthrough when the director of civil aviation, Sir Sefton Brancker, was asked by the government to travel to India to see about setting up Empire air routes for both aeroplanes and airships. With typical government lack of foresight he was expected to travel by P and O ocean liner; the government would not run to the cost of hiring a plane and pilot. Alan begged and pleaded, and the government relented slightly on the price if part of the money came from the civilian aircraft industry. Every aircraft company in Britain knew the value of the publicity so they readily stumped up the money. The flight from Croydon to Rangoon and back caused a sensation. When Alan landed back at Croydon on 17 March 1925 it was to a world that was finally seeing aviation as a viable transport enterprise and not some novelty or wartime necessity. Next Alan decided to fly to Cape Town. He had made a little money writing about aviation and although his wife Gladys was a successful actress, he still had to beg and borrow in order to get all he needed for this new venture, for he was going to be doing this without either the wealthy Mr Sharpe or the Minister for Aviation in tow. Taking a mechanic and a Gaumont cinema cameraman with him, the flight was a great success and his share of the film they produced netted him £8,000.

On his return on 13 March 1926 he was almost immediately sent for by King George V, who had been keenly following the flight and was passionate about new innovations. Alan almost immediately announced that his next flight would be to Australia. He made it in a converted De-Havilland which had been fitted with floats to land on water. As he was passing over Basra on the return journey, there was a loud bang behind him, caused by a pipe bursting. The burst injured his great friend and mechanic Elliot, who had accompanied him on all his long distance flights. Realizing that Elliot was losing blood, Alan pushed on for their next landing point near a British RAF base where medical assistance could be found, but despite this Elliot died two days later. When the plane was inspected it was discovered that someone on the ground, probably a desert tribesman frightened or feeling threatened by the plane, had fired his rifle at it. The bullet had pierced both of Elliot's lungs. The RAF base commander therefore allowed one of his own mechanics to accompany Alan, who then completed the journey. Although this achievement saw him knighted for services to aviation, because of the death of Elliot it didn't feel like the triumph he had hoped for. He was also physically exhausted, and he now had two young sons and had missed both their births and one family Christmas. Maybe it was time for another change.

Technically he was employed as an air taxi pilot for De-Havilland, but he was also a knight of the realm and famous enough to be mobbed wherever he went, and feted by celebrities and captains of industry. His friends thought he should be a company director or at least some sort of manager and he approached the De-Havilland board with this suggestion, but they declined his proposal that he join them and he thought about leaving the company. But where would he go? Then De-Havilland did something he couldn't forgive them for. His faithful DH 50, serial number G-EBFO, veteran of all his long distance flights, was sold to another air taxi firm. Alan felt this should have been marked as an historic aircraft, not just shunted off like a secondhand car. Alan tendered his resignation the day after its sale.

His next project was to set up Alan Cobham Aviation Ltd, an airline company that would set about opening the air routes of both Africa and the Empire. Imperial Airways already had government backing but only had an informal agreement regarding routes in Africa, and this was where Alan decided to focus his attention. For this venture Alan decided that a float plane or flying boat would be the ideal aircraft. There were still large parts of Africa that were undiscovered and Alan reasoned that a float plane landing on a lake or lagoon would be a safer option than trying to find runways in the jungle. Next he needed to find the right aircraft. Short Brothers of Rochester were the leading seaplane manufacturer and they had just finished trialing a Singapore MK1, a large twin-engined aircraft with a revolutionary metal hull. Alan felt it was perfect as it afforded plenty of room not only for his crew, but all their supplies. When the plane took off on 17 November 1927 it had a crew of six – Alan, second pilot Worrall (a highly experienced New Zealand seaplane pilot), two engineers by the names of Green and Conway, Mr Bonnet, a cameraman on loan from the Gaumont cinema chain, and Alan's wife Gladys, who was to act as secretary and take care of all the paperwork.

The journey was supposed to be a three month tour of Africa, but vagaries of the weather and metal fatigue which caused damage to the engine crankcases, necessitating a three week wait for repairs, meant that the trip was to eventually take six months. Alan was seriously worried that instead of showing the world how convenient air travel was for getting around the globe, he might have had the opposite effect and highlighted the problems associated with air travel. In an effort to repair not only his image but the cause of aviation in general, immediately on returning to the UK Alan began to organise a grand tour of the country in the hope that if civic leaders and citizens could see up close the seaplane that had circumnavigated Africa, they would once more be fired with a passion for aviation. He decided to start the tour in Rochester, as the home base of Short Brothers, but the aircraft began vibrating alarmingly and they had to make an emergency landing. The engine mounting bolts were found to be at fault and they had to call on Rolls Royce for help. This was the third time the Rolls Royce Condor engines had given trouble and the firm decided to stop production and suggested another engine was fitted, the only problem being that this was

Advertising poster for Alan Cobham's National Aviation Day Display in Llandrindod Wells in 1932. (© Powys County Archives)

going to take three months to complete. Alan therefore turned to one of two other projects he had in mind.

He had the idea that every small town in Britain should have its own aerodrome so that flying would be as common as travel by bus. He therefore set up the Municipal Aerodrome Campaign. He reasoned that as most town councils wouldn't have a clue about aviation, he could be their advisor (for a small fee). He would get local dignitaries in each town to identify a suitable field, then, on a pre-advertised day, he would land in it, and in the morning give a lecture or an educational speech to the assembled councillors and take some of them up free of charge. This would then be followed by some sort of civic lunch and in the afternoon Alan would be free to take up fare-paying members of the public for a joy ride. It might also lead to more consultancy work.

The project was helped considerably by Sir Charles Wakefield, who advanced enough money to the project to give 10,000 school age children a free flight. Sir Charles, like Alan, felt that aviation was the future and that getting children up would be a good way to spread the word. Alan bought a De-Havilland DH61 and christened it the 'Youth of Britain' as a tribute to Charles Wakefield. Between May and October 1929, Alan Cobham visited 110 towns and cities trying to encourage his aerodrome scheme, a project that kept him busy until 1931. Councils countrywide appeared interested, but there was never any money.

Alan's next project was that of National Air Days, which were to herald the beginning of what became known as the Flying Circus. Alan collected together a motley group of aircraft with crews to go with them. There were to be stunt pilots performing aerobatics, daring wing walkers and even parachutists. He had pilots like Fl/Lt Geoffrey Tyson, who would swoop so low that he could pick up a handkerchief from the ground on a hook at the end of his wing, and planes such as a windmill plane, an early type of helicopter. Some pilots would fake near crashes, or emerge from the crowd pretending to be a novice and make a comic turn out of getting in and starting the engine before giving a faultless display – all in the cause of thrilling people in the crowd into wanting more and deciding that they

Alan Cobham's aircraft 'Youth of Britain'.
(© Flight Magazine)

must be the next person to travel by air. Everything from the ticket booth to the toilets was packed into the back of Alan's fleet of vehicles, which included his own little Ford, often driven by Gladys, and a converted bus complete with cocktail bar which housed the mechanics. There were posters and banners and rolls of tickets, photographs that could be signed by pilots, and souvenir badges. The arrow man would set off early to place a series of large arrows directing the public to the airfield; his was also the last job at night as the arrows were collected for reuse.

All this paraphernalia arrived in Radnorshire in the summer of 1932. It was met with a mixture of excitement and awe, but not the fear that Gustav Hamel had encountered nearly 20 years before when the crowds had stampeded as his aircraft had swooped over. Now groups of young men would comment on the planes as their girlfriends queued for a flight; some were veterans themselves and would offer their expertise to those waiting. The children would excitedly beg their parents to be allowed to go up, and the old excuse of 'it's too expensive' couldn't be used thanks to Sir Charles Wakefield, whilst that of 'it's too dangerous' was thwarted by Alan's hiring of Earl Bateman Fielden.

Fielden was born in Skipton in Yorkshire in 1899 and joined the RFC as a flight cadet on 2 February 1917, becoming a qualified pilot in August 1918. He was assigned to 24 Squadron and sent out to France where he flew on the western front. Fielden became well and truly bitten by the flying bug and at the end of the war, although there was a place for him in the family business, he, like Cobham, was determined to keep on flying.

In 1922 he joined the staff of Northern Aviation as a junior pilot. Fielden quickly became known as a steady and safe pilot and was often requested by repeat passengers. Although not famous like Alan Cobham, he had his admirers in the aviation world. This

Councillors of Builth Wells UDC who were taken aloft by E.B. Fielden in 1933 from what is now the Royal Welsh Showground.
(© The late Mr E. Turner, via the author's collection)

Sir Alan Cobham's Flying Circus on the move.

may have been why Alan Cobham picked Fielden to fly the 'Airspeed Ferry', one of the larger planes Cobham used in the National Air Days displays. The plane was capable of taking up ten people at time.

By 1931 it was estimated that Fielden had flown more passengers than any other pilot, a number that reached 200,000 by 1934, earning him the nickname of 'Safety First' Fielden. He had, however, suffered two crashes. The first was in September 1931, when the aircraft he was piloting came down on the Moortown golf course in the East Riding of Yorkshire. Although the aircraft burst into flames, everybody got out safely. The second crash was reportedly during his time with Sir Alan Cobham. On 25 August 1933, Fielden, along with two other pilots – Clifford Jones of Blackwood and Frederick La Croix of Finchley, London – was almost at the landing ground of the Scunthorpe Air Pageant, having left Kidderminster earlier that morning, when the aircraft was seen to get into difficulties and

Complimentary Ticket.

Llandrindod Wells
AERIAL PAGEANT

SATURDAY, AUGUST 27th, 1932

ADMIT BEARER
TO THE AERODROME.

Llandrindod Wells
AERIAL PAGEANT.

SATURDAY, AUGUST 27th, 1932

Free Flight Voucher.

This Voucher must be handed in at the Booking Office Tent in exchange for which a Flight Ticket will be issued.

A complimentary ticket and free flight voucher for the Llandrindod Wells Aerial Pageant on 27 August 1932. (© Radnorshire Museum)

crash a short way from the landing ground in a field of sugar beet. Fielden was able to jump from the cockpit as the plane overturned. Officials and spectators from the landing field ran to help and the other two men were dragged from the plane. All three were taken to Scunthorpe hospital. Fielden was back at the display later the same day and his two companions left hospital the next day with nothing but cuts and bruises.

Shortly after the second accident Fielden left Cobham's circus and joined a rival organisation, the British Hospitals Air Pageants (BHAP). This group not only promoted aviation but gave ten per cent of takings at any event to local hospitals. Private and commercial pilots would be invited to form up as a flying circus, using either their own or hired aircraft. The BHAP would organise all the advertising, the landing areas and crowd control – all the pilots would have to do was turn up and perform. Cobham took the view that this was rather a scam operation with very little monitoring of exactly how much was made and handed over.

Cobham and his pilots were a big hit with the public, but Alan was to sell his flying circus just two years later to Charles Scott. But before Scott could visit the Ddole Airfield, another pilot was advertising his wares.

On Easter Monday 1935 the world famous glider ace Robert Kronfeld appeared in the town. Rather austere two-tone posters had announced that 'Mr Robert Kronfeld the famous Austrian gliding ace' would be the next visitor to the Ddole airstrip. Whilst Kronfeld was as well known as his predecessors, his gliding display did not have the romance of previous air displays.

The son of an Austrian Jewish dentist, Kronfeld had become interested in flight from an early age when during a trip to Germany he had seen the many gliding clubs that had been set up following the First World War. He joined Austria's only gliding club and, not content with just flying, started to build gliders to his own design.

In the late 1920s the German newspaper *Grüne Post* launched a competition with a 500 deutschmark prize for a glider that could successfully fly 100 kilometres. Kronfeld befriended an Austrian meteorologist and together they explored the use of thermals (hot air currents) to help a glider fly more successfully. Kronfeld duly won the competition in 1929 at the age of 25 and used the money to build a super sailplane with a wingspan of 30 metres, a glider not matched in size until the end of the 20th century.

On 20 June 1931 he became the first person to fly a glider across the English Channel, and soon held a great many height and distance records. But at the beginning of 1933 the German Nazi government prohibited Jews from flying and Austria still only had one gliding club, so he decided to come to England where both military and civilian companies were experimenting with glider construction. The British Aircraft Company (BAC) were fitting small motorcycle engines onto gliders to make

Robert Kronfeld. (Courtesy thetartanterror.blogspot.com)

them more manoeuvrable and Kronfeld was with the company when its chief test pilot and owner, C.H. Lowe-Wylde, was killed on 13 May 1933. Kronfeld then took over the company and renamed the glider the 'Drone'. Twenty 'Drones' were built (and presumably sold) before Kronfeld again modified the design and turned it into the 'Super Drone'.

It was this glider that made an appearance in Radnorshire on Easter Monday 1935. The Super Drone had been designed to be compact, easy to handle and cheap to run. Even the purchase price of £275 was similar to that of a standard car of the day. The glider would get airborne by means of a small motorbike engine mounted above the wings and once up would rely on the wind, just like any other glider. This ability to take off without the complicated winch mechanisms that other gliders used and the tiny amount of fuel that the motorbike engine used were chief selling features. Although it would be nice to think of a Super Drone still squirrelled away in a Radnorshire barn, there are no records of any being sold from the Ddole air display. (In 1939 Kronfeld became a British citizen – he had already been joined in Britain by his father – and early in 1940 he joined the Royal Air Force. He eventually became a squadron leader and was attached to the experimental glider unit. Some of the Drones made it onto operational squadrons, but not quite for the purpose Kronfeld had intended. No.609 Spitfire squadron camouflaged a Super Drone deluxe and, armed with a 12 bore shot gun, the pilots would often go out on duck hunting expeditions. Kronfeld was killed on 12 February 1948 when testing a new glider.)

(© Radnorshire Museum)

(© Author's collection)

DAILY FLYING

At **LLANDRINDOD WELLS**

Commencing FRIDAY, AUGUST 3rd (until further notice)

SEASON 1933.

SEASON 1933.

THERE are now many provincial aerodromes in existence but not until this year has it been possible to establish regular flying in the heart of the Principality, although the Premier Welsh Spa has been gradually forging ahead in developing this exhilarating and modern form of travel.

Llandrindod Wells now possesses a centrally situated compact aerodrome (adjoining the Rock Hotel) of twenty-five acres and 550 yards long complete with hangarage to house a number of machines. Owners of private aeroplanes are therefore able to fly to Central Wales and even make it their base for daily tours over country so famous for its beauty. The landing fee is 2/6 per machine and the cost of hangar space per twenty-four hours 5/- Fuel and oil supplies available on landing ground.

Commencing on Friday, August 3rd, Messrs. Universal Aircraft Services Limited will experiment with a daily flying service and are prepared to make short or extended air tours at reasonable charges in addition to providing joy rides over the immediate neighbourhood at very popular prices. For this purpose the following machines will be placed in commission :— (1) " Avro " 504K biplane seating pilot and two passengers ; (2) " Bristol " biplane fitted with 275h.p Rolls Royce Falcon engine, seating pilot and one passenger. **Rates :** in the " Avro " (two passengers) 9d. per mile each passenger or if one passenger 1/- per mile. In the " Bristol " (one passenger) 1/3 per mile. *JOY RIDES from 5/-*

The SCALE set out enables comparison to be made of flying and road mileages from which it will be observed that the cost is really no greater than car hire.

To	Return Flying Mileage.	Return Road Mileage.	AVRO BIPLANE Two passengers (each) at 9d. Mile.	AVRO BIPLANE One passenger at 1/- Mile.	BRISTOL BIPLANE One Passenger at 1/3 Mile.
ABERYSTWYTH	66	95	£2 9 6	£3 6 0	£4 2 6
BIRMINGHAM ..	142	164	£5 6 6	£7 2 0	£8 17 6
BORTH	68	98	£2 11 0	£3 8 0	£4 5 0
BRISTOL	134	2)4	£5 0 6	£6 14 0	£8 7 6
CARDIFF	108	144	£4 1 0	£5 8 0	£6 15 0
CHESTER	140	170	£5 5 0	£7 0 0	£8 15 0
ELAN VALLEY LAKES *A spectacular flight of extreme interest.*	24	40	£— 18 0	£1 4 0	£1 10 0
HEREFORD ...	62	80	£2 6 6	£3 2 0	£3 17 6
LONDON ...	276	344	£10 7 0	£13 16 0	£17 5 0
SHREWSBURY ...	86	110	£3 4 6	£4 6 0	£5 7 6

For further information and booking of flights apply to Manager, The Aerodrome, Llandrindod Wells.

"Travel the Skyway for Business and Pleasure."

An advertisement for the air taxi service that operated from the Ddole airstrip between 1932 and 1934.
(© Radnorshire Museum)

Advertising poster for the Jubilee Air Display in Llandrindod Wells in 1935.
(© Powys County Archives)

By 1935 the days of the Ddole aerodrome were waning. The field was small, boggy and surrounded by trees. When the first aeroplane had landed there nobody could have dreamed how big and powerful aircraft would become, and the aerodrome was no longer suitable. Even so, that May saw the Silver Jubilee of King George V and Queen Mary, and among the celebrations 180 towns around Great Britain were to be visited by the 'Jubilee Air Display' led by none other than Owen Cathcart-Jones.

A poster for the 1935 Jubilee Air Display. (© Radnorshire Museum)

Some of the aircraft involved in the 1936 air display run by Scott and Campbell-Black on the Ddole airfield.
(© P. Davies)

A simple poster for the air display's visit to the Ddole airfield simply enticed the audience to 'Fly with Cathcart-Jones in his Monospar Monoplane'. Owen Cathcart-Jones was the star attraction at the display that June, and although aircraft were now commonplace even in Radnorshire (the town had had a taxi service for two years) the display still commanded a good turnout.

Shortly after he thrilled the crowds in Radnorshire, Cathcart-Jones left Britain. In July he looked for a sponsor to help him build the world's fastest plane, but this came to nothing. He next appeared in the national newspapers having flown a borrowed plane to Spain, where, it seems, he sold it and disappeared. The owner sued but got nowhere.

Members of the town council had still not given up on the idea of an airfield in the district, and with the threat of war hanging over Europe, the council now approached both the army and the Air Ministry in an attempt to bring some prosperity to the town. But 1936 was to see the last air display in Llandrindod Wells, this time organized by C.W.A. Scott with fellow aviator Tom Campbell-Black.

Scott had joined the RAF in 1922 and quickly became one of their best aerobatic pilots. He was singled out from others in the display team by being allowed to paint his aircraft bright red and having a certain amount of freedom in the type and height of the display he conducted. Scott held several speed records and in 1931 he was awarded the Air Force Cross for breaking the England to Australia solo flight time. In 1932 he took and then retook the title. He was also instrumental in setting up QANTAS airways.

Tom Campbell-Black had joined the Royal Naval Air Service on his 18th birthday on 22 August 1917; he transferred to the RAF in 1920. In 1922 he went to join his brother in Kenya raising horses on a ranch about 110 miles from Nairobi. He maintained an aircraft while in Kenya and with the help of the wealthy Mrs Wilson, whom he had taught to fly,

C.W.A. Scott (left) and Tom Campbell-Black.
(© Royal Aero Club)

set up Wilson Airways. In 1932 he left Kenya and returned to England to be the personal pilot of a wealthy horse breeder.

Scott and Campbell-Black met at a cocktail party in 1933 after the England to Australia air race and there and then decided to get sponsorship for the next year's race. It was little wonder that they made a record-winning team, flying one of three purpose-built De-Havilland DH88 Comet racers, in what is still considered by many today to be the world's greatest air race, garnering £10,000 in prize money in the process. Scott used part of his winnings to buy Alan Cobham's flying circus. Although many of Alan's pilots stayed with the circus, Scott asked Campbell-Black to join him as well.

Thus on 17 August 1936 the two record-winning long distance pilots and their circus entertained the crowds at Llandrindod Wells. By now displays were becoming a bit old hat, but they were still a chance for many to get their first ride in a plane. Scott did not have the advantage that Cobham had enjoyed in having Sir Charles Wakefield not only backing his campaign but also funding the 'Youth of Britain' free flight project. It is almost impossible now to calculate the impact of both the Cobham/Wakefield project and flying circuses in general on the young folk of Great Britain. As the 1930s progressed the RAF embarked on a major expansion programme and many of the fresh-faced young men and women who stepped forward to keenly fill these new roles did so because they had had their first taste of flying with Alan Cobham or had marvelled at the skill of the pilots on National Air Days.

The last air display on the Ddole Airstrip, August 1936.
(© Radnorshire Museum)

An exceptionally poor summer, however, meant that the 1936 air displays were nowhere near as successful as the previous year's. Scott considered folding the flying circus. Then, on 19 September, Tom Campbell-Black announced that he would be entering the England to South Africa air race under the sponsorship of John Moores, the Littlewoods tycoon. The Percival Mew Gull (a single seater racing aircraft constructed of wood) had just been renamed 'Miss Liverpool' in a ceremony at Speke Airport and Campbell-Black was waiting on the tarmac to take off when Flying Officer Peter Salter, the assistant adjutant and chief flying instructor of 611 Squadron, came into land and started taxiing along the runway. Salter was flying a Hawker Hart light bomber, a cumbersome biplane with not much forward visibility when on the ground. Salter's propeller sliced through the cockpit of Campbell-Black's plane, causing him fatal injuries. Salter was unhurt.

Hearing the news, Scott sold the flying circus and later that month in a Percival Vega Gull he won the very race Campbell-Black had been about to enter. Scott then struggled with depression for some time but at the outbreak of the Second World War he volunteered his services to the RAF. He was informed that he could start as a pilot officer (the lowest commissioned rank) and might be able to carry out ferry pilot duties after some further aviation instruction. This attitude outraged Scott – he was after all a world famous Air Force Cross winner who had also been part of the RAF's own crack display team. Scott withdrew his offer of service and went and joined the London ARP as an ambulance driver.

During the years that the air displays continued to be held at the Ddole airfield, Llandrindod Wells Urban District Council continued to try to get a plot of land on the south side of town turned into a landing strip. Dolberthog common, a large flat and open piece of land, ran alongside the railway line and close to the main road which made it an

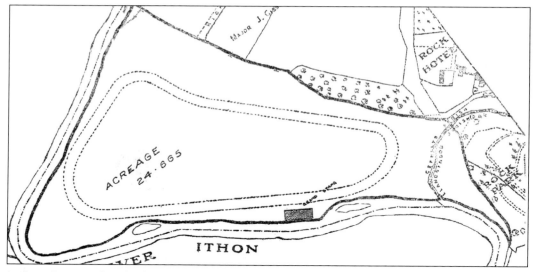

Plan of proposed airfield on the Rock Park Ddole as drawn up in the late 1920s or early 1930s.
The site had been a racecourse and aircraft landed and took off on the long straight
in front of the grandstand. (© Radnorshire Museum)

ideal site and a far better proposition than the old Ddole airfield. Plans were drawn up and the cost was announced as £38,500. On 22 May 1944 the idea was finally shelved as the air ministry were making plans for the invasion of Europe, and very little building of new airfields was now taking place in Britain.

In the meantime Scott had donated the trophy he and Tom Campbell-Black had won in their epic England to Australia race to the Red Cross for melting down. Eventually he did join RAF Ferry Command. He also worked for the Canadian branch of De-Havilland, testing and eventually instructing on the Mosquito – a plane developed from the DH88 Comet that Scott and Campbell-Black had flown in the 1934 air race.

Scott's personal life had always been turbulent. His first two marriages failed due to drink and absences from home. His only child, a daughter, Rosemary, lived in Australia with her mother. With the war ending and his fame and ability to command vast crowds as an air race hero gone, Scott slipped into deeper and deeper depression. Estranged from his third wife and whilst stationed with the United Nations in Germany he was told by his mistress that she would never leave her husband and so he decided to take his own life. On 15 April 1946 he shot himself.

As for Owen Cathcart-Jones, he will make another appearance in Chapter 5.

5 Training Recruits in the Second World War

Although many schools and youth organizations had been operating cadet forces for several years, usually conducted along military lines, it was not until the 1930s that the government decided to take control and organize the cadet forces properly and set about forming a coherent training program for young men between the ages of 14 and 18. Junior branches were formed for each service, the Army had its cadets, the Navy had the sea scouts and the Air Force had the Air Defence Cadet Corps (ADCC). The outbreak of the Second World War saw many boys rush to join all branches of the cadet force.

Initially those joining the ADCC wore the same uniform as the army cadets, but with an armband identifying them as RAF cadets. They met in schools, church and village halls, and even sports pavilions. By 1940 cadets could be out training every night and most of Saturday. It was hoped that the Air Defence Corps cadets would join either the Royal Air Force or the Fleet Air Arm, the Navy's Flying wing, as the sea cadets purely focused on turning out potential ship board personnel. The cadets also patrolled with air raid wardens, manned first aid stations, served tea and filled sandbags, among many other useful roles. In 1941 the government finally realised just how valuable the cadet corps was and started to reorganise them along stricter military lines. As a result, on 5 February 1941 the ADCC became the Air Training Corps, with King George VI their Air Commodore in Chief. The boys were given uniforms in RAF blue closely resembling their fully fledged counterparts, but with white metal buttons and a badge depicting a falcon and the words *Air Training Corps*. The cadets also wore their flight number on their shoulders. There was a rush to form new ATC squadrons and in March 1941 the headmaster of Llandrindod Wells County School, H. Gordon Garratt, applied to set up a cadet force at the school, proudly telling the Air Ministry that he had 55 boys ready and willing to start. The headmaster duly received a commission as a pilot officer in the RAFVR.

The Llandrindod Wells Air Training Corps was designated No.579 Flight and went from strength to strength, averaging around 40 cadets through most of the war years, the majority coming from the senior years. Gordon Garratt was succeeded by Pilot Officer D.T Evans later in 1941, ably assisted by two other masters – Pilot Officer S.E Sobey and Pilot Officer K.N. Lobb. Pilot Officer H.A. Peter joined the staff in 1943.

Land adjoining the prestigious Llandrindod Wells Golf Club, situated on high ground overlooking the town lake, was used by the 124 Officer Cadet Training Unit (OCTU) of the Royal Artillery, based in the town until 1944. A flat field was used as an airstrip by aircraft from 1943 onwards, when the whole area was requisitioned and used by the Americans, army spotter planes observing the range and accuracy of artillery fired either from the Cambrian battle school at Llangurig west of Llandrindod, or from the Mynydd Epynt artillery school to the south. The results would be radioed back to headquarters and the guns could be recalibrated if the target had been missed. The OCTU meanwhile annoyed members of the golf club by damaging the road that passed the clubhouse with their trucks and large vehicles and as a result, shortly after the start of the war the manager of the golf club was moved to write to army headquarters in Brecon. He received a very short, sharp reply reminding him that there was a war on and further advising him that the whole area was marked down for requisition by the military and that any repairs would be paid for at the end of hostilities.

The OCTU would help instruct the cadets in drill and weapons training as well as aircraft and tank recognition. The young cadets were also taught maths, signalling, wireless engineering and navigation to enable them to pass the air crew proficiency exams. Cadets also worked on RAF bases before they were able to either join up full time or get a place

No.579 Llandrindod Wells County School Flight of the ATC in 1942. (© Mr G. Price)

No.1822 Knighton Flight of the ATC in 1942. (© No.579 Squadron ATC)

on an apprentice course, and many of 579's cadets indeed went on to join the RAF. One, D.H. Evans, excelled at aircraft recognition and achieved top marks in a test with the Royal Observer Corps. He was the only cadet in Wales to do so and came to the attention of the Air Ministry who expressly asked if he would join adult Observer Corps members on board one of the ships crossing the channel on D-Day. Evans had not yet reached the age of 16 so could not be called up, and his parents refused to allow him to go as they thought it would be far too dangerous.

The Royal Observer Corps is an often overlooked branch of the services. Originally formed in 1925, in recent years it has often been portrayed as a group of part-timers, boys or retired old men who just stood outside wooden huts drinking tea and waiting for something to happen. Although radar coverage improved with each passing year of the war, there were always gaps in the system. Even late in the war it was still relatively easy for a lone enemy intruder to sneak in under the radar, and the ROC was often the first to provide an alert regarding enemy aircraft in a given area. The ROC was also responsible for tracking allied aircraft and alerting the emergency services of a downed aircraft, and many an airman in a lost or damaged aircraft was guided home as a result of their actions. Many a crash was located quickly enough for lives to be saved, simply because the stricken aeroplane had passed over an ROC post. Radnorshire had five ROC posts – all opened in August 1939 – in Knighton, Llananno, Llandrindod Wells, New Radnor and Rhayader. They formed part of No.25 Group, which was formed in 1938 in Cardiff.[1]

The Royal Observer Corps post in Llandrindod Wells. (© P. Williams)

Llandrindod Wells becomes a home for recuperating servicemen

During the Second World War, Llandrindod Wells came to the attention of the war office for several reasons. Due to its rural location and surplus of large buildings and hotels, the town was deemed eminently suitable both for the stationing of troops under training and for turning many of its large hotels into hospitals and convalescent homes. There was a small county war memorial hospital that had been built in the town before the war, but at least four hotels and several large houses were also turned into hospitals. The largest of these was the Pump House Hotel, an impressive Victorian building that went through several changes of use from luxury hotel to wartime hospital to residential deaf school and council offices before being knocked down in the late 1980s. The Powys County Council Hall building now stands on the site.

Nurses accompanying recuperating soldiers, sailors and airmen were just as familiar a sight as the young trainee officers who were also billeted in the town. Ernest Morley and Cyril Mould were just two of the men who came to Llandrindod for medical attention.

Ernest John Morley was born in about 1905, the son of Joseph Henry and Hannah Morley of 17 Pennant Terrace, Walthamstow in Essex. Ernest had enlisted in the Royal Air Force Volunteer Reserve in April/May 1940 and had become an Aircraftsman First Class. He was being treated at the Ministry of Pensions' hospital (the Pump House Hotel) when he died on 31 December 1944. Ernest's family (it is not clear if he was married) decided he should be buried in Llandrindod Wells cemetery. Ernest had served

Doctors and nursing staff of the Ministry of Pensions hospital at the Pump House in 1940.
(© P. Williams)

The gravestones in Llandrindod Wells Town Cemetery of Ernest Morley (top) and Cyril Mould (bottom) (© Author's collection)

four years in the RAF and records do not tell where he served or what he did; it may never be known if his death was the result of illness or an accident or wound, but this 39-year-old airman rests in the town's cemetery, the words 'at the going down of the sun and in the morning we will remember him' inscribed on his headstone.

Cyril Chardin Mould was born in Surrey in 1908; his father was a commercial traveller who worked for a biscuit manufacturer. Cyril was married to Ada Lillian Mould and they lived at 25 Prince Road, Selhurst in south-east London. Cyril joined the Royal Air Force Volunteer Reserve in the summer of 1941 and became a leading aircraftsman. What led to Cyril being admitted to the Ministry of Pensions hospital and his eventual death on 27 March 1945 is not recorded. Like Ernest, Cyril was buried in the local cemetery and their war grave commission RAF service headstones stand side by side. Cyril's family had the words *Vitae Summa Brevi Spem Nos Vetat Incohare Longam* – 'The brief sum of life prevents us from hoping that we may endure for a long while' – carved on his headstone. The words are from Horace's ode 1.4, which was used by Ernest Dawson as a title for the poem which contains the well-known phrase, 'They are not long, these days of wine and roses'.

Slight mystery surrounds a third airman who might have been treated in Llandrindod Wells and who also might have had some other connections with Radnorshire. Frederick Pritchard, the son of David and Edith Pritchard, was born in Shrewsbury on 20 November 1906. Frederick went to work for the Midland Bank and was to spend nearly 20 years with them, working at the Colwyn Bay branch between 1937 and 1941. He married Lilian Powell. In November 1941 he enlisted in the RAFVR and a year later was an aircraftsman second class serving with 543 Squadron, a photo reconnaissance unit based at RAF Benson in Oxfordshire. On 13 November 1942 Frederick was among 200 passengers on a train that was travelling in heavy fog on the Oxford to Didcot line. At 1.45am at Appleford near Didcot the train collided with a goods train that was on the same line due to a signalling error. Both trains were derailed. The driver and fireman of the goods train were killed, a porter was killed on the passenger train and sixteen people were injured, one of them, Frederick Pritchard, seriously. He died of his injuries a week later on his 37th birthday and was buried at All Saints Church in Newbridge-on-Wye, but the reason for his being buried there is unclear. A family link with Radnorshire has not been traced and his wife was still living in Colwyn Bay, where he is remembered on the war memorial. It may well be that Frederick had been transferred to the hospital in Llandrindod Wells that specialised in spinal injuries.

Another Radnorshire airman who had connections with Llandrindod Wells' wartime hospitals was Alexander Montgomery Bryan Smith, known as Monty. His widowed grandmother ran the large Ye Wells hotel in the town and during the First World War had petitioned the War Office to excuse her son Ernest (Monty's father) war service after she had already lost both another son Clement and her stepson Howard in France, arguing that Ernest was needed to help her run the hotel. As Ernest was subsequently found to have a heart condition, his military service was in any event deferred. Ernest had married Beatrice Mary Griffiths, the daughter of Newbridge-on-Wye vicar James Griffiths in 1913 and both moved into Ye Wells hotel, where Monty was born in 1914. On the outbreak of the Second World War Monty joined the Royal Air Force, training to become an RAF medic. Meanwhile, in June 1940 Ye Wells hotel was commandeered as a hospital, while Monty's sister Sheila was working as a nurse at the hospital based in the Pump House Hotel. Not content with serving as a medic, Monty applied for and was accepted to train for aircrew. By June 1942 he was at Scarborough and then was sent to Canada to complete his training. Whilst it is known that he became an air gunner and flew several times to Germany, details of his career are sketchy. He survived the war and returned home to Llandrindod Wells. His family had decided not to reopen the hotel once the military had relinquished it, and the building become a further education college. Monty, who had trained as an artist before the war, set up an art gallery and bookshop in the town, but later contracted polio and became confined to a wheelchair. He died in 1980.

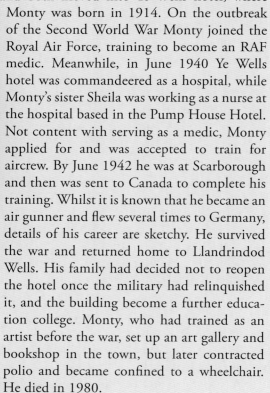

Alexander 'Monty' as a medical orderly at Halton Camp in 1940 (top) and (above left) during his training in Canada.

Throughout the war, civilian instructors were also drafted in to give a variety of lectures to the air cadets, sometimes relating to their own experiences in the First World War. An important part of the training was conducted at the annual summer camps, and cadets from 579 Flight spent time at RAF stations in St Athan and Fairwood Common, as well as gaining flying experience at RAF Madley in Herefordshire.[2]

In due time the golf course at Llandrindod Wells was indeed requisitioned. In 1943 an American field artillery battalion moved in and used it as a small landing strip for L4 Piper aircraft (known as Grasshoppers), remaining there until the summer of 1944, when the golf course was returned to its former use.

The only other wartime airstrip in Radnorshire was at what is now the Royal Welsh Agricultural Showground in Llanelwedd. For a short time during 1942, 651 Air Observation Post (AOP) Squadron was based there, essentially doing the same job as the Americans up on the golf course in Llandrindod Wells. The AOP units were small and compact and could operate out of farmhouses and village halls; they only needed a fairly flat strip of land to act as a landing strip and they kept in touch with their home bases via a radio. The units were mostly manned by army pilots and on 6 March 1942 Captain Rogers arrived in Llanelwedd by road to survey the site. Rogers and Captain Nielson from B flight then commenced spotting flights from the showground. Just eight days later Captain Rogers was killed when his Taylorcraft Plus aircraft crashed in a field in Garth in Breconshire. He is remembered on a plaque in Llangammarch church. Four days later Captain Nielson packed up and left.

The training that an RAF recruit as opposed to a cadet received is well illustrated in the case of Thomas Henry Anthony of Clyro. The son of Richard and Elizabeth Anthony, Thomas was born on 6 March 1914, one of eight children. He became a clerk for the Prudential Insurance Company, before joining the Royal Air Force Volunteer Reserve a year after the outbreak of the Second World War on 3 September 1940. On 15 May 1941 he married his fiancée Dorothy Freda Woodley (Freda) of Hay-on-Wye at Christchurch, Weston-Super-Mare.

Thomas's initial training was at Cardington in Bedfordshire, and then, on 23 October 1941, he was posted to the Blackpool radio school. Here he would have been taught all the skills necessary to become a wireless operator, but that was not the end of his training for he was destined to become a combined wireless operator and air gunner in a bomber crew – it was usual for the wireless operator to also be an air gunner in one of the bomber's turrets. He therefore spent a further three months at signal school and another month at an air gunnery school. Then in July 1942 he was promoted to the rank of pilot officer, a rank that confusingly does not indicate he was now a qualified pilot.

It might be useful at this point to set out the order of seniority of ranks that will be encountered in this and the following chapters. The lowest rank was that of aircraftsman 2nd class (Ac2), with progression to aircraftsman 1st class (Ac1) and then leading aircraftsman (LAC) before the ranks of corporal (Cpl) and then sergeant (Sgt). Next in seniority, but still non commissioned officers, were flight sergeant (Flt/Sgt) and warrant officer W/O), the latter being a separate class and normally awarded to someone as a result of long service or particular expertise in a given field. With the next rank of pilot officer (P/O) one entered the ranks of the commissioned officers, even if the actual name was a slight misnomer. Then, in ascending order of seniority, came flying officer (F/O), flight lieutenant (Flt/Lt), squadron leader, wing commander and group captain, beyond which lay air commodore and then the various ranks of air marshals. A rank might well be initially awarded for a probationary period.

Most of those who sought to join the RAF wished to become pilots, and during what was to become known as the Battle of Britain their wish would probably be satisfied, as there were not enough trained pilots ready to take the places of the young men who were being killed. But the RAF had need of more than just pilots and once that crisis was past would seek to ascertain where a recruit would be most usefully employed. Take the case of David Colville Price, of whom more will be told in Chapter 11. He was just 16 years old when war broke out; he had just taken his school certificate and was unsure what exactly he would do with his life. The Secretary of State for War (Leslie Hore-Belisha) had introduced a limited form of national service on 27 April 1939 whereby all fit single men between the ages of 20 and 22 could be called up to train alongside the regular army. This was amended on the outbreak of the war for possible conscription of all men between the ages of 18 and 41.

Although still too young to be called up, David decided that when the time came he would like to try for the Royal Air Force. In July 1941 at the age of 17 he was asked to attend for the first stages of his recruitment. David recounted in a letter to his grandchildren how he first had to attend a medical which included rigorous tests on his hearing and eyesight. He and his fellow hopefuls were then given a whole series of exams, including mathematics, at which he was very good, and problem solving. A panel of RAF officers then assessed the results and decided on which course to enrol them.

Many of those who became pilots undertook some of their training at an Elementary Flying Training School (EFTS). This was the case for Chris Peirson Jones, of whom more in Chapter 7, who attended the EFTS at Wolverhampton. Here he was taught the rudiments of flying, and his carefully kept logbook details his first air experience flight with Sgt Lowther as pilot on 15 December 1941. During the 20 minute flight in a DH82 (Tiger Moth) Chris was expected to familiarise himself with the cockpit but he would not have done any flying. The next day he was up again with Sgt Lowther, this time for 30 minutes, and he was actually allowed to get the feel of the controls. On a second flight later that same day he was allowed to taxi the aircraft and once airborne to do a bit of straight and level flying and even climbing, gliding and a few turns. Chris continued flying with Sgt Lowther until 27 December, all the time being assessed as to what sort of pilot he would make.

A trainee pilot would then normally progress to a Service Flying Training School (SFTS) where, if successful, he would gain his 'wings', and then go on to an Advanced Flying Unit (AFU).

Whether destined to become a pilot or another member of a bomber crew, such as the flight engineer, navigator, wireless operator and/or air gunner, and having completed the relevant training, pilots and crew would then attend an Operational Training Unit (OTU). These were situated away from the 'front line' but would enable crews to fly under conditions as close to actual operational circumstances as possible. Bomber and fighter OTUs operated differently from each other, and there were cases such as on the 'thousand bomber raids' when instructors and more advanced pupils from bomber OTUs were sent on operations.

The training varied as war progressed and it became common for a bomber pilot in the later stages of his training to go on a raid with an experienced crew as a second pilot before taking his own crew on operations.

Pilot Officer Thomas Anthony RAFVR.
(© The Anthony Family Archive)

During 1943 the drive to recruit more RAF personnel was starting to turn what had been a shortage of servicemen into a surfeit, and pilots and aircrew who had been judged more than competent to fly found that they had nowhere to go. So the Air Ministry started to increase the length of some courses and designated some training units as holding units where all aircrew were kept in a state of preparedness whilst waiting to be posted to an operational squadron.

Returning to the training of Thomas Anthony, who we left just having been promoted to the rank of pilot officer in July 1942, he was then posted to an operational training unit (No.19 OTU in his case). Following this, in November 1942, he joined a conversion unit. Here he trained on the aircraft that he would be flying in operationally. From here he was posted to 57 Squadron in Scampton in Lincolnshire. The squadron had been flying Wellingtons but was in the process of moving to Lancasters; the MkI and MkIII Lancasters had started arriving at Scampton in September. When he arrived on 12 January 1943 the crews were still carrying out familiarisation exercises with the new aircraft as well as flying the aircraft at night, using instruments only.

On the night of 27 January 1943, just fifteen days later, Thomas and his crew were on a cross-country exercise. The night was moonless and very dark, but their pilot Sgt W.H. Wood was experienced, having 298 flying hours under his belt, 68 of which had been at night. However he had only flown Lancasters for a total of 32 hours and only ten of these had been at night. During the course of this night's exercise he would be called upon to use the blind flying instrument panel. The aircraft flew across the Lincolnshire countryside, passed over Caistor heading north-east, but crashed into the ground two miles beyond the town. Sgt Norman Long, an air gunner, managed to bail out and survived the crash, but the other crew members – pilot Sgt W.H. Wood, flight engineer R.B. Wetterell, Sgt E.W. Campbell, the navigator, Sgt R.A. Chapman, the bomb aimer from the Royal Canadian Air Force, Sgt S.C. Bradley, another air gunner, together with the wireless operator/air gunner Pilot Officer Thomas Anthony – were all killed.

As it was a night-time cross-country exercise and not a combat mission, a court of enquiry was set up to investigate the circumstances of the crash. The short and rather damning report found that the pilot was unable to use the blind flying instrument equipment properly; it further concluded that the pilot had 'lost his head'. It is not clear if Sgt. Long, who survived the crash by bailing out, gave evidence to this effect or if Thomas was able to radio back to base the trouble they were in. Sadly events unfolded too quickly to allow all the crew members to bail out.

On 2 February 1943 his family brought Thomas's body back to Clyro for burial. Thomas Anthony was not the only Radnorshire airman to be killed during his training.

Thomas Morgan was born in Rhayader in the summer of 1917 to Thomas and Catherine Ellen Morgan. He attended Llandrindod Wells County School before enlisting in the Royal Air Force Volunteer Reserve at Uxbridge in 1939. He rose to the rank of sergeant and in early 1941 was sent to No.25 Operational Training Unit which provided the final polishing of crews for the both the Hampden and the Anson (a multi-role aircraft), conducting both day and night time exercises before the crews became fully operational.

The Hampden had first entered RAF service in 1938 with 49 Squadron. At the outbreak of the war they were used for reconnaissance duties and light daylight bombing raids, but the ponderous and not very manoeuvrable Hampden soon proved to be no match for German fighters and by December 1939 Bomber Command decided to switch the Hampden to a night bomber role. The Hampden had been nicknamed the flying suitcase by crews who found it a very cramped aircraft to fly. Wing Commander Guy Gibson, who led the successful Dambusters raid, spent his first two years flying the Hampden and his book *Enemy Coast Ahead* (published posthumously in 1946) details some of the trials and tribulation of flying the aircraft.

No.25 OTU was based at RAF Finningley in South Yorkshire, a satellite base for RAF Scampton. Here Thomas teamed up with Sergeants Billy Halbert and Edward Dawson, and with Flying Officer Peter Dixon-Spain as pilot they made up the four-man crew of a Hampden. (Finningley would host the Vulcan bomber during the 1960s and eventually enter private hands and become the Robin Hood Airport.)

On 18 May 1941 Thomas and his crew were on a night time navigational exercise. The exact route and duration of the flight they took that night is unknown, for nothing more was heard from the crew after they took off from the base. No wreckage was found and they were listed as lost without trace. All the crew are commemorated on the Runnymede memorial for those with no known grave, whilst Thomas Morgan is also remembered on the memorial in his home town of Rhayader and on the Llandrindod Wells County School memorial. He was 23 years old.

Like Thomas Anthony, William Cyril Williams, known to his family as Cyril, was also to attend the Blackpool radio school. Born on 31 July 1921 to John and Sarah Williams, who ran the Llanbadarn Hotel in Crossgates (now the Builders Arms), Cyril

Sgt William Cyril Williams, RAFVR.
(© Mrs S.E. Goodwin)

attended Llandrindod Wells County School. On 11 July 1941, just before his 20th birthday, he enlisted in the Royal Air Force. His initial request for aircrew training was turned down, but he was told to re-apply three months later for trade training, presumably in maintenance. Three months later he was duly sent to Blackpool and by 31 December he had the rank of aircraftsman first class, was judged to be of very good character with satisfactory marks in all his tests, and was informed that he would be an aircraft hand on general duties.

Although happy just to be in the RAF, Cyril had not completely given up on his dream of flying. Many young men who wished to be aircrew were given the opportunity to train with the service to make up for gaps in schooling. Whether or not this was Cyril's route it is impossible to say, but it seems that in December 1941, six months after being turned down for aircrew, he was posted to No.14 Service Flying Training School at RAF Ossington, Nottinghamshire. This school was redesignated No.14 (Pilot) Advanced Flying Unit on 26 January 1942, and it was here that Cyril gained his pilot's wings on successful completion of his course.

It seems that Cyril's career then took a strange turn. On 15 April 1942 he was posted to RAF Hereford to complete a drill course, and from there was sent to the Technical School of Physical Training for possible training as a PT instructor, whilst September found him awaiting an interview with the Air Crew Selection Board. Whether the next move was the decision of the selection board or of Cyril himself is not known, but in December 1942 he was posted to the No.2 Air Gunnery School – but not as a pilot, instead training to be an air gunner.

It is easy to jump to the conclusion that Cyril in some way failed at pilot training. This may not have been the case. Many young men who passed initial training found places on an operational training unit so difficult to get, that rather than wait and do even more training (often in places like Canada away from the action) they would apply for other duties in an aircraft.

Cyril duly qualified as an air gunner on 29 January 1943 and then entered on a period of further intensive training. Between 31 January and 5 July 1943 he moved seven times, but always flying in heavy bombers. He started in Stirlings, then moved on to Wellingtons and spent three weeks with a target towing unit. Then he was posted to a Lancaster conversation unit. At all of these units he was judged to be proficient in his trade and to have an excellent character. He was next based in RAF Swinderby near Lincoln with No.1660 Heavy Conversion Unit. It was here, on 6 July 1943, that Cyril, while still under training, took off as part of the crew of Lancaster Bomber R5736. The crew consisted of Pilot Officer E.A. Orchard, Flight Sgt B.A. Cook and Sergeants C.P. Lucas, R.E. Sadleir, R.W.A. Dipple, and Sgt William Cyril Williams as air gunner. The pilot had 243 solo flying hours to his credit, but only four of these were on Lancasters. The weather was poor so the crew had been warned to maintain a safe height, especially as they were to be flying over the mountains of north Wales. During the flight the navigator believed they had crossed over the high ground, but may have asked the pilot for a visual fix. The aircraft descended into the gloom of thickening cloud and rain; even at an altitude of 100ft they were still not able to see the ground. Minutes later the aircraft struck the ground at Llangernyw in Denbighshire and exploded on impact. Everybody on board was killed. A subsequent court of inquiry concluded that 'an error of captaincy' had been to blame.

Pilot Officer E.A Orchard and Sergeant R.W.A Dipple were given military funerals. The remaining crew members were taken home and buried by their families; Cyril Williams was buried in St Michael's churchyard, Beguildy, where his parents commissioned a stained glass window in his honour. He is also remembered on the Llandrindod Wells war memorial and on the war memorial in Penybont.

Cyril Williams might have turned down the chance to go and train in Canada, but several men did take that opportunity, or to train in the US under what became known as the Arnold Scheme. This scheme had been instigated in May 1941 when American General Henry H. Arnold had offered the services of several bases in the country to help train new RAF recruits. At this stage in the war the British were finding it increasingly difficult to keep up with the demand for new airmen and keep RAF bases operational. One of the men trained under the Arnold Scheme was Alfred Thomas Lloyd, the son of Mr and Mrs James Lloyd of New Radnor.

In 1941, at the age of 18, Alfred applied to join the Royal Air Force, was accepted and sent for pilot training in America by the American Army Air Corps under the Arnold Scheme. Alfred was posted to Carlstrom airfield in Florida. Alfred arrived in late 1941 and on 5 January 1942 was judged able to take his first solo flight, which was completed successfully. One favourite trick at the airfield was to perform a small initiation ceremony on a newly soloed pilot, which involved dunking the cadet. Carlstrom had a swimming pool on its base and that night, once Alfred was asleep, four of his classmates crept into his bedroom, picked up his mattress and quietly conveyed him towards the pool and threw him in. As the seconds ticked by the horrified cadets realised that Alfred was not showing any signs of surfacing, and dived in to pull him out, but barely seven hours after experiencing the thrill of his first solo flight, Alfred was dead. There was a court of enquiry, but no blame was laid at anybody's door – it was judged a case of high spirits that had gone tragically wrong. Alfred was buried in the Arcadia Cemetery in Oakridge, Florida.

One pilot who had paid a fleeting aerial visit to Radnorshire shortly before the war was to turn up in Canada in 1940 and join the Royal Canadian Air Force (RCAF). This was Owen Cathcart-Jones, last seen having absconded with an aircraft which he flew to Spain and sold. It would seem that he lay low in the interim, possibly having moved to the States. In any event, by 1942 he was a squadron leader in the RCAF, but between April and July that year he was listed as Being Absent Without Leave, being brought back under escort from California, where he had had a brief stint in the movies. He had served as technical director on a James Cagney film *Captains of the Clouds* in which he even gained a small acting part as the chief flying instructor. The film was described by *Flight Magazine* as 'First class in every respect'. A second film, Errol Flynn's *Desperate Journey*, was not so well received. He became friendly with Errol Flynn but got mixed up in a court case between Flynn and the 15-year-old Peggy Satterlee.

It was also while he was serving with the RCAF that Cathcart-Jones designed a board game entitled 'Be an Airman', being responsible for the design and the artwork (art being another string to his bow). It was a success and was sold to raise funds for the RCAF benevolent fund.

In September 1942 he retired from the RCAF. He was subsequently rumoured to have served as a Lieutenant Commander in the United States Naval Reserve, where he commanded his own ship, and was even reputed to have joined General MacArthur's staff at Lake Sentani above Hollandia in New Guinea. (He was next to be found raising polo ponies on a ranch in Santa Barbara where he became president of the polo club and spent most of the rest of his life. Aged 79 in 1981 he was knocked off his horse, but survived to die peacefully at his California home in 1986.)

Another man with a rather chequered background was Vivian Newton Ashton. Vivian was born in 1918 to Harold and Florence Mary Ashton (née Gooch) who lived in Spalding, Lincolnshire where Harold was a corporate accountant and the family were considered somewhat 'well to do'. In the early 1920s they moved to Ivydene, a tall Victorian town house in Alexandra Road, Llandrindod Wells. Very little is known about Vivian's early life and it seems he took pains to keep his adult life secret as well.

Vivian was tall, good looking and well educated – he was fluent in both French and German. His talent for languages would have probably given him access to any branch of the services he wished to join and he chose the Royal Navy. Contemporary photographs show him with a cheeky boyish smile and a seemingly happy demeanour, but Vivian hated his time in the Navy. In fact he hated it so much that on the eve of the Second World War he deserted and a warrant was issued for his arrest. Although the government had stopped shooting deserters in 1930, his actions would still carry a stiff penalty.

Vivian was unable to come back to Llandrindod and, according to his nephew Hugh Webbon, his parents moved to the Golders Green area of London in order to help and support him. It would be easy to jump to the conclusion that Vivian was just shirking his duty at a time when so many young men were being killed, but this was not entirely the case. Whatever had led to his decision to desert, it had not been a hatred of the sea or ships because Vivian next had a spell with the Merchant Navy. He enlisted as the lowliest of lowly deck hands under the name of Eric James Ashton and became a crew member on the *Doric Star*. The *Doric Star* was a refrigerated cargo ship carrying frozen meat as well as eggs and cheese; also stacked in the hold were several hundred bales of wool.

The German pocket battle ship *Graf Spee* caught up with and captured the *Doric Star* on 2 December 1939, firing warning shots across her bow and threatening to sink her if a radio message was transmitted. German officers then boarded the ship and took the entire crew prisoner. The leader of the boarding party had only taken a cursory glance into the hold and didn't notice all the food, only the wool. The order was given to sink the ship. The *Graf Spee* had been one hundred days at sea with very little fresh produce left on board and when its captain learned of the sunken food, he was apparently less than pleased.

Vivian Newton Ashton.
(© The late Miss J. Ashton)

Vivian, now a prisoner of war, was transferred to the converted tanker the *Altmark*. By February 1940 there were 299 prisoners on board the vessel. On 14 February 1940 the *Altmark* was spotted in a Norwegian fjord by an aircraft of British Coastal Command. Two days later, *HMS Cossack* reached her and a skirmish ensued. Eventually, late in the evening, Royal Navy personnel boarded the *Altmark* and in the hand to hand fighting the last recorded use in anger of a cutlass by an officer of the Royal Navy took place. The *Altmark* was run onto the rocks. Seven German officers who tried to flee across the ice were shot and the rest taken prisoner.

HMS Cossack returned to Britain a few days later and reporters were on the quayside to photograph the rescued prisoners. Ashton family legend tells that Vivian's photograph was among the first to appear in the newspapers the next day. In fact that was not the only reference to Vivian, as the Pathé News team was also on the quayside and to this day a smiling and waving Vivian can be seen disembarking from *HMS Cossack*. It must have been quite a shock for a deserter to know that his face was all over the cinema screens.

There was still a warrant out for his arrest and rather understandably Vivian was no longer overly keen on the Merchant Navy, so he decided to disappear a second time. This time he enlisted legal help and changed his name by deed poll. The *London Gazette* for 27 January 1942 records that Vivian Newton Ashton would henceforth be known as James Ashton. Not a great change, but probably enough in the pre-computer days for him not to be found.

James Ashton, as he was now known, decided to join the RAF, enlisting in the RAFVR under the name of Eric James Ashton, the name he had used when enlisting on the *Doric Star* (although there is no official record of a change to Eric). Sadly the details of his time in the RAF are as sketchy as the rest of his life. What is known is that he reached the rank of sergeant pilot in the RAFVR, had 112 flying hours under his belt, 39 of these on the Airspeed Oxford, a twin-engined training aircraft. On 21 May 1943 flying an Oxford he crashed near Little Rissington, Gloucestershire, home of No.6 Pilots Advanced Flying Unit. Vivian had been practising a glide approach and landing, not a difficult manoeuvre, when the aircraft was seen to spin into the ground from the relatively low height of 500 feet. The crash report simply states that the cause was obscure, but that there may have been a physical reason, suggesting that Vivian blacked out, but in truth nobody will ever know.

James Ashton is buried in Cheltenham Cemetery, Eric James Ashton is listed as killed in the advanced flying unit's records and Vivian Newton Ashton is commemorated on the war memorial in Llandrindod Wells. They are all one and the same man, a 24-year-old with a wide smile who deserted from one service, was captured while serving in a second service and was finally killed while flying with a third. His family have described him as being secretive, and he was apparently reluctant to visit or write to them, but this may have been because there was still a warrant out for his arrest.

Like Vivian/James Ashton, Hugh Douglas Bryson was not born in Radnorshire; in his case his place of birth was Rutherglen in Lanarkshire, Scotland. Born in 1921, he was the only son of William and Margaret Bryson, who moved to Bailey Mawr House in Penybont in 1938 when his father became a land agent for Lord Ormathwaite.

Hugh joined the RAFVR in the winter of 1940/41. Details of his time in the service are sketchy, but by late July 1943 he had gained the rank of flight sergeant and had logged up 333 flying hours, 147 of them spent on Tiger Moths. He was then based with No.15 EFTS (Elementary Flying Training School) at Redhill in Surrey, and it would appear that he had either become a flying instructor, or was training to become one. On 23 July he was flying Tiger Moth, serial number T6498, with Flight Sergeant T.R. Furber, who had logged up over 1,000 flying hours. After flying for 1¾ hours the pair were over Westlington in Cumberland, when the plane spun into the ground during a slow roll manoeuvre. Hugh was killed and Furber was seriously injured. A report into the incident concluded that there was no blame to be put on the pilot for the aircraft had suffered a structural defect, with the fin and rudder becoming detached from the fuselage – the rudder had been unable to stand the abnormal strain put on it during the execution of a half roll.

William and Margaret buried their son in their home town of Rutherglen, but he is also remembered on the war memorial in Penybont.

Another RAF recruit with Radnorshire connections, though also not born in the county, was Joseph Widger Murphy Macdonald. Born in Yorkshire in 1913, Joseph married Knighton girl Phyllis Rimmer in 1933 when they were both 20 years old. By 1934 they were living in Yorkshire where they had a son, Roy William.

In 1941 Joseph joined the Royal Air Force Volunteer Reserve and was soon training to become a bomber pilot. In August 1943 he was at No.1654 Heavy Conversion Unit at RAF Wigsley in Nottinghamshire learning to fly the Lancaster. On 12 August Joseph received a commission and was made a pilot officer. On the night of 1 September he took part in a night exercise. The rest of the crew were Flight Engineer Sgt G.R. Joyce, Flying Officer W.S. Jobling as navigator, Sgt E.N. Jones as bomb aimer, Sgt G.H. Tough as the wireless operator and air gunner, Sgt Hutchinson who was a member of the Royal Auxiliary Air Force as an air gunner, and Fl/Sgt R.W. Rashbrook of the Royal Australian Air Force who was also an air gunner. The navigator, F/O Walter Steven Jobling, was probably tour expired and instructing; he had previously served with 50 Squadron and had been awarded the Distinguished Flying Cross on 12 August 1943. The Lancaster was due to be back at its base in Wigsley at approximately 2.40am but at 3.26am, almost 50 minutes after they should have

landed, the plane was flying at 1,500 feet near the neighbouring airbase of RAF Syerston, about 18 miles from Wigsley. Also in the air was another Lancaster that was returning from a bombing raid on Berlin. It was an extremely dark night with heavy cloud cover at 4,000 feet, and some mist reported below that height, although visibility at ground level was reported to be approximately 4 miles. Neither Lancaster bomber radioed its base and although they would both have been showing navigation lights, these did not prevent the head on crash that happened

IN LOVING MEMORY OF
WILLIAM BRYSON
BELOVED HUSBAND OF MARGARET CLARK
DIED 3RD SEPTEMBER 1943, AGED 53 YEARS
AND THEIR DEAR SON
DOUGLAS BRYSON, FLIGHT SERGEANT, R.A.F.V.R.
KILLED ON ACTIVE SERVICE 23RD JULY 1943, AGED 21 YEARS
ALSO THE ABOVE
MARGARET CLARK
DIED 4TH JULY 1979, AGED 89 YEARS
ALSO THEIR DAUGHTER
GRETA GORDON
DIED 12TH NOV. 1993, AGED 79 YEARS
AND HER DEAR HUSBAND
BILL
DIED 11TH MAR. 1988, AGED 80 YEARS

*The commemorative text on the Bryson family grave
at Rutherglen Cemetery.
(© Author's collection)*

four miles outside Syerston. There was an explosion and all members of both crews were killed. Joseph was brought back to his home town and buried in the family grave, leaving a wife and young son.

The accident report concluded that there had been a failure in both crews to keep an adequate look out while flying in a congested area. It was concluded that if some of the navigation lights on the aircraft had been flashing they might have attracted more attention and given either one or both pilots time to take evasive action. All aircraft the world over now have to carry flashing lights by law.

Joseph Widger Murphy Macdonald remembered on the family plot in Birkdale RC Cemetery. (© aircrewremembered.com)

And then there is the rather sad story of one airman for whom little information has been found. Alfred Edward Evans was born to Oscar and Maude Evans (née Woosnam) of 29 Wye View Terrace, Builth Road, Rhayader in 1921, Oscar being a signalman on the railway. Alfred attended Llandrindod Wells County School and enlisted in the RAFVR in April or May 1940, becoming an aircraftsman 2nd class. On 9 September 1943 he died in the South Wales Sanatorium in Bronllys near Talgarth in Breconshire. The sanatorium had been turned over to the military in 1940 and treated, among other things, infectious diseases such as tuberculosis and this may have been the cause of death. Alfred had not married; his body was brought back to Radnorshire and buried in the churchyard of St John's Church, Cwm Bach Llechryd, Builth Road. He is remembered on the Roll of Honour in St John's Church and on the County School memorial in Llandrindod Wells.

6   Blenheims and Beaufighters

The Blenheim was a twin-engined light bomber used largely in daylight bombing raids in the first two years of the war, before they were shown to be easy prey for the German Messerschmitt fighters and were replaced by other aircraft. The Beaufighter was a more successful derivative of the aircraft used as a night fighter.

One of the Blenheim pilots was the grandson of a Radnorshire labourer and had a colourful parentage that brought him to the county as a young boy. John Henry Hanne, known as Jack, was born in Lambeth on 15 February 1913. His mother, Elizabeth (née Langford), had been born in 1888 to a Radnorshire labourer and his wife of 4 Denham Terrace at the Ridgebourne in Llandrindod Wells. Elizabeth had entered service as a house-maid and it was whilst working in Cardigan that she met Henry Hanne. Henry was a German immigrant who had come to England in November 1907 having worked as a waiter in several large hotels in Germany and soon became the butler for the eccentric American, Dr John Walter Pritchard (one time dentist to the Prince of Wales). Pritchard had served as a captain in the American civil war leading the 160th New York Volunteers, then moved to London before buying, for the princely sum of £1,325, the Priory Estate in Cardigan.

According to Henry Hanne, Dr Pritchard was an eccentric woman-hater who would only allow men servants in the house. This seems an odd statement in view of the fact that several female servants are recorded at the Priory both before and during Henry's time. When exactly Henry started work at the Priory is unclear, but it is how he came to meet Elizabeth Langford. They were married on 24 January 1911.

At the outbreak of the First World War, Henry Hanne (along with thousands of other foreign nationals) was interned at Knockaloe Camp on the Isle of Man. Elizabeth now had three children by Henry – daughter May (born in 1912), John Henry 'Jack' and his younger brother Frederick (born in 1914). Life must have been very hard for a young Welsh woman married to a man considered to be an enemy alien, but far more serious concerns were to arise.

Elizabeth may have been subject to certain restrictions herself as the wife of an alien as well as finding herself in financial hardship. It seems that she tried to get some form of legal document from the Swiss embassy in order to get monetary help from the German government to support her children while their father was interned. During the First World

War Switzerland remained neutral and through its connection with the International Red Cross would act as a go-between in such cases. The document she did get back was not at all what she had been expecting, for Henry, it seems, had another wife and child in Germany.

When questioned about this by the camp commander, Henry claimed that the wife of his former employer, Dr Pritchard, had not wanted the men-only servant arrangement to continue on her husband's death and had urged Henry to marry, even apparently persuading him that nobody would find out in Wales about his German wife if he never mentioned her. There were many holes in Henry's story and he attempted to defend himself by claiming that some years previously he had been knocked off his bicycle and had suffered memory loss. He was able to tell the camp commander in almost forensic detail about every hotel he had worked in throughout Europe with precise dates but became very vague on the subject of his first wife, eventually admitting that after the girl had become pregnant, his own mother had persuaded him to marry.

Henry Hanne, Jack Hanne's German father. (© Peter Hanne)

Elizabeth decided to move back to Llandrindod Wells with her children and rather bravely did not call for her marriage to be annulled, but chose instead to prosecute Henry for bigamy, a course of action that could have led to the whole story becoming public. With the help of her solicitor, Elizabeth was able to prove that Henry had not been free to marry, and that her marriage was void. She did not pursue Henry and he disappears from record. Those who knew her story felt she had been taken advantage of and by and large she did not suffer any stigma for what she had been through. Elizabeth did find happiness again when she married Mr Frank Floyd of Rhayader in 1920.

Just short of his 17th birthday, on 14 January 1930 Jack Hanne decided to enlist in the RAF. With one war far behind and another one not yet on the horizon, this must have seemed like a glamorous and exciting career. Jack may even have been inspired by seeing one of the flying displays on the

Elizabeth Langford, Jack Hanne's mother (note the brooch in the shape of the RAF wings). (© Peter Hanne)

Ddole airfield. Having successfully passed some tough entrance exams, Jack entered the service as a boy aircraft apprentice and was sent to RAF Halton in Buckinghamshire where he trained with No.2 Wing.

Halton was the primary establishment for boy trainees, who became affectionately known as the Trenchard Brats, after Lord Trenchard who initiated the scheme. Many of the Brats went on to become non commissioned officers and were praised for their high standard of training. The apprentices were trained not just in technical trades but in all aspects of military discipline. Initially as a boy apprentice Jack would have had an 8.30am to 4.30pm day in a classroom or workshop, outside of which there were activities such as gliding, participating in a project to build and fly a small light aircraft as well as all manner of sports, music, literature and debating societies.

Halton (a country estate initially requisitioned from the Rothschilds, then eventually purchased at Lord Trenchard's insistence) was chosen specifically for its close proximity to London and all the main train routes. Lord Trenchard felt that it would benefit the possibly homesick boys if their parents could visit them on the weekends. Presumably he did not expect apprentices like Jack to come from so far away. Also he was not averse to allowing them the use of the cinemas and dance halls on the weekends, provided they conducted themselves in an appropriate manner. Photographs of the time show the young Jack Hanne as a suave and debonair young man who carried himself with an air of easy confidence. He was only of average height (5 feet 5½ inches), but he had a distinctive shock of auburn hair, brown eyes and a fresh complexion.

On his 18th birthday he enlisted in the RAF full time and for the duration of 12 years.

Jack may not have received many visits from Llandrindod Wells but it seems quite likely that he found time to get back there from time to time, as it was where he found his wife. Jack Hanne and Nancy Vera Gilford had grown up in the same street and many of the photographs in Nancy's album show the two of them enjoying time together in and around the town, some dated as early as 1932. Maybe Jack was waiting to 'pop the question' until he was sure of his prospects. They were clearly in love and Jack would write her long letters, often including poetry.

He completed his training at Halton as a qualified fitter and armourer and with the judgement that he had the technical ability of a non commissioned officer. On 1 April 1935 his dream of becoming a pilot was finally realized when he was sent to RAF Wittering for the start of his pilot training.

The following January he was awarded a good conduct stripe, and later in 1936 he was promoted

Jack Hanne in training, 1929.
(© Group Captain Clive Coombes.
OBE)

Nancy and Jack Hanne.
(© Group Captain Clive Coombes. OBE)

to sergeant, unpaid – it was not uncommon for a rank to be awarded for a probationary unpaid period – and then took what was probably his first trip overseas. He was sent to RAF Hinaidi in Iraq (just outside Baghdad) to serve with No.70 Bomber Training Squadron, who were flying twin-engined heavy bombers. Hinaidi was a former First World War British army base that had been taken over by the RAF in 1922. In March 1937 he was in Karachi where he was finally examined and confirmed as a fully paid sergeant; his results show he was considered skilled in his trade and proficient as a pilot.

On 29 August 1938, after a good five years of courtship, Jack and Nancy tied the knot at Holy Trinity Church in Llandrindod Wells. Nancy was given away by her father, and her sister June and Jack's sister May acted as her bridesmaids. Jack's only brother Fred was his best man. Jack's mother (now

J. Hanne (on the right) 'Bombing Up' (i.e. preparing bombs for arming an aircraft)
at RAF Catfoss in Yorkshire prior to his pilot training.
(© Group Captain Clive Coombes. OBE)

Pupils at No.11 Flying Training School at RAF Wittering in 1935.
Jack Hanne is on the far right.
(© Group Captain Clive Coombes. OBE)

No.70 Bomber Training Squadron at RAF Hinaidi.
Jack Hanne is third from the right in the back row.
(© Group Captain Clive Coombes. OBE)

Mrs Floyd) also attended. The reception was held in the Louis café in Llandrindod Wells, before Jack and Nancy left for a honeymoon in Skegness. The couple then moved to 7 Edgar Avenue in Stowmarket in Suffolk, 6 miles from where Jack was now stationed at RAF Wattisham. From here he flew Blenheims, an aircraft he both liked and was proficient in flying.

On 24 July 1939, Jack took off from Wattisham in a Blenheim he was ferrying to Hullavington, but his aircraft started to lose power somewhere around Debden. His approach was baulked by a Hurricane fighter plane and in turning away he was unable to avoid overshooting what was now a very tight landing area, finishing up in a wood.

By September, Britain was at war. For some, this period known as the Phoney War was little different from their peace-time activities. For Jack, however, the war was to start almost immediately. At 4pm on 4 September, the day after war was declared, Jack was part of a raid on the Kiel Canal led by Squadron Leader Kenneth Doran. This was officially the first RAF bombing raid of the Second World War. Jack and four other Blenheims from 110 Squadron were accompanied by Blenheims from 107 and 149 Squadrons as well as Wellington bombers from 9 Squadron. Not all the aircraft returned safely, and among the dead was Sgt Pilot Albert Stanley Prince, who was the first Canadian (serving with any of the forces) to be killed in the war.

A few days later Jack was included in a small group of airmen presented to King George VI by Sir Kingsley Wood, the Minister for Air. His Squadron Leader K.C. Doran was awarded the Distinguished Flying Cross.

There is then a period of mystery in Jack's life. An undated note in a scrapbook kept by Nancy, written by Squadron Leader K.C. Doran, suggests that Jack had in some way been judged unfit to fly and disagreed with the decision. A search of the operational record book can shed no light on why he had been posted unfit. However, this was during a period when life for 110 Squadron was very quiet and a combination of bad weather and lack of enemy activity led to very few operational sorties. The squadron spent the next few months on standby but not doing very much. Their flying mainly consisted of bombing practice and training flights.

Jack was back on flying duties by 9 January 1940 with Sgt George Llewellyn Williams as his navigator and Aircraftsman first class Edwin Vick as his wireless operator/air gunner, the crew flying a Blenheim MkIV, serial number L4859. By now Jack was a very experienced pilot with 568 flying hours under his belt, 212 of which were on Blenheims.

By this date, the role of 110 Squadron was to fly over the Channel and North Sea looking out for enemy ships or aircraft in what was known as a sweep. On 10 January, Jack along with 11 other Blenheims set out on a sweep over the North Sea during which they were attacked by five Messerschmitt 110s, aircraft that had four 7.92mm mg 17 machine guns in the upper nose and two 20mm ff/m cannons fitted in the lower part of the nose. The Blenheims dived to sea level and tried making it back to base, the dog fight lasting for 25 minutes. The air gunners in the Blenheims fought back, quickly damaging one of the Me110s, whilst another was seen to crash into the sea and a further badly damaged one landed in Denmark. (Leading Aircraftsman John Tippet, a wireless operator /air gunner was to be awarded the Distinguished Flying Medal for his efforts that day in keeping the Me110s at bay.) Meanwhile Jack's Blenheim was hit and lost one of its engines, its reduced speed causing it to fall behind the rest of his squadron. Seeing his chance, Hauptmann Wolfgang Falck of 2/ZG76 (the German equivalent of a fighter wing) attacked again and the Blenheim with Jack, Williams and Vick still on board was seen to crash into the sea and explode. Initially the crew were reported as missing. The news must have been almost unbearable for Nancy, who was now three months pregnant. She kept the newspaper cuttings both about him being listed as missing and eventually telling of his death. Probably the scrapbook was intended to show the unborn child how brave its father had been. She returned to live with her parents in Llandrindod Wells, while the local paper tells of Jack being Radnorshire's first airman to be killed in the war. Radnorshire Urban District Council sent a letter of condolence both to Nancy and to Jack's mother.

Nancy gave birth to Jack's daughter, Jacqueline Anne on 14 July 1940. Sadly the baby only lived for two days and is buried in Llandrindod Wells cemetery. Nancy lived on and married again (Mr Sidney Morgan) but she had no more children. She was buried with Jacqueline in 1996 when she was 82 years old.

Wolfgang Falck

Wolfgang Falck was three years older than Jack Hanne and like Jack he had joined up before the war. Germany was only allowed a small army under the Treaty of Versailles and next to no airforce, a restriction that it partially got round by setting up many glider schools. Wolfgang along with 29 other bright young army officers was sent to a secret Luftvehrschule (flying school). He began flying in 1932 although still officially an army officer, and would go on six week flying refresher courses.

In March 1935 (just before Jack started his pilot training) Wolfgang was appointed a flying instructor in the fledgling Luftwaffe. On 1 April 1936 he was made Oberleutnant and was sent to be a staff captain at the squadron formed by and named after Manfred Von Richthofen (the infamous Red Baron).

With the start of the war, Wolfgang saw action early on in Poland, gaining three victories over Polish aircraft. He survived the war, being briefly imprisoned by the Americans in early 1945, and on release he took several jobs including becoming a civilian officer working for the British army operating the depot stores for the 47th Royal Engineers. He remained interested in aviation and in 1961 he took a job advising the North American Aviation Company before being employed in 1966 by McDonnell Douglas aviation. He retired in 1986 and died on 13 March 2007 aged 96. The many men who knew him, both during and after the war felt that Wolfgang Falck was one of the last chivalrous pilots, who liked to see fair play and honour above all else.[1]

Wolfgang Falck. (© The late W. Falck)

Jack, having crashed into the sea, has no known grave but is remembered on panel 15 of the Runnymede memorial.

Another airman who flew on Blenheims in the early stages of the war was George Percy Moore, though in his case he flew as the observer/navigator. George was born in Wooton in Oxfordshire in 1910, the second son of Harry and Miriam Moore. His connection with Radnorshire came through his wife, Mabel, who hailed from Llandrindod Wells and who returned to the town after their marriage in 1936.

George had enlisted in the Royal Air Force in the 1930s as an aircraft hand through the RAF apprentice scheme, as had Jack Hanne. Whilst many apprentices were more than happy to serve their country with their feet planted firmly on the ground, George was among those who were not going to be content with a ground role and as war broke out he was training to be an observer.

LLANDRINDOD WELLS WELCOME HOME FUND.

Llandrindod Wells,
18th November 1946.

Dear Mrs Hanne,

The above Fund is now being distributed, and it has been decided that a Certificate should be sent to the relatives of each of those Service men who lost their lives during the late World War recording the sincere and heartfelt sympathy of the people of this town with them in their great loss, together with a cheque for £7, the same amount that is being given to all Service men and women who have returned home. We accordingly send you the enclosed Certificate and Cheque, and sincerely trust you will accept same in the spirit in which it is sent, that is, that those who have made the supreme sacrifice are not forgotten.

Yours sincerely
J Watkins
W H Powell.

Joint Hon. Secretaries.

Many towns organised collections to help dependant relatives of those killed in the war; this being a time before the Welfare State was established. This letter shows that Nancy Hanne was awarded the same amount as the servicemen and women who returned home to Llandrindod Wells at the end of the war.

He was then posted to 82 Bomber Squadron and joined the three man crew of a Bristol Blenheim.

Based at RAF Watton in Norfolk, in early 1940 82 Squadron were employed conducting day time bombing raids over France. In May, as the evacuation of Dunkirk got under way the squadron carried out missions bombing the columns of enemy troops heading for the allies trapped on the beach. On 17 May the squadron was almost wiped out during a raid on Gembloux, for of the twelve planes involved, not one returned. As the Battle of France turned into the Battle of Britain in June, the Blenheims of 82 Squadron conducted night-time bombing raids on the invasion barges in the Channel ports as well as continuing their day time operations. Eleven Blenheim squadrons from No.2 Group Bomber Command were on 24 hour alert; they were bombing round the clock and it was impossible for anyone to get a good night's sleep. As soon as the weary aircrew landed and headed for bed the ground crew took over to repair or re-arm the aircraft before the next wave of bombers took off. The Blenheims were taking off night after night and the sheer number of sorties they conducted meant that they were bound to suffer heavy losses, and were being supplied with fresh aircraft and crews.

The Germans had designated 13 August 1940 as Adler Tag (Eagle Day), when they planned a massive assault on RAF bases in England in order to soften the country up for an invasion. No.2 Bomber group had meanwhile been tasked with hitting the gathering German planes on the ground and 12 Blenheims from 82 Squadron headed for the German held airfield at Aalborg in the north-east of Denmark to hopefully stop the Ju88 fighters from leaving the ground. The commanding officer, Wing Commander E.C. de Virac Lart led the raid, which was almost at the limit of the Blenheim's range. As they crossed the coast, Sgt Baron, flying Blenheim R3915, checked his gauges and decided he would not have enough fuel to reach the target and get back home. He may have been flying with his mixture on rich and using more fuel than the rest of the squadron, or he may have just misread his gauge, but either way he took the decision to turn back. For this action he was ordered to appear before a Court Martial, but he was lost on another raid before his case was heard. In the meantime some of the observers in the other Blenheims thought that de Virac Lart was off course. As there was to be strict radio silence, one or two of the other Blenheims tried to attract the attention of the CO using their Aldis signalling lamps, but all to no avail. Due to a two degree miscalculation by his observer, de Virac Lart was almost 50 miles off course, meaning they would be approaching Aalborg from the wrong direction giving the Germans plenty of warning that they were on their way. As the airfield came in sight the German anti-aircraft batteries opened up and almost immediately five of the Blenheims were shot down. Nine Me109s from 5/JG-77 (also based at Aalborg) had taken off as the Blenheims came into view and now pounced on the rest of the formation. Not one of the Blenheims survived the attack. George Moore, the observer in Blenheim MkIV serial R3829, was killed along with the wireless operator Sgt T.E. Girvan. The pilot, Squadron Leader R.N. Wardell, bailed out and became a prisoner of war. Of the 33 crewmen who attacked the Aalborg airfield, 20 were killed and 13 became prisoners of war, of whom eight had been seriously wounded and would suffer long term health problems. The Germans turned the raid into a propaganda exercise and widely published photographs of the military funeral they gave the airmen in the cemetery at Vadum in Denmark. After the war a memorial wall was built by the Danish with the names of all the airmen engraved upon it, including that of 30-year-old Georg Moore.

Derrick Gordon Masters was born in Knighton on 13 June 1921 and enlisted in the RAFVR in Birmingham in 1941. By April 1943 he had reached the rank of pilot officer and was a navigator/wireless operator on a Bristol Beaufighter serving with 488 (RNZAF) Squadron based in Ayr in Scotland. This squadron had been formed under the Empire Air Training Scheme which allowed young men from all corners of the Empire to train to be air crew in their own countries before coming to Britain to form squadrons that would ultimately join the RAF. Although the new squadrons came under the command of the RAF, squadrons that had been formed by aircrew from predominately one country were designated with their home nation's insignia, thus RNZAF stood for the Royal New Zealand Air Force. (New Zealand sent 2,743 fully trained pilots over to the UK during the course of the war. It also set up an initial training programme which saw almost that number again start their training in New Zealand before finishing it in Canada, whilst hundreds more trained as wireless operators, air gunners, bomb aimers, navigators and flight engineers.) Although

488 Squadron's personnel largely came from New Zealand, all Empire squadrons did have a quota of British RAF crew members.

No.488 was split into two distinct sections, a Daytime Fighter Force flying Hawker Hurricanes and a Night Fighter Force flying the Bristol Beaufighter. Derrick as navigator/wireless operator and New Zealander Pilot Officer Rupert Clark O'Gara as pilot took off in the early afternoon of 2 April 1943 in Beaufighter MkVIF serial number X8263 on what was to be a routine training flight. The weather was bad with very poor visibility, but O'Gara was an experienced pilot with around 413 flying hours under his belt, over 100 of which were on Beaufighters. However minutes after take-off the Beaufighter crashed into a hilltop at Balig farm, 3 miles South of Ayr on the road to Dunure. Both men were killed.

The men were buried together in the cemetery in Knighton. Derrick's parents, Charles Albert and Dorothy Gertrude Masters, wished their son to be laid to rest in his home town and the New Zealand High Commissioner sanctioned O'Gara's burial in Knighton. Derrick is also remembered on the Knighton War Memorial.

Derrick Masters & Rupert O'Gara's grave in Knighton Cemetery. (© Author's collection)

7   Fighter Command

Most of the Radnorshire men who joined the RAF during the Second World War ended up as members of bomber crews, but a few were fighter pilots. Jack Royston Hamar was one of them. He was born in Knighton on 2 December 1914 to Arthur Hamar; his father and his uncles Alfred and Richard had been dubbed the 'Mad Hamars' for careering around the lanes of Radnorshire on motorcycles. Alfred and Richard had both lost their lives serving with the Royal Flying Corps in the First World War (see pages 39-41).

Jack attended Knighton primary school and then went on to John Beddoes Grammar School in Presteigne before joining the family grocery business. Expanding the animal and poultry feed side of the business, he used the increased revenue to buy himself an Ariel 250cc motorcycle. This was soon traded up for an Ariel Red Hunter motorbike on which he competed successfully in a number of hill climbs. He then progressed to sports cars, buying first a three-wheeler Morgan, then an Aero Minx and finally an MG. It wasn't long before he progressed to aeroplanes and took flying lessons at a civilian flying school, and in May 1938 joined the Royal Air Force Volunteer Reserve (RAFVR). He gained his licence to fly 'Private flying machines' on 17 June 1938 at Yatesbury in Wiltshire and went on to further pilot training with the RAF volunteer reserve. Having successfully completed his flying training he went on a fighter pilot's course before reporting to 151 (fighter) Squadron at North Weald in Essex on 4 March 1939, a squadron equipped with the Hawker Hurricane. On 16 May 1939 Jack Royston Hamar was commissioned as a pilot officer.

Less than four months later, on 3 September, the Second World War was declared but Jack and his squadron did not see any action until well into 1940. However, on 11 February 1940, Jack did have a bit of a shake up. Coming into land at Debden Airfield he stalled the Miles Magister he was flying and crashed into the runway. The aircraft's undercarriage collapsed and the propeller was smashed. Jack, however, was unhurt.

There were, at this time, far fewer Spitfires than Hurricanes in Fighter Command and it was decided to keep the Spitfires in Britain and only send some of the Hurricanes over to France. Some Hurricane squadrons would be permanently based in France whilst others would hop over the Channel, refuel at an allied base and conduct their sortie from there. His squadron was for the time being going to remain based in England.

At 10am on 17 May, led by Squadron Leader Teddy Donaldson, 151 Squadron went on an offensive patrol of the Lille to Valenciennes area. An hour later they came face to face

151 Squadron. Jack Hamar is fourth from the right;
his friend Teddy Donaldson is fourth from the left. (© Author's collection)

with the enemy for the first time when Donaldson spotted a couple of Stuka dive bombers some distance away and took one section with him to investigate. There turned out to be 20 Stukas and the entire squadron joined the dog fight. The Hurricanes definitely destroyed six of the German aircraft with another two claimed by Jack but not confirmed. On landing it was discovered that Jack's Hurricane had ten bullet holes in it.

The following day Jack's squadron were back in France and at 3.30 that afternoon they took part in what Jack described as a colossal dog fight. Jack chased two Me110s, getting close enough to fire and seeing his own tracer bullets entering the wings of one aircraft, but his own aircraft had been hit and oil was covering his windscreen, so he turned back to base as he was unable to see clearly.

On 22 May Jack was over France again, tangling with a couple of Ju87s. This time Jack definitely shot down one aircraft and severely damaged another, ripping off the part of the port wing and opening the fuselage, before having to high tail it out of the dog fight as five other Ju87s turned their attention on him.

Jack was back in action on 25 May, this time over Calais. He fired at a lone Junkers 88 which jettisoned its bombs, but Jack didn't observe any damage to the aircraft.

On 29 May 1940 Jack was patrolling the Dunkirk area protecting the seemingly endless lines of allied soldiers from attack. A lone Ju88 appeared, probably as a decoy to get the fighters to chase it leaving the soldiers vulnerable to air attack. Only Jack and Squadron Leader Donaldson took the bait, destroying the plane between them. The squadron were to fly as many as seven sorties a day as the British forces were evacuated from Dunkirk.

Within days the German Luftwaffe was flying from the bases in France at which Jack and others like him had landed when refuelling not many days before. On 9 July, 151

Squadron was involved in a dog fight with nearly 100 German aircraft, during which Jack damaged a Messerschmitt 110 (Me110) fighter. The Battle of Britain officially began the following day and on the 14th Jack claimed an Me109.

On 23 July, word was received that Jack Hamar had been recommended for the Distinguished Flying Cross. The Citation read: 'Since December this officer has participated in all operations and most of the patrol flights undertaken by his squadron. He has shown coolness and courage of a high order and has personally destroyed six enemy aircraft.' Squadron records, however, show that Jack had brought down three confirmed enemy aircraft and damaged six.

Sadly, though Jack knew of his award, he was not to receive it in person. Squadron Leader Teddy Donaldson was to recall that he and Jack had been extremely close. Of the eight pilots who had started sleeping in a dugout at North Weald to be ready for a scramble only he and Jack were left. The night before he was killed, Jack told Donaldson 'Sir, we have been to hell and back and we are still here. I think we will get through this.' Donaldson told him not to talk like that as it would bring bad luck. The next day was one of filthy weather with rain and mist right down on the deck. 151 received a call about an unidentified aircraft in the area of Felixstowe and because of the weather they were asked, but not ordered, to investigate. Donaldson told Jack about the call and his reply was 'Let's get the bastard.' Three aircraft took off, the third flown by Sgt Atkinson, but no sooner were they airborne than the aircraft was identified as friendly.

As Donaldson's wingman, Jack and he flew back side by side at the relatively low speed (for a Hurricane) of 120mph flying about 60 feet above the ground. Jack was flying with the canopy of his aircraft open to improve visibility in the fog as in such bad weather the main hazards were the 100 foot high radio masts that were positioned close to the airfield. The two men used to have a routine on coming in to land – as they approached the airfield they would always break, one would go left and the other right, and would each perform a roll before landing. Donaldson saw Jack start the manoeuvre and shouted 'Don't' over the radio, only to see Jack commence an upward roll. The aeroplane was flying too slow and too low for such a manoeuvre and Jack crashed into the ground. Donaldson was on the ground besides him in minutes, but the open canopy had left Jack completely unprotected and he died instantly.

Jack was buried with full military honours on 28 July 1940 in the cemetery in Knighton. A firing party from North Weald attended at their own request. His parents received over 100 floral tributes and many letters from friends and fellow officers who told of their dismay at being unable to attend.

Jack's mother attended Buckingham Palace on 17 September 1940 in order to collect Jack's DFC, but the air raid sirens went off shortly before the ceremony and she received Jack's medal from the king in the plainly furnished air raid shelter underneath the palace. It is not known if Jack's father, Arthur attended. Perhaps the loss of two brothers and now his son were just too much for him to bear. This was the first Distinguished Flying Cross to be awarded to a native of Radnorshire.

Richard Atheling Sanders was another fighter pilot. Though not born in Radnorshire – he was born in Leicester on 20 April 1920, the son of Flight Lieutenant James Sanders of the Royal Flying Corps and Mary Sanders – his parents moved to Llandrindod Wells early in the war. Whether this was just for the duration of the war or whether his horticulturist father had some business interest in the area is not known.

After he had finished his education at the prestigious Dixie Grammar School in Market Bosworth, Richard followed in his father's footsteps and joined the Royal Air Force. Richard received his commission as pilot officer on 1 April 1939 and after he had completed his training at No.11 Flying Training School (FTS) he joined 145 Squadron based at Croydon as a pilot flying the Mk1 Hawker Hurricane.

Early in May 1940, 145 Squadron began flying over France acting as air cover for the evacuation of Dunkirk. On 10 May the squadron was moved to Tangmere in Sussex and in the middle of the month he was sent with five other pilots to take Hurricanes to Lille Marcq, an airfield near Lille in France, to replenish 87 Squadron, which had suffered many recent losses. The six pilots had no clear instructions as to what to do after delivering the aircraft and seeing how badly the squadron had been hit and that there were no spare pilots to fly the new aircraft, they decided to stay and help. The Allies however, were now pulling out of France and on the morning of 20 May 1940 the order was received at Lille Marcq to withdraw. Richard was already airborne and involved in combat with some German BF110s over the airbase when his aircraft was badly shot up and he crash-landed near Arras. Badly wounded, Richard was taken to an ambulance train heading for Dunkirk. The train was strafed by German aircraft, but again Richard survived, to be put on board the hospital ship *Worthing* which headed towards Shorncliff military hospital in Kent. On 23 May he died of his wounds; he had just turned 20 years of age. Of the six ferry pilots who had taken the new planes to France, only two made it back to England (P/O Comely and F/O Ward).

His parents had the words 'Lest we forget; One of England's gallant sons who died that we might live' carved on his headstone at Shorncliffe Military Cemetery in Kent. Richard Sanders is also remembered on the Roll of Honour of his old grammar school in Market Bosworth.

Of the 415 RAF pilots who were lost in the Battle of France, Richard is among only six who were buried in England. All the others were either buried on the Continent or commemorated on the Runnymede memorial for those who have no known grave.

Paul Clifford Webb's connections with Radnorshire only came in his retirement. Born in Greenock in Scotland on 10 March 1918, Paul was educated in Glasgow at the Kelvinside Academy and then worked for the Royal Bank of Scotland. In late 1937 he joined the auxiliary branch of the Royal Air Force, which was rather like the volunteer reserve, with men being taught to fly on a part-time basis, and became a sergeant with No.602 (City of Glasgow) Auxiliary Squadron based at RAF Renfrew. Paul was commissioned as a pilot officer on 23 January 1938, and was awarded his Flying Badge (or Wings) on 4 July 1938. He was made a flying officer on 23 July 1939 and transferred to full time RAF service a month later on 24 August.

A Spitfire pilot, at the start of the war Paul and the rest of his squadron were engaged in protecting shipping in the Glasgow and Edinburgh shipyards. On 16 October 1939 they were scrambled to attack nine German Ju88s that were heading their way on a bombing raid. The seven members of 'D' flight, who had the names of Snow White's seven dwarfs as their code names, took off from their base at Drem to intercept the enemy raiders. Paul

(Dopey) and the rest of the flight intercepted the Ju88s led by Helmut Pohle as they started to attack the cruisers *HMS Southampton* and *HMS Edinburgh* in Rosyth harbour. This was the first time that German bombers had been seen over the coast of the UK during the war, and people on the sea front at Kirkcaldy had a grandstand view of the dog fight. Paul and Flight Commander George Pinkerton chased the Ju88s at low level over the sea, forcing one plane to crash into the water; Helmut was the only survivor. Paul was to share in the destruction of another enemy plane before claiming his first solo aerial victory on 1 July 1940. Flying Spitfire N3119, he attacked a Ju88 of 1/KG51 approximately three miles east of Dunbar, and the aircraft crashed at Melun-Villarochein in France.

The Battle of Britain soon intensified, and on 13 August 1940, 602 Squadron was sent south to Westhampnett just outside Chichester. Within days Paul had helped to destroy an Me110 over Arundel. On 25 August he destroyed two more Me110s near Dorchester, and the next day he shared in the destruction of an He59 float plane just south of St Catherine's point. On 4 September the now Flight Lieutenant Webb damaged an Me110 near Beachy Head, and on the 7th he shot down another Me110 ten miles to the south of Bembridge. On 9 September he was himself attacked and after a fierce fight with a German Bf109 over Mayfield, he had to force land his Spitfire in a wood at Crocker Hill near Box Grove in Sussex. He suffered a broken wrist and minor cuts and bruises in the crash, the damage to his wrist being enough to keep him out of the rest of the Battle of Britain.

On 11 March 1941 he was posted to No.58 Operational Training Unit (OTU) where he acted as an instructor. On 25 May he was attached to 123 Squadron based at Turnhouse to the west of Edinburgh. On approaching the airfield to land his Spitfire R7151 on 7 July, he realised that he was unable to lock his undercarriage securely in place, but landed anyway, leaving himself uninjured, if bending his aircraft.

Paul was next posted back to 602 Squadron, now based at Kenley in Surrey, but he was only with them for a month before heading back up to Drem, where he served as a flight commander with 123 Squadron. His next stop was with 416 Squadron, where he became the commanding officer of this newly formed Royal Canadian Air Force Squadron. Still based in Scotland, this time at RAF Peterhead in Aberdeenshire, Paul was made a squadron leader in December 1941, commanding 416 Squadron from November 1941 until March 1942 when he headed for the Middle East. Here he flew offensive missions over the western desert before being transferred to Malta to undertake a training role. He became the commanding officer of 253 Squadron on 25 May 1944, the squadron flying Spitfires MkIX in the Mediterranean theatre, mostly from Foggia in Italy. They also carried out sweeps along the Yugoslavian coast and in July the squadron became part of the Balkans air force, using the small island of Vis off the Adriatic coast as an advanced landing ground. As well as leading attacks against German rail and road networks, Paul also flew escort sorties to the Dakotas that were dropping supplies to the partisans loyal to Tito. In September Paul took command of No.281 Wing which included not only his old squadron but also two newly formed Yugoslavian squadrons. The wing was heavily involved not only in ground attack missions but also in armed reconnaissance. On 17 October 1944 he was awarded the Distinguished Flying Cross for having 'caused considerable destruction and damage to the enemy when his personal example set a very high standard of efficiency and enthusiasm'. His later career is detailed in Chapter 15.

Of the ten Peirson Jones children born in Nantmel at the beginning of the 20th century, two were destined for the flying services. Their experiences, however, would be very different and they would start on opposite sides of the world.

The children's grandfather was the vicar of the local church. The youngest child, Chris (born in 1917), was only one year old when his father died. The pressure on a family with ten children and no father must have been quite considerable and in 1928 the two oldest boys Humphrey and Martin (born in 1909) decided to emigrate and start new lives for themselves. Martin's story is told in Chapter 10, but here we pick up the tale of Chris's life.

In 1930, shortly after Humphrey and Martin had emigrated, the boys' mother took the rest of the children to live in Llanigon near Hay-on-Wye. It was here that Chris grew up and developed a love of the countryside and farming. He attended the Llandrindod Wells County School and on leaving found work as a shepherd. This job took him to various parts of Wales and the Cotswolds before he decided to do a short course in agriculture at Aberystwyth University.

When the war broke out he was working on a farm in Talgarth and could have avoided, at least initially, being called up as farming was considered a reserved occupation. Although the Women's Land Army were on hand to work the farms, many men were eligible to stay at home. On 28 April 1941, Chris volunteered for the air force and was sent to an initial training school where he applied to become a pilot. His next stop was No.28 Elementary Flying Training School (EFTS) at Wolverhampton. In May 1942 he was selected to join the Arnold Scheme, and was posted to Tuscaloosa Primary Training School in Alabama, USA for further training.

Although Chris had to start almost from scratch showing his new instructor Mr J.R. Mayer (the Arnold Scheme utilised both military and civilian flying instructors and

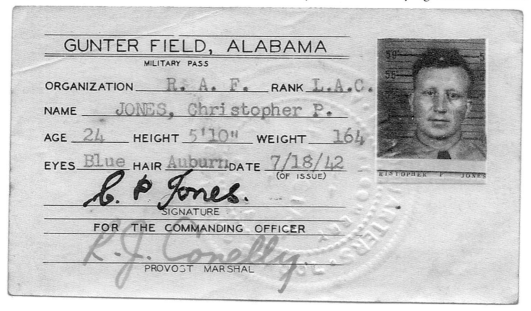

Chris Peirson Jones's pass for Gunter Field, Alabama. (© P. Eckley)

bases) all the manoeuvres that he had been put through in England, it would not be long before he took his first solo flight. This he did on 22 May in a PT 17 Stearman; his log book has the capital lettered FIRST SOLO underlined in red. Day after day his log book details longer solo flights and cryptic descriptions of his activities such as Chandelles (a 180 degree climbing turn) or lazy eights (a sweeping manoeuvre consisting of turns and climbs) and circuits and bumps (repeated take off, short flight and landing). Mr Mayer only joined him now on occasions when some new manoeuvre was tried out or to check Chris's progress on instrument flying. Chris was still a long way from becoming a fully-fledged combat pilot, however, and his next stop was the Gunter Field Air Force base, also in Alabama, where he arrived on 4 July 1942. Although the course was listed as basic it was a step up from primary and consequently the aircraft were more advanced. His training was now on the Bt13 Vultee, a two seat single winged trainer, which would have had a more powerful engine and been faster and heavier than anything Chris would have been used to.

His first flight on 6 July with Pilot Officer J. Rodgers lasted 85 minutes and by 13 July he was once more going solo. Throughout the summer Chris flew almost every day. The usual pattern was a first flight with an instructor, then flying solo to practise whatever had been taught. A small amount of night time flying was also added to the course. On 7 September he was moved to the advanced flying school at Craig, near Selma, Alabama. Here he was confronted by an even more powerful aircraft on which to train, the North American AT-6. The orientation period was shorter this time and soon Chris was taking longer flights. Navigation and air gunnery also appear more frequently in his log book and there was the beginning of formation flying and high altitude flying necessitating the use of oxygen. By the end of November he had flown 208 hours and was now routinely flying for one or two hours at a time solo, performing aerobatics and mock combats, flying at night, navigating and taking part in formation flying.

On 30 November he headed back to the UK and to Harrogate and the No.7 Personnel Distribution Centre. After spending Christmas in Yorkshire, he was posted to No.7 Pilots Advanced Flying Unit (PAFU) in Peterborough. Here he flew Ansons and Masters under constant supervision, for it wasn't uncommon for potential pilots to be rejected at even this stage and be transferred to another crew trade. Chris, however, passed this course and his next stop was the No.6 Air Observer School at RAF Staverton near Gloucester. After only a week he headed to No.3 Air Gunnery School at RAF Mona on Anglesey. Here he moved onto the Miles Martinet, before heading to Wiltshire and the No.1 Beam Approach School at RAF Watchfield, one of the first airfields in the UK which taught blind or beam approach techniques. The first stages of this training would take place in a simulator, where he would familiarise himself with the instruments and pay close attention to audio signals over the radio. Once a pilot was judged proficient in the simulator he would be blindfolded and expected to perform the same manoeuvres in an actual aircraft. In theory, once trained these pilots would be able to land at any airfield whatever the visibility or weather conditions. After completing the course he was sent back to No.3 Air Gunnery School at RAF Mona. Although he had been judged proficient in all exercises and had flown for 576 hours and 5 minutes there was still no operational flying in sight.

Instead, his next stop, in November 1943, was Castle Kennedy in Scotland, from which the No.3 Air Gunnery School were now flying. Here he flew the Martinet, conducting various wireless, air and weather tests.

Finally, in November 1944, Chris was judged ready to join an operational training unit. He had been judged as an above average as a pilot and would now be able to prove himself at No.71 OTU based at RAF Ismailia in Egypt, flying single seat fighter aircraft such as the Harvard and the Hurricane. Being an operational training unit it meant that the men were situated behind the lines and away from the action, but at the same time its purpose was to train men for battle. Thus it was while in Egypt that Chris joined a formation that, as he put it, 'whistled off in search of a U-boat'. It was also here that he had his first chance to fly a Spitfire, the aircraft that more than any other has come to symbolise the role of fighter pilot. The MkV Spitfire with its machine guns and cannon was a formidable weapon of war, and in tests of his shooting skills Chris scored an A- and two A+, but his instructor remarked on a tendency to skid (side-slip) when attacking.

Chris looked destined to be a good fighter pilot, but not on the Spitfire, for his next posting was back to the UK, where he joined No.55 OTU at Chedworth, Gloucestershire and embarked on a short conversion course onto the Hawker Typhoon. Known affectionately as the Tiffy, this aircraft was a fighter bomber which was not only capable of high speed but also had an impressive range of armament. Chris spent March 1945 putting the Typhoon through its paces, skimming low over the British countryside. Then finally in April 1945 Chris saw action.

He was posted to 137 Squadron based at Helmonde in Belgium. After an initial recce of the base area on 4 April 1945, Chris was ready and on the 5th took his Typhoon to Germany for the first time. The weather was bad and although he saw no action as he flew over the Rhine he was able to return with some reconnaissance photographs. On the 8th he headed for Loningen in Germany but was not happy with his shooting skills, and it was the same the next day. By the 11th, when he attacked a German army target outside the village of Bethem in Holland, he was feeling more confident in his accuracy. The next day in Rottenburg he also hit his target. The aircraft would have been fitted with wing mounted cameras and if a pilot made exaggerated claims of success they could be easily checked. During the month of April he flew 19 times, 12 of these on operational sorties over Belgium, Holland, Germany and Hanover. He attacked airfields, trains, towns and even conducted a strike on shipping near Lauenburg, mostly with success. He was involved in two operational sorties on 1 May, the second of these to the Schwelin area of Germany he described as the best yet, the squadron as a whole destroying 7 aircraft with another 20 described as damaged. The next day Chris returned to base with some debris lodged in his port wing, which seems to have been the first time he was fired at and hit. 3 and 4 May saw Chris's 16th and 17th sorties, both conducted on shipping in the bay of Lübeck. A note in his log book reads 'looks like being the last trip for a while' and two days later Chris was off to Denmark. For the rest of May and all of June Chris practised and gave demonstration flights in Denmark.

By now the war in Europe was over and the clean up was beginning. As politicians and servicemen alike had time to wander around the ruined cities of Europe they could see for themselves the damage those five years of war had inflicted. One British pilot, the fighter ace Johnnie Johnson, was with a group of Danish businessmen when they passed the site of a ruined school. The sight affected Johnnie greatly and he made a note to get Air Vice Marshal Basil Embry, the minster for air, to visit the site and console the relatives who had lost children and the nuns who had run the school. The idea of a visit grew into a plan to hold a charity air show for victims of the bombing. What was to become known as 'The Big Show' on 1 July 1945 at Copenhagen was a mixture of aerobatics and combat manoeuvres; part pre-war air pageant and part show of air force skill. Almost every type of aircraft that had been used in the war had some part to play. Chris took to the skies as

137 Squadron in 1945.
In the top photograph Chris Peirson Jones is standing behind the propeller blade of the Typhoon, in the lower he is on the right of the front row. (© P. Eckley)

part of a formation of 16 Typhoons and staged a mock rocket attack on two seaplanes in Copenhagen Harbour. Over 250,000 people flocked to Copenhagen for the spectacle and a few days later a very sizeable cheque was handed to the king of Denmark.

Chris continued flying his Typhoon throughout July and August. On 11 August when the plane started developing engine trouble at 8,000 feet over Germany, he descended ready to make a forced landing, but the engine picked up again and he continued to head for home. Then the engine cut out completely and he made a forced landing in a field about a mile outside the town of Havighorst, around 30 miles from Lübeck. It turned out that an engine bearing had failed due to loss of engine oil.

On 20 August he headed back to England to RAF Warmwell in Dorset. In September he flew back and forth to Holland, then from 11 October 1945 he was based at Fairwood Common near Swansea at the No.1 Armament Practice School. Here he was back to flying the Martinet as a tug pilot towing a target at which new pilots could practise firing. December 1945 saw Chris about to finish four years of flying with barely a blemish on his record when on Friday 14 December he took a Typhoon up for a practice flight. His log book entry has a scribbled 'Black Friday' with two exclamation marks followed by the words 'pranged on landing'. His sector commander added the words 'overshooting, carelessness'. So it was back to target towing for Chris until he left the service in April 1946. In a little over four years he had flown 17 operational sorties, become proficient on eleven different types of aircraft and had spent 1,087 hours and 55 mins in the air.

Chris headed first to Builth Wells and then set up in Talgarth, where he farmed for the rest of his life. Chris Peirson Jones died in 1983.

8   Bomber Command

At the start of the war many British bombing raids took place in daylight with often fairly light bombers such as the Bristol Blenheim, as recounted in Chapter 6. Another stalwart of the early years of the war, especially as regards bombing missions from UK soil against targets in Germany, was the Handley Page Hampden medium bomber. This was retired from service during 1942 to be replaced by heavier bombers such as the Lancaster and the Halifax. One of the pilots of this aircraft in late 1940 was John Raymond Bufton, one of four sons of James and Florence Bufton of Llandrindod Wells three of whom were to serve in the RAF during the Second World War. More will be told about the family and of the other two sons in subsequent chapters.

John attended the county school in Llandrindod Wells, from where he won an open scholarship to study mathematics at the University of Southampton. In 1935 he gained a BSc before completing a first class diploma in engineering, following this up with a first class certificate in applied aerodynamics. He gained intensive and practical training at some of Britain's leading aircraft firms before becoming the joint designer of an aircraft that went on to win a competition organised by the Chelsea Aeronautical College, a competition that attracted over one hundred entries.

James and Florence Bufton
with sons Hal (on the left) and John,
and daughter Mary (Mel).
(© Bufton family archive)

John Bufton.
(© Bufton family archive)

John had already 'gained his wings' by the time war broke out, for he had learned to fly while still at college. At least one aircraft company pressed him to undertake 'war work' with them that would have exempted him from service, but John would have none of it. Despite all his academic qualifications, John decided that the best way to help his country would be to fly.

He made rapid progress through the ranks of the RAF and in October 1940 was posted to 49 Squadron based at Scampton in Lincolnshire as the pilot of a Handley Page Hampden. On the night of 7/8 October he flew his first operational sortie, as second pilot, on a successful bombing raid on Lorient, a port in Brittany. After his one acclimatising flight, he was in command of his next sortie on the night of 12 /13 October. On 20/21 October he led a bombing raid to Berlin. He subsequently wrote to his father that his greatest wish had been fulfilled.

On 24/25 October he teamed up with Pilot Officer K. Ballas-Andersen and Sergeants R.F. Robertson and F.J.W. Bichard on another raid. Not being able to accurately identify their chosen target, John diverted to a secondary target and they photographed and then bombed a canal bridge near Meppin.

On the night of 27/28 October 1940 he was off again with the same crew. That night 49 Squadron was part of a raid conducted on the towns of Hamburg and Bremen. John Raymond and his crew were returning home along with another Hampden from the same squadron, when German night fighter ace Lt Heinz Volker, flying the night fighter variant of the Junkers 88, attacked both aircraft. The other Hampden although damaged managed to get back to base, but that piloted by John Bufton was far more badly damaged. Even so he managed to successfully ditch the Hampden in the sea, about a mile off Skegness.

All British beaches were now blocked by barricades of barbed wire in order to prevent the enemy sneaking ashore, but that night it would hamper a rescue. Members of the Skegness lifeboat station had heard the crash landing and immediately played a powerful searchlight over the water. However, the local army captain in charge of the barricade immediately ordered the light to be doused as he had received reports that enemy raiders were still in the area. The men complied but tried to launch their lifeboat and requested that the army move aside the barricade. An argument ensued between the captain and the lifeboat men, both trying to do their jobs under difficult situations.

It was said that the crew's cries for help could he heard from the seafront in Skegness, but it would be nearly 8am the next morning before the lifeboat set out. Tragically, the delay and the freezing sea had proved fatal and everybody who had been on board perished.

Lieutenant Heinz Volker

Heinz Volker was a leading fighter ace in the Luftwaffe night fighter unit NJG2. He was born on 3 February 1914, so was just a year older than John Bufton.

An experienced pilot flying the night fighter version of the Junkers 88, he specialized in picking off large heavy bombers at night; he was credited with nine aircraft destroyed. Bringing down John Raymond Bufton's aircraft was not his first victory and would not be his last. In May 1941 Volker had begun leading night raids over Cambridgeshire, patrolling along the east coast at night in search of inexperienced Wellington bomber crews from the many operational training units in the area. It was on one such raid on the night of 21/22 July 1941 that Volker caught up with and began to destroy a Wellington. The heavily damaged Wellington turned sharply to starboard to get away, a manoeuvre Volker had not been expecting, and they collided in mid-air over the village of Ashwell. Locals described a noise like a thunderclap as both planes exploded. Both crews were killed.

The body of Pilot Officer Ballas-Andersen was never found and he is remembered on the memorial at Runnymede.

John Raymond Bufton's body was returned to Llandrindod Wells and he was buried in the town cemetery with full military honours. To this day the lifeboat station at Skegness maintains a memorial to the crash; they retrieved one of the plane's propellers and have mounted a brass plaque beneath it with the men's names engraved on it.

A few days before he died he had written to his fiancée Jenny a letter that included these lines: 'If anything happens to me I want you to go and have a perm, do up the face, put the hat on and carry on ...' adding later 'Over the last three months I have got used to the idea of sudden accidents. They have happened so often to friends and acquaintances that the idea doesn't much startle one now.' His words sum up the feelings of many young men at the time.

As mentioned in the previous chapter, most Radnorshire airmen ended up in Bomber Command as opposed to Fighter Command. This was to be expected as during the war 125,000 aircrew passed through Bomber Command, whilst that for the other Commands, including Fighter Command, was 60,000. A good example of the possible career of a pilot in Bomber Command as it geared up for a protracted bombing offensive against Germany is provided by John Naughton Rowland. Though born in south Wales, he was to make Radnorshire his home in later years, managing the Rock Park Hotel in Llandrindod Wells for five years, and then buying a property near Rhayader in which to live.

Born in 1919, he was a brilliant student, excelling at mathematics, and after leaving college he joined the Atlas Insurance Company in London. While here he became friendly with a fellow worker who had joined the RAF Volunteer Reserve and was learning to fly. John accompanied his friend down to the airfield at Redhill to see what the RAFVR was all about and, liking what he saw, he applied and was accepted, and took his first flight in a De-Havilland Moth on 1 October 1938. This was a time when the RAF was expanding in the run up to the Second World War, and when he next turned up at Redhill he found he was to fly a brand new Miles Magister monoplane trainer.

John began to consider joining the RAF full time, but he needed to obtain a scholarship to RAF Cranwell to fund the course. While still working and training with the reserves he therefore set about preparing madly for his entrance exams, enlisting the help of a firm of 'crammers' – tutors who specialised in getting young men through the entrance exams to the military colleges of Woolwich, Sandhurst and of course Cranwell. Hundreds of young hopefuls would apply to the college and many would fail at the first interview before even being given a chance to take the exam. Even then only the top 20 would be taken and only the top four of those would be granted a scholarship. John flew solo for the first time in the Miles Magister on 14 February 1939, had a successful interview and was allowed to take the entrance exam in March – finishing with the top score. He was the only entrant who had chosen higher maths and he had impressed not only by joining the RAFVR of his own volition but also by having already gone solo.

John loved everything about Cranwell. He thought the building fabulous, had a room to himself and shared a batman with just three other cadets. He also made friends easily, not just with the other 20 cadets who had passed the same exam but also with the eight young men who had come from various parts of the world under the Empire Air Training Scheme.

This scheme was set up in the early months of the war by the British, Australian, New Zealand and Canadian governments. Many British airfields were subject to German attack and also needed to fly constant sorties, making it difficult to train pilots and crew consistently, a problem further complicated by the variable weather. Thus the scheme called for facilities in the Dominions to train British and each other's aircrews to the standard of the RAF. The plan aimed to train nearly 50,000 aircrew a year, 22,000 from the UK, with the final stages of training being completed in Canada.

Having already gone solo, John was unsurprisingly the first of the new Cranwell intake to do so on the course. The term ended in July and the cadets were not due to report back till the autumn, but as the situation in Europe deteriorated they were recalled in August. With the declaration of war on 3 September the course was shortened, as any subjects not immediately connected with flying were dropped.

By January 1940 John had finished his flying training and was sent to Stranraer in Scotland for practice on the air firing ranges. After a short course John and his fellow cadets were commissioned on 6 March 1940. Although all the cadets had hoped to become fighter pilots, only two of John's year joined fighter squadrons. Along with ten others, John was posted to Old Sarum near Salisbury to the School of Army Co-operation. Most of the pupils grumbled that instead of flying Spitfires and Hurricanes they were expected to trundle around the skies in Hawker Hectors and Lysanders. Rumours began to abound that things were not going all that well in France, and the first casualties were reported among the men who John had been with at Cranwell. Although this was a shock, the boys in the army co-operation unit thought they were safe enough with their artillery spotting, aerial photography and mock gas spraying exercises. Then in May, as the evacuation of Dunkirk was under way, the order came for six Hawker Hectors to head to Calais to bomb German gun placements. The raid was a success and the next day another six were sent over the Channel, and this time John was at the controls of one of the planes. They flew in two groups of three planes and had been ordered to disrupt the German troops as much as

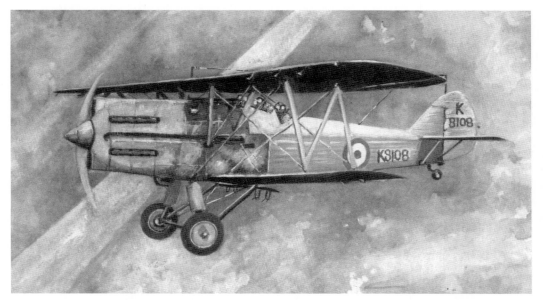

Hawker Hector K8108 painted by Peter Haughton, an air gunner on the Calais trip.
(© J. Rowland)

possible by dropping their bombs and shooting at anything that moved. John and his rear gunner, LAC R.V. Brown, arrived back safely, but one of the Hectors crashed as it reached Dover. John told his commanding officer that everything had been very quiet, though when they had landed they noticed a bullet hole in the aircraft. This was the first and only time that the Hawker Hector was used operationally, for the elderly aircraft was already obsolete by the outbreak of the war.

After Dunkirk, John along with all the squadrons who had been given army co-operation duties were switched to patrolling the coast from dawn to dusk to act as an early warning system watching for attack. Their allotted patrol route was from Filey in Yorkshire to the Humber, then from the mouth of the Humber down to the Wash in Lincolnshire. John spent the whole summer flying up and down the coast, and never had to report any approaching attack. Then, on 21 September, he was posted to the central flying school to do an instructor's course, on the completion of which he was given a choice of three instructor postings – join the Empire Air Training programme and go to Canada, or Montrose in Scotland or Sealand in Flintshire.

John chose Montrose and found to his delight when he got there that the chief flying instructor was his old flight commander from Cranwell, with whom he had always got on well. Training was initially given in the Miles Master followed by the Mk1 Hurricane, but soon it was decided that as the pupil pilots would be going on to Spitfires once they had left Montrose, that the instructors ought to have go at flying them. John was to spend two and a half years as a flying instructor before, on 16 February 1943, he found himself posted to No.30 Operational Training Unit at Hixon near Stafford, a Bomber Command station. John was teamed up with a crew who had lost their pilot, he having broken his leg playing

131

rugby. John was now a Wellington pilot and having flown over 1,600 hours he managed to go solo on the Wellington after only three hours dual instruction. John soon realised that while he had been an instructor he had been somewhat sheltered not just from the war but also from the technical advancements that made target finding and night flying so much more accurate. John completed the course and was then posted to No.1656 Heavy Conversion Unit at Lindholme, where he was to convert to the Lancaster bomber with the same crew as he had trained with on the Wellington with the addition of a flight engineer.

On 20 June 1943 John and his crew arrived at 12 Squadron at Wickenby just outside Lincoln, a night bombing squadron that had lost five aircraft the previous night. For the first month John and his crew familiarised themselves with the local territory but by 23 July the crew was fully operational. On the first bombing mission, the usual form was either for an experienced pilot to take the rookie pilot along for a trip, or for an experienced pilot to take a rookie crew. In John's case he accompanied an experienced crew. His aircraft was part of a wave of a hundred bombers that would soon join a force of six hundred all heading to Germany in close formation, for Bomber Command had a policy of trying to swamp the German defences. Their target was Gelsenkirchen, a centre of coal mining and oil refining. As they approached, the sky in front of him was filled with twinkling flashes, a combination of flak spread over an area of about 10 square miles and lights dropped as target indicators by the Pathfinders (for whom see the following chapter). As they closed on the target the activity increased as the searchlights tried to pick out the bombers. He could see the bombs and incendiaries dropped by other planes explode below and then the bomb aimer in his aircraft suddenly shouted 'bomb doors open' then 'left, left' and 'bombs gone'. John felt the huge lurch in the aircraft as the bombs dropped and the lightened Lancaster rose in the air, after which the pilot had to keep the aircraft straight and level for a whole minute while a photograph was taken to show, hopefully, that they had dropped their bombs on target. This was a controversial system that had been introduced not only to stop crews just dumping their bombs in the sea and returning to base but also to calculate results. The camera was activated when the bomb was dropped and because it was night-time a small flare was released as well to provide additional light. The system often failed, but without the photograph a mission would not count towards the total needed for a crew to complete a tour. At the beginning of their service bomber crews were usually told that they would be expected to do a 'tour' consisting of 30 trips, but trips only counted if they reached their intended target. Assuming they survived their tour, the crew would then be taken off operations and employed in instructing roles or other duties within the RAF, usually for six months before becoming 'available' for operations once more. This notwithstanding, many crews and individual airmen did volunteer for more tours.

John was now ready to command his first operational mission, and was given an 'easy' run for his first trip – to drop parachute mines in the mouth of the Gironde river. It was known by the code name of 'gardening', with the mines given the names of vegetables as the crew's job was to 'plant' them in a shipping lane.

This operation was successful and on the night of 3 July they joined a successful mission to Cologne and arrived home after a fairly uneventful trip. During July and August John continued making successful raids over Germany, and then the beginning of September brought a welcome period of leave. On 22 September, John was selected to take a new crew on their first trip. The drawback with this system was that this mission, added to that he took as second pilot, meant that John had done 18 trips and his crew had only done 16, meaning he would finish his tour before the rest of his mates. There were many cases when a pilot in this position would fly the last trip with his crew when he didn't have to and end up being killed on a raid he needn't have flown. John and his crew completed 20 trips together almost without incident, at which point Charlie, their flight engineer, who had already served with Coastal Command, was eligible to leave as he had done more trips than the rest of them. It seemed as if his luck left with them, for the day after Charlie left they flew to Munich with a new flight engineer and were almost over the target when they got caught by a searchlight. Soon other lights homed in on them and the flak batteries started firing. The aircraft rocked, then all of a sudden there was a blinding flash and everything went dark. For a moment John thought he was dead, then as the seconds ticked by he realised that the flak had actually hit the next Lancaster along, which had been flying only about 100 yards away, and it had exploded. Thinking that the explosion had been from the Lancaster they were focusing on, the Germans had turned off the searchlight and waited for the next plane; it was a very near miss.

Their next trip was to Frankfurt and they were barely over the French coast when Pete the gunner reported that his turret was non-operational. This had happened before, and the crew knew that Pete would be in for an uncomfortable time constantly turning around in the cramped space trying to keep a look out. They followed the Pathfinders but were glad to turn for home. When the turret went u/s again on the next flight they jettisoned their bombs and turned for home as they were all getting fed up with this recurring problem.

On 8 October the crew headed for Hanover but hadn't reached the target when Pete suddenly yelled over the radio 'Fighter, Starboard Go'. This was a sign to John to quickly dip the starboard wing and turn sharply to get out of range of a German night fighter, and John had barely started the manoeuvre when a line of cannon tracer passed his window, followed by the sound of a dull thud from somewhere in the back of the fuselage. John asked if everybody was OK, but there was no reply from Pete and the flight engineer went back to see what was wrong. A cannon shell had hit the turret and killed Pete outright, but they decided to fly on as they were only a few minutes away from the target.

The crew had a week's leave after Pete's death and for his first trip back John was again chosen to take a new crew, taking with him his own mid upper gunner, Robinson, who had lost a trip and didn't want to fall too far behind in his tour tally. They reached their target and as they dropped their bombs they came under heavy fire. John called up everybody on the intercom and this time it was

Squadron Leader John Rowland DSO, DFC & bar.
(© J. Rowland)

Robinson who didn't answer. The flight engineer went back to check on him and found Robinson alive but with a nasty head wound. As the ambulance men were attending to Robbie on their return (he did recover), the new pilot, Birchall said, 'There is something wrong with my back.' John pulled up Birchall's shirt and saw a nasty wound; a bullet had gone through his back and lodged in his lung. They also discovered that the flight engineer had had a lucky escape. Just before they were hit he had had his head up in the perspex observation window or bubble keeping a lookout, and it had been holed by a bullet.

John had now flown 28 operational sorties, slightly short of a full tour, and was told that he had been recommended for a DFC – he had no idea why – and promoted to squadron leader. He was also told that he and his crew had been assessed and found perfect for acting as an instructional crew on a heavy conversion unit. He was sent back to Lindholme where he became the officer commanding A flight with five instructors under him. At Lindholme the pilots were trained using a Halifax, an aircraft John hated, so he was more than glad that he spent more time flying his desk than he did in the air.

Technically, when a crew had finished an operational tour they were given six months rest either as instructors or on other duties before they were asked to do another tour. John had flown his last sortie on 10 November 1943 and he was posted to 625 Squadron on 12 May 1944, almost six months to the day since his last flight. He was a flight commander and back flying his beloved Lancaster bombers. Again John's first few sorties were successful and relatively quiet, and during this period, on 26 May, he married Jean McMichael, a Scottish WAAF he had met at the Central Flying School in 1942.

A few days later all leave was cancelled in readiness for D-Day on 6 June. John was airborne that night, flying to Vire close to Normandy, but he did not fly again until 22 June. Bomber Command were now sending out much smaller groups of aircraft, with smaller targets such as the doodlebug sites which were launching the pilotless flying bomb (V1).

During this second tour, John was asked to serve on two courts of enquiry, the first to look into the reasons why two Lancasters had collided on the ground in the dark while taxiing around the edge of an airfield. His commanding officer told him in no uncertain terms not to provide a whitewash report as he would only get a black mark himself and the case would have to be heard again. Nobody had been hurt, but the two Lancasters had been badly damaged. John found that men in

Newly married John Rowland and Jean McMichael with their dog Bonnie.
(© J. Rowland)

both aircraft were responsible for the accident. The second case concerned the reason why six aircraft had landed back at their base after being informed that due to adverse weather they should all land at other bases. It did not take John long to discover that five of them had crew members who had dates that night and wanted to get back, whilst the sixth had a new navigator who could find his way back to his own base but was not very confident about finding another airfield.

John was to leave the RAF in December 1944, but how this came about is told in Chapter 15.

Another Radnorshire airman whose RAF career took him to Bomber Command was Ronald Alfred William Beaumont.[1] Born in Knighton on 14 November 1919, the only son of Josiah and Gladys Beaumont of No.5 High Street, Ronald loved aircraft and flying but unlike most of his aviation-minded counterparts in Radnorshire, rather than seeking to join the RAF, he took a civilian route into aviation. Just after his 18th birthday he started an apprenticeship with Air Dispatch Ltd at Croydon airport, Surrey as a trainee ground and flight engineer. At the outbreak of the Second World War civilian flying was severely restricted and the company moved their operation to Pengam Moors near Cardiff and Ron went with them. It was not until the autumn of 1941 that he sought to join the RAF.

It seems likely that Ron's time with Air Dispatch worked in his favour, as an air crew selection board recommended him for pilot training almost immediately. The first stage of Ron's training was conducted in England, but as already noted in Chapter 5, due to the pressure on airfields and the risk of attack at any moment the RAF had started sending aircrew abroad to train, mainly to America and Canada, and it was to Monckton RCAF

Ron Beaumont (on the right) and crew at Air Dispatch Ltd. (© H. Lambert)

Ronald Beaumont standing in front of a Junkers aircraft at Pengam (Cardiff) airport before the start of the war, the aircraft being a popular civilian airliner and freight carrier. (© H. Lambert)

Ronald Beaumont while on flight training in North America. (© H. Lambert)

base in New Brunswick that Ron was sent to further his training. He arrived on 2 July 1942 and on 20 February 1943 was awarded his flying badge (RAF wings); he was now a qualified pilot. His next move was to No.11 Pilots Advanced Flying Unit for further training.

Ron soon acquired the nickname 'Butch' Beaumont and in October he was given the probationary rank of pilot officer; he was still listed as Sergeant Beaumont when he arrived at 57 Squadron in December 1943. Based at East Kirby in Lincolnshire, 57 Squadron was involved in night-time Bomber Command operations over Europe. The Berlin bomber offensive had started in November 1943 and Beaumont would spend the next few months flying long dangerous missions at night into the heart of some of the most heavily defended cities in Germany. The losses were high, with almost ten percent of crews lost on every raid. The raids continued all through the winter with only the severest of weather grounding the bombers.

The flights to Berlin and back would take approximately eight hours in pitch darkness often under radio silence, the crew half expecting at any moment to be shot down or suffer engine failure or some other malfunction that would lead to bailing out over the sea or hostile territory, perhaps to be wounded or killed; the strain on crews could be enormous.

A new crew would often find their first raid was a long flight in poor visibility straight into the path of the waiting German night fighters. For many crews their first sortie would be their last. Out of the total of 125,000 aircrew in Bomber Command over the course of the war, 55,573 were to lose their lives, a loss of 44.4%. A further 8,403 were wounded and 9,838 became prisoners of war. During the Second World War a member of Bomber Command aircrew had a worse chance of survival than an infantryman in the First World War; John Rowland was one of the lucky ones.

Butch's first sortie was to Berlin on the night of 16/17 of December 1943, when he joined the crew of Lancaster bomber JB725 as second pilot; pilots often teamed up with another crew for one flight to get the feel of an actual mission before taking their own crew out. A week later it was Butch's turn to take his own crew to Berlin. The sortie on the night of 23/24 December wasn't a success, as the navigator Flight Sergeant M.A. Johns fell ill and Butch had to turn back. This was the first sortie he flew with a man who was to become a good friend, mid upper gunner Sgt R.I. Hudson (known as Allen).

There were no more sorties for Butch and his crew in the last week of December, and they were also able to have a quiet January with their only flight recorded as a 'bulls eye' exercise for the 23rd. (This type of exercise was meant to simulate an actual bombing raid, the aircraft intending to deliver its bombs as close to the centre of the target – the bull's eye – as possible. Aircraft would fly through searchlight beams and even be subject to mock attacks from other RAF planes.)

February saw far more action when flying in Lancaster bomber serial number ND506, the crew consisting of the now commissioned Pilot Officer R.A.W. 'Butch' Beaumont as pilot, F/Sgt M.A. Clark as flight engineer, F/Sgt D.J. McCrudden as navigator (replacing Johns who had been ill on the first sortie), F/Sgt T.H. Mayne RCAF as bomb aimer, Sgt F.P. Robinson as wireless operator, Sgt R.I. Hudson as mid upper gunner and Sgt A.R. Muir as the rear gunner. On the night of the 15/16th they flew successfully to Berlin, on the 19/20th they successfully bombed Leipzig, the 24/25th saw another completed sortie this time to Schweinfurt (a centre for the manufacture of anti-friction bearings) and on the night of the 26/27th they bombed Augsburg.

March saw the same crew and the same Lancaster fly another six successful missions over Germany. During this time it was common practice for Allen Hudson and Sgt A.R. Muir to swap positions.

The crew were back over Germany on the night of 10/11 April. The next night they flew another Lancaster, serial ND405, perhaps because their plane was undergoing maintenance, but it did not hamper the crew's safe return. Back in Lancaster ND506 for the night of the 18/19th, they took along Pilot Officer J.B. Spencer as second pilot to gain experience. It was only three short months ago that Butch was himself being shown the ropes.

Twice more they would conduct successful raids over Germany; then on the night of 26/27 April 1944 things went disastrously wrong. Butch was among 14 aircraft that were dispatched to bomb Schweinfurt. The headwinds were far stronger than had been anticipated and the bombers arrived late over the target, and whilst the red spot fires and the green target indicators could be seen by the crews, they had also attracted the attention of German night fighters. Allen was to recall later that as the aircraft turned on the final leg of the bombing run they all became acutely aware that the German fighters knew exactly where they were heading. The German night fighter activity was hotting up all around them and the anti-aircraft fire was becoming more and more intense. Sgt Muir in the mid upper gun position reported that a Lancaster up ahead had been caught in the searchlights and was getting some serious attention from a flak battery, so Butch started to weave the Lancaster around, hopefully keeping her in the dark part of the sky and away from trouble. Muir then spotted a night fighter on the port side and Allen immediately turned his attention to the starboard, for a favourite German trick was for one fighter to fly just out of range of the Lancaster guns and attract attention while another fighter sneaked up on the other side and attacked, and sure enough Allen spotted another German closing in. A solid stream of 20mm cannon fire hit the Lancaster running down the main fuselage. The bursts were so bright that Allen was temporarily blinded; he later recalled how the sound reminded him of a child running a stick along a metal fence. The aircraft started to corkscrew wildly and Allen could hear explosions inside the fuselage. The whole aircraft shuddered with the impacts and Allen felt it was time to get out.

Pilot Officer Ronald Beaumont.
(© H. Lambert)

The gunner's parachute was stowed inside the plane as his turret was so small and he set about crawling back to retrieve it. The aircraft was diving steeply and he was struggling forward just as the Lancaster gave a violent lurch which shot him up into the fuselage with a sickening crunch. One boot, his flying helmet and more importantly his oxygen mask were torn away. He was relieved to see in the utter chaos of the fuselage that at least two crew members were still aboard. Sgt McCrudden appeared to be still in his position and Sgt Robinson had managed to get the rear door open and was preparing to jump. Robinson had also lost his oxygen mask and was beginning to feel the effects of oxygen starvation. He had clipped his parachute haphazardly across his chest by only one clip and had managed to pull the 'D' ring release so that the silk was billowing around his feet – it would have been suicide to jump and Allen yelled at him and pushed him until he got away from the door. The aircraft levelled out slightly and it became obvious that Butch was still up front and in control if only barely. Mayne, the Canadian bomb aimer, appeared with an oxygen bottle and between them they sorted out Robinson. A few seconds later there came another series of explosions and Allen felt as if he had been hit across the back with a sledgehammer and fell to the floor. The plane started bucking about and Allen was thrown from side to side dazed, in pain and terrified – he was convinced that the end had come. Once again Butch got the aircraft under control and dropped to a lower altitude, making breathing easier for the men who had lost oxygen. Allen was injured and in shock but he resisted attempts by Mayne to move him to a more comfortable position.

Allen suddenly realised that the other gunner – Sgt Muir – hadn't moved out of his turret; he could see Muir's legs dangling from the turret but he wasn't moving. The flight engineer F/Sgt Clark came to see how Allen was doing and Allen indicated that they should see to Muir. Clark just shook his head indicating that Muir had already died in his turret and there was nothing they could do for him.

Butch nursed the Lancaster homeward whilst Allen drifted in and out of consciousness, hardly aware of the journey or if any of his other mates had been injured. A grey light started filtering into the aircraft as they crossed the coast of England. Clark and Robinson came to Allen and announced they would crash land at the first airfield that would take them and with that they picked up the protesting Allen and dragged and carried him to the rest position next to the main spar where they both held on to him in preparation for the landing. Apart from being shot up they were now low on fuel and Butch flew the spluttering aircraft straight on to the runway. The plane hit the ground with a resounding crash, leapt 20 feet into the air and then landed again. Part of the fuselage broke away and the Lancaster came to rest in the marshland alongside the airfield. They had landed at Tangmere.

Allen's last memory of that night concerned the Canadian, Mayne. They were all being checked out in the sick quarters and Mayne was pointing out the shattered left-hand clip of his parachute harness, assuming it had got damaged when they had been thrown about inside the aircraft. He proceeded to unbuckle his harness and take off his jacket and pullover, and as the latter came off there was a clunk and there on the floor for all to see was about two-thirds of a 20mm cannon shell; he must have been hit by shrapnel and saved by his harness.

Two of the 14 aircraft had been lost, whilst Butch and another Lancaster flown by P/O Nicklin made emergency landings at Tangmere that night. Once on the ground the extent of the damage could be assessed. The Lancaster was riddled with holes; mid upper gunner A.R. Muir had been killed; Allen Hudson was so badly injured that he would spend the next five months in hospital; whilst Sgt Robinson and the Canadian bombardier Mayne sustained lesser injuries.

Despite this harrowing flight, just over a week later, on the night of 7/8 May, Butch took to the skies once more. Clark and McCrudden were still with him as his flight engineer and navigator, but all the other crew members had to be replaced. The crew completed another sortie and even damaged an Me110 night fighter in the process. By 19 May, Mayne, having recovered from his injuries, was back with the crew.

Butch Beaumont continued to fly sorties with his new crew comprising F/Sgt M.A. Clark, Pilot Officer D.J. McCrudden, wireless operator T.H. Mayne RCAF, wireless operator C.H.T Hurley, F/Sgt G.R Ansdell and F/Sgt E.H Goehring RCAF. They completed four more successful sorties in May, and another seven in the first half of June.

Their eighth sortie in June was Butch's 30th as a pilot. Their mission was to bomb the synthetic oil plant at Wesseling. Butch took off from the airfield at East Kirby at 11pm on the night of 21 June 1944, and after that, nothing more was heard from the aircraft. Aircraft on this raid reported being attacked as soon as they started their bombing run. There was heavy anti-aircraft activity and the German night fighters kept up a near constant attack, following the bombers back over coast after the bombing had finished; 36 Lancasters were lost. It was thought that Beaumont was attacked by a night fighter or hit by flak on his way into the target, still with his full bombload on board. Some details of what happened to the aircraft only emerged after the war was over and will be recounted later.

Another Radnorshire airman involved in the Berlin bombing offensive was Philip Charles Knill Bennett, the son of William and Mary Frances Bennett (née Knill), who was born in Builth Wells in the summer of 1924. The family moved to Gate Farm on the outskirts of Llandrindod Wells and it was here that Philip grew up, attended Llandrindod Wells County School and joined the school flight of the air cadets, before applying to the Royal Air Force.

Philip joined the RAF Volunteer Reserve (RAFVR), became a flight sergeant and joined a seven-man Lancaster bomber crew. After a spell at No.1656 Bomber Conversion Unit he was posted to 514 Squadron on 21 September 1943. The squadron had only been formed at the beginning of the month, and was moved to Waterbeach in Cambridgeshire on 24 November. Philip and five others who had been with him at No.1656 formed the crew, their pilot P/O J.R. Laing arriving from No.1678 Conversion Unit on 18 November 1943. No operations were listed for the crew until 29 December 1943 when P/O Laing along with navigator Sgt A. Vickers, bomb aimer Sgt J. Knight, wireless operator Sgt G.E. Hydes, Royal Canadian Air Force mid upper gunner Sgt R.B. McAllister, rear gunner Sgt C.A. Salt and flight engineer Sgt Philip Bennett took off in Lancaster bomber 'C' LL625 to bomb Berlin. Although the crew was late over the target their mission was successful.

1 January 1944 saw them over Berlin again, another completed mission, although the formation they had been flying in had been scattered and the raid was not wholly successful. The same crew took off in the same Lancaster to bomb the same target the next night, the squadron records showing that the bombs had been on target and the concentration of bombing had been good.

The crew had a few nights off, then, again in the same Lancaster though now with Sgt G.E. Scott as wireless operator, they headed off for Brunswick on 14 January. Although they completed their mission, 12 of the 30 incendiary bombs they had been carrying failed to release. 20 January saw another raid on Berlin, as did 27 January, on which night they encountered heavy flak. The next night, after completing a raid on Berlin, Laing, the pilot, wrote in his report 'Best Prang I have been on' – the crew had encountered enemy aircraft but had fought them off successfully whilst the Pathfinder force had been bang on target. (Pathfinders had been introduced in August 1942, and are the subject of the next chapter.)

Their seventh and final sortie for the month was on 30 January. On the outward journey at approximately 8pm the rear gunner reported the presence of a twin-engined aircraft on the starboard side about 1,000 yards away. Being visible in silhouette against a white cloud, they soon identified it as a Ju88 German night fighter which the gunner thought was shadowing the Lancaster. Under instruction from the gunner, the pilot started a series of sweeping turns in order to shake off the Ju88 but the gunner reported that the enemy aircraft was closing in on them. When it was about 700 yards away the gunner, sensing that the Ju88 was getting ready to fire, ordered a sharp corkscrew to port. The enemy aircraft fired just at this moment but the bullets streamed past the Lancaster, causing no damage. All the while the enemy aircraft was closing in. The rear and mid upper gunners in the Lancaster both let fly bursts of machine gun fire, the port engine of the Ju88 was seen to burst into flames, and the aircraft began diving out of control. Both the gunners and the wireless operator saw an object they believed to be a parachute leave the aircraft before it spun out of sight. They carried on and reached Berlin without seeing any searchlights or flak and dropped their bombs at 8.25pm from 20,000 feet. The pilot reported seeing no results in the target area, but fires were seen as they left.

The crew were then rested for a fortnight, but the night of 15/16 February saw them off to Berlin again. This time the target was completely covered in cloud and the flak was far more intense than usual, but no enemy planes were seen.

After another night sortie on 19/20 February, Pilot Officer Laing reported that there had been a good exhibition of sky marking and on leaving the target the red glows were immediately visible. He further added that the route markers home had all been seen and used and were in fact very helpful; he commended the Pathfinders' exceptionally good effort in finding them a quieter route.

The crew took out another Lancaster on the night of 25/26 February – 44, 'F' DS842 – and this time they headed for Augsburg. Again the route was marked clearly by the Pathfinders and visibility was good, but Laing reported that the Monica had gone useless – Monica was a tail-borne warning system that the bombers used to detect an enemy aircraft homing in on them from behind. The Germans eventually managed to use the system to their advantage, using it to track aircraft. It is impossible to tell how many aircraft succumbed to this device before it was discovered when a German bomber landed by mistake on a British airfield and on inspection of its radios the system was uncovered.

The crew were back in LL 625 on 1 March for a raid on Stuttgart. Six days later they took along Sgt Macdonald as second pilot for him to gain experience, flying to Le Mans but did not drop their bombs as their target could not be accurately identified. They completed a successful mission to Frankfurt on the night of 22/23 March 1944. On 24/25 March they were back over Berlin carrying an 8,000lb bomb which they dropped on their target. They were returning home when the Lancaster crashed in Germany about 12 kilometres east-north-east of Dresden, near the village of Worlitz. The Canadian, F/Sgt McAllister, was the only member of the crew to survive and was taken prisoner. Phil Bennett and his crew had flown 15 sorties, ten of them to Berlin, all at night and all during the most intense period of bombing of the war. The Berlin bombing offensive ceased six days later.

Philip Bennett and the other crew members were buried in the local cemetery in Worlitz near where they crashed. After the war they were taken to Berlin and re-buried in the city's 1939-45 war cemetery. Philip is also remembered in the town cemetery in Llandrindod Wells and on the town's war memorial.

Whilst Butch Beaumont had survived 29 bombing missions, and Philip Bennett 14, it has already been noted that many an aircrew did not survive their first mission, and this was the case for Frank Haines. The son of John and Elizabeth Haines of Cardiff, Frank was born in about 1916. As a young man he lodged with the Sissons family of Hillcrest, Llandrindod Wells before joining the Royal Air Force Volunteer Reserve in Birmingham in June 1941. After his initial training he became a navigator and was commissioned in December 1942 as a pilot officer. It is unclear exactly when Frank became operational or even if he changed trade and had an extra period of training, but in the summer of 1943 he was with 51 Squadron based at Snaith in Yorkshire. The squadron were equipped with Handley Page Halifax bombers and were, like Butch Beaumont's squadron, involved in the bombing offensive on Germany.

Pilot Officer Frank Haines was teamed up with a crew of five men that arrived at the squadron on 19 June from No.1658 Conversion Unit, the seventh member of the crew being Sgt R.V. Boyd, an air gunner. There is no record of Frank at the base till 28 June. That night was therefore the first time that the crew had flown together, with D.W. Sigourney as pilot. The Halifax MkII serial number DT513 MH-N took off from Snaith just before midnight, their mission to drop their 7,000lb bombload on the city of Cologne. Nothing more was heard of the crew. It is believed that the aircraft was shot down off the coast of Holland by Oberleutnant Victor Sarko, a German night fight pilot. (Sarko claimed four victories before being killed in action on 6 March 1944.) Sigourney's body was recovered from the North Sea and buried in Bergen Cemetery in the Netherlands, but the other crew members are remembered on the Runnymede memorial for airmen with no known grave. Frank Haines is also remembered on the war memorial in Llandrindod Wells.

At the opposite end of the survival scale was Victor Griffiths Hope, who started to fly operational bombing missions a good year before the Berlin offensive was launched. Born in Llandrindod Wells on 22 November 1918, he was the youngest son of Harry Hope of Beechgrove, Tremont Road. He attended the National Primary School and then completed his education at the Llandrindod Wells County School. His first job was as a messenger with the town's post office and then he secured a job with an aircraft company in the Midlands. He joined the Royal Air Force in 1938, becoming a flight engineer on Halifax bombers.

He was initially posted to 405 RCAF Squadron, then to 158 Squadron based at Driffield in Yorkshire. It had originally been equipped with Wellington bombers but was in the process of converting to the Halifax when Sergeant Victor Hope arrived on 20 May. On 6 June the squadron moved bases to RAF East Moor north of York and was now ready to take part in operations.

On 25 June 1942 Victor was on the first raid that 158 flew with the Halifax; it was Bomber Command's third raid using 1,000 bombers. They took off at 11.30pm in Halifax W7745 and reached their target over Bremen on time, but the bombs failed to be released – the aircraft had been hit by flak over Germany which damaged the bomb release gear in the nose as well as the starboard outer engine; the fuselage was also scarred. The crew were uninjured, however, and the aircraft made it back to base.

The aircraft was repaired and on 8 July it was back over Germany for a bombing mission to Wilhelmshaven. The mission was a success, as was their trip to Vegesack on 19 July. On 23 July they bombed Duisburg and their navigator F/O Fairbairn was commended for his first class performance. On 26 and 31 July they bombed Hamburg and Düsseldorf, both missions again deemed a success. Victor was next up on 2 September when he and his crew took off with five other Halifaxes to bomb Karlsruhe. They could see the town alight and commended the work of the Pathfinders in pinpointing the target. Soon, however, German night fighters were bearing down on them. One Ju88 came towards Victor's aircraft; the gunners could see a light in the nose, so they fired towards it and the light went out. Another Ju88 came up on the starboard side and both the rear and mid upper gunner opened fire as the pilot, Wing Commander P. Stevens, took successful evasive action.

On 16 September the aircraft was scheduled to take off, but it was discovered that one of the gun turrets was useless because of an electrical failure, so all they could do was walk away from the aircraft as the rest of the squadron took off. On 23 October the crew took a Halifax on a raid to Genoa in Italy. This seems to have been Victor's last trip for 1942 as he does not appear in the squadron records again that year.

On 19 January 1943 Victor received a commission to the rank of pilot officer. On 2 February the crew joined a raid on Hamburg. The Pathfinders laid flares but by the time Victor and his crew were over the target there was almost complete cloud cover. They could see the glow of several fires in and around the city but could not identify their own target. In the end the pilot dropped his bombs in the area of the brightest glow after circling around the target area for 17 minutes. His bombs scattered over a wide area, something that the pilot was unhappy about, as indeed were the crew, from the squadron records. On the same raid they dropped Nickels, a code name for the propaganda leaflets that the British dropped on German cities.

It was 26 February before Victor was airborne again, this time heading for Cologne in Halifax DT703. They were part of a large formation of bombers that night and as they reached the target area they could see that the Pathfinders had clearly marked the area with green flares. The pilot reported that the bombs dropped by the rest of the formation were so concentrated that they could not pick out the explosions from their own bombs. This comment shows the valuable contribution made by the Pathfinders, who by arriving in a given area ahead of the main force would pinpoint the target with coloured (usually green or red) flares, so that the bombers coming behind would bomb only strategic targets of military or industrial significance.

For most of his previous raids Victor had flown with the squadron's commanding officer, Wing Commander Robinson, as pilot, but Robinson was posted to 138 Squadron, so for his tenth raid on 12 March Victor joined the crew of Halifax DT700 flown by Wing Commander T.R Hope (no relation), the new squadron C.O., for a raid on Essen.

Although Victor had only just reached the rank of pilot officer, on 24 March 1943 he was granted the temporary rank of acting flight lieutenant. He also had the title of squadron flight engineer leader, which explains why he flew comparatively few sorties at this time. Interestingly, a close look at his sorties shows that Victor was teamed up with high-ranking officers in almost any crew he joined. Fl/Eng Victor Hope and Wing Commander T.R. Hope teamed up again on 29 March, although the other five members of the crew had changed yet again. The target was Berlin, but the Halifax turned back before it reached the target area as heavy flak from the Esbjerg anti-aircraft battery had put the port outer engine out of action. There were also numerous holes in the fuselage, port wing and mid upper turret. They jettisoned their bombs near Helevad in the east of Denmark.

On 3 April the two Hopes set off again, this time for Essen and again with a new crew. The raid was not a success, as the target indicators seemed to be all over the place, the wing commander suggesting that dummy flares had been laid in order to confuse the bombers.

King George VI presenting Victor Hope with his DFC. (© P. Davies)

Victor went through an unusual number of crew changes which may indicate that the senior pilots wanted to instil confidence in novice crews, not just by having an experienced pilot fly the aircraft, but also in having an experienced flight engineer on board.

On 16 April Victor headed for Pilsen. It was a clear night and buildings could be identified by the light from flares. Wing Commander Hope did a preliminary run over the target before turning for the bombing run. He concluded in his report that the bombing mission had been successful, although the area was almost immediately obscured by smoke haze. Duisburg was the target on 12 May, Essen on 27 May, Düsseldorf on 11 June and Aachen on 13/14 July – all missions being judged a success.

At the last minute on 10 August 1943, P/O G.J. Macrae replaced Victor as flight engineer to Wing Commander Hope; the crew were heading for Nuremberg when the aircraft was shot down. Although Macrae, Wing Commander Hope and P/O I. Hirshbein survived, the rest of the crew were killed.

Victor flew his 18th sortie with P/O D.C. Cameron as pilot in Halifax HR 715 to Hamburg, but this was to be his last sortie with 158 Squadron as on 31 August he was posted to No.1663 Conversion Unit, possibly for instructor duties. He was awarded the Distinguished Flying Cross for his work with 158 Squadron and subsequently became the chief ground instructor for the Canadian bomber force in England, aged just 26.

Victor achieved the rank of squadron leader and then, at his own request, left the Royal Air Force on 27 October 1947. It is believed that he settled near Harrogate in Yorkshire. He passed away in 1991.

James Spencer Lang was a different type of bomber pilot from Butch Beaumont, and indeed flew completely different types of missions from the air crew mentioned above. James was born in Axebridge, Somerset in early 1923 to Ernest and Bertha Lang (née Crane). His 49-year-old father died in 1930 and his mother in 1937, leaving James as a 14-year-old orphan. His mother's brother, Walter Crane brought the boy to live with him in Llandrindod Wells where he ran a chemist's shop.

In early 1941 James enlisted in the RAFVR, probably on or about his 18th birthday. After initial training he was selected to train as a pilot, becoming a qualified bomber pilot on the American made Douglas Boston. The Boston, with its crew of four, was a medium bomber used in daytime. In 1943 he was posted to 107 Squadron based at RAF Hartfordbridge in Hampshire. The squadron had gained quite a reputation for daring low level bombing raids in France, a reputation that it seems James was keen to uphold. During a raid on the Pont à Vendin power station in July, James was jumped on by a German Focke Wolfe 190 which he managed to evade by performing a very sharp corkscrew manoeuvre into the cloud cover, a feat that would involve being suddenly plunged into almost zero visibility but still keeping flying on course. James and fellow Boston pilot Wing Commander England used this trick of flying in cloud frequently, both for arriving unnoticed in a target area and for escaping quickly afterwards. It involved not only skilful flying but quite a lot of stress on the aircraft – the Boston might have been small as a bomber but she was not a sleek aerobatic fighter.

Exactly how many missions James flew with 107 Squadron is hard to determine, but it seems he enjoyed flying Bostons for on 20 April 1944 he and his three crew members joined 88 Squadron which was moving to Hartfordbridge and would be still flying Bostons, whilst 107 Squadron was moving to nearby RAF Lasham where they were to be equipped with the new Mosquito. No.88 Squadron specialized in daylight bombing raids, usually in the early morning or late afternoon, on coastal targets and enemy shipping.

On 6 June 1944, James and most of the squadron were called for a very early morning briefing. It was D-Day and the squadron were going to be accompanying the first wave of men landing, laying a giant smoke screen across the French beaches. At 5am the first Bostons were over Le Havre, led by Wing Commander Maher, releasing their aerial smoke screen, but strong winds dispersed the haze almost immediately. James was flying in the third Boston of the group; he too released his smoke screen and although they encountered some flak got back safely. Wave after wave of Bostons took off ten minutes apart.

As each crew landed they were told to be ready to take off again. Of the 12 aircraft in that first wave, one piloted by W/O A.J. Boyle failed to return and a second piloted by Fl/Lt Smith overshot the runway and crashed. Smith suffered internal injuries and his navigator F/Sgt Allen was killed, whilst the other two crew members were shaken but unhurt.

Throughout the coming days 88 Squadron were on round the clock readiness and bombing missions were conducted from dawn to dusk. On 10 June James was among 16 aircraft that attacked the marshalling yards at St Sauviour, and on the evening of 15 June among the 24 Bostons that headed for Portillion, 12 Bostons from 88 Squadron and 12 from 342 Squadron; this latter squadron, which shared the airfield at Hartfordbridge, were crewed by Free French. Their target was the headquarters of the First Panzer Corps. Although some of the bombs had landed a bit wide of the mark, the raid was deemed a success and the aircraft only encountered a small amount of inaccurate flak.

Another successful raid was carried out on 20 June, but the next day's was unsuccessful as the fighter plane base at Bois Coquerel they were sent to attack was completely obscured by cloud, and all the aircraft brought their bombs back home.

On 9 August James left Hartfordbridge at 10.25 in the morning for a raid on an ammunition dump at Lyons La Fôret near Rouen, his crew comprising F/O J.R. Haynes as navigator, F/O R. Holmes as wireless operator and F/O Ken Jones as air gunner. James was leading his section, and as they neared the target a flak battery between Senarpont and Aumale opened up with intense and accurate flak. Several aircraft were hit and the section scattered. James's Boston received a direct hit on the starboard wing, between the fuselage and the engine, causing the wing to fall off, and the aircraft was seen to go into a spin before bursting into flames. None of the aircraft in the area reported seeing any parachutes and the crew were all killed.

On 11 August 1944, two days after he was killed, James was awarded the Distinguished Flying Cross. The citation had been drafted when James had completed 30 sorties and read: 'This officer has completed many hazardous high and low level attacks on enemy occupied territory and has on occasions led his section. During one sortie his aircraft was repeatedly attacked by the enemy, causing some damage, but, displaying fine airmanship, he flew the aircraft safely back to base. In times of stress Pilot Officer Lang has always shown a high degree of coolness and courage.' Ken Jones and Jack Haynes, who were part of James's crew, were also awarded the DFC at the same time.

All of the crew were buried at St Léger-aux-Bois Cemetery.

Another bomber pilot who was to see action late on in the war in Europe was John Anthony Norton, known to his family as Tony, who was the son of Llandrindod Wells

John Anthony 'Tony' Norton when a sergeant as an aircrew cadet (top) and when a pilot officer (bottom). (© Y. Norton)

businessman and flight enthusiast Tom Norton. Tom had been instrumental in trying to set up an aerodrome in the town, and above Tom's 'Automobile Palace' the word 'aircraft' was emblazoned in moulded stone with a ceramic coating for all to see. Born in 1922, Tony joined the RAFVR in November 1941, gaining a commission on 6 August 1943 when he was made a pilot officer. Becoming a pilot on the four-engined heavy bomber, the Short Stirling, he completed his training at No.1665 Heavy Conversion Unit.

In February 1944 Tony was further promoted to the rank of flying officer and in September he was posted to 196 Squadron, based at RAF Keevil in Wiltshire. Tony and his crew arrived at the base on 22 September and their first mission was to deliver supplies to the paratroops surrounded at Arnhem. The mission was a success, but they were hit by heavy flak over the target area, the flight engineer was injured and the propeller was blown off the port outer engine. Tony nursed the aircraft back over the Channel and landed at RAF Manston. The flight engineer Sgt F. Gill was taken off for medical treatment, but the rest of the crew were unhurt and returned to Keevil the next day.

On 4 November Tony and his crew were engaged on an air sea rescue and flew back and forth over the search area, but sighted nothing.

On 9 November Tony headed for Holland again in formation with another seven bombers. He was carrying 24 containers and three panniers of supplies to the 'Draught's Seven' drop zone at Venhuizen near Enkhuizen along the west bank of the former Zuider Zee. This was a Special Operations Executive mission, dropping supplies under the cover of darkness. What happened next nobody knows for sure, as the Stirling (serial no EP234) was lost without trace. None of the other aircraft in the area reported seeing an aircraft go down and the register of aircraft lost over Holland doesn't mention the plane. Although aircraft are recovered from drained Polders from time to time, the area around Enkhuizen is still under water.

Flying Officer John Anthony Norton, aged 22, has no known grave and so is remembered on the Runnymede memorial, together with his crew: Flying Officer D.W. Eves, navigator, 21 years of age; Flight Sergeant H. Rushton, bomb aimer, 27 years of age; Sergeant J.V. Thompson, wireless operator, 21 years of age; Flight Sergeant C.A. Myers, flight engineer, 34 years of age and Sergeant M.A Goult, air gunner, 19 years of age. His name also appears on the war memorial in his home town of Llandrindod Wells, where he is also remembered on the family grave at the old parish church.

It would be surprising if everyone subjected to the knowledge of the rate of loss in Bomber Command, the continual possibility of accidents, or being hit by flak or a night fighter, managed to survive the war without showing some mental strain. In the case of Ronald Habgood Hamer, one particular episode seems to have taken him beyond his limit; perhaps he found some restorative calm in Radnorshire after the war.

Born in Yorkshire on 3 October 1918, Ronald grew up at Easingwold near Ripon and was educated at Bury Grammar School in Manchester. On leaving school he was granted a scholarship to Lancaster University, and on the outbreak of war he enlisted in the RAFVR and trained to be an observer. The role of observer was the second oldest in the air force. Initially in the First World War only pilots wore a distinguishing brevet – what became known as the RAF 'wings' badge still worn today – and this rankled with the men in the second seat who were not only facing the same dangers as the pilot, but also acting as lookouts, navigators, air gunners and bomb aimers. In September 1915 the RFC issued an observer badge (brevet) which took the form of an embroidered letter O with one white feathered wing attached. When the larger bombers started to join the air force extra men were needed to man them, leading to the creation of new trades or roles. Each new trade was granted its own brevet and meanwhile the role of observer began to change, to the extent that by 1942 it was decided to scrap the title and classify such men as navigators. Men who then wore the observer brevet were expected to hand them in and replace them with the new navigator's brevet (a winged N), but many refused, wishing to continue a tradition dating back to the early days of the RFC.

Ronald took part in his first operational sortie barely a year after joining up, when as part of a bomber crew he flew to Bremen on 13 July 1940. Before the month was out Ronald and his crew were to fly to Germany three more times. August saw the crew take to the skies a further nine times, on the ninth actually flying twice; the first flight only lasted 25 minutes and may have been to test some part of their equipment before they made the full sortie to Knapsack in Westphalia. September saw no rest as the crew flew another seven times to targets ranging from Boulogne to Berlin and Ostend to Mannheim.

October saw the same level of action as night after night Bomber Command despatched missions over Germany, France and Belgium. Eight times that month Ronald and his crew conducted successful sorties over the Continent. The crew flew over Hamburg on 5 November, and on 11 November they took off to bomb Gelsenkirchen, returning to the town on 13 November, but the mission failed and they turned back. On 14 November they were over Berlin, at the time among the most heavily defended of German cities; for

Ronald Hamer with his sister Irene at her wedding. (© C.A. Griffiths)

many crews their flight to Berlin was their first and last sortie. The crew then had quite an extended break and didn't fly again until 12 March 1941.

By now Ronald had flown a total of 32 trips. He certainly did a spell of instructing, but the records go quiet and there is not much information on exactly what his role was. It is known that he was promoted to the rank of pilot officer on 7 August 1942, and to flying officer on 7 February 1943. Then in June 1943 he was back on operational duties and once more flying to Germany at night with a bomber crew. Ronald had joined a Canadian squadron, No.432 RCAF, formed on 1 May from 18 crews from 427 Squadron. Based at Skipton on Swale in Yorkshire, he was now near his wife, for Ronald had married Edith Jarvis in the autumn of 1939 just after joining up. Ronald was acting as bombing leader for the squadron and on 24 June he flew in one of the squadron's Wellington bombers to Eberfeld. On 26 June he flew to Brest but the mission was not successful. Between June 1943 and July 1944 Ronald was to fly another 10 missions. In that time the squadron went from flying the Wellington MkX to flying the Lancaster MkII, to which they converted soon after moving to the RCAF station at East Moor on 18 September 1943. In January 1944 they changed again, now flying the Halifax MkIII. Ronald flew another mission on 28 July 1944 to Hamburg, and on 7 August he was promoted to flight lieutenant.

So far Ronald had gone through the war relatively unscathed but he did suffer one incident that landed him with a spell in hospital. On one of his bombing missions the last bomb failed to be properly released from its mechanism in the aircraft. Although the arming mechanism would not activate until the bomb was actually falling, if the bomb had been hit by either anti-aircraft fire or a German night fighter this would have proved fatal to their aircraft, so Ronald attempted to release the bomb by hand. The bombs should have been released when the bomb-bay doors opened and a 'catch' was activated allowing them to fall; the doors were open but the catch had got stuck. Ronald's only option was to lean out over the open bomb-bay door and pull and push the catch until it released. In the dark and with the slipstream whistling through the open bomb-bay doors, Ronald nearly lost his footing. There was nothing between him and a 20,000 foot drop, for he was not wearing a parachute; these were only donned immediately before jumping from an aircraft. That incident may have lived to haunt him. It is not clear on which raid this happened but his family attested that he had spent some time in Norbreck Sanatorium in Blackpool, possibly for nervous exhaustion. This is quite possibly why Ronald did not finish his last tour of duty.

On 14 November 1944 Ronald was awarded the Distinguished Flying Cross. The *London Gazette* published a citation on the day of the award which read: 'Completed numerous operations against the enemy, in the course of which he has invariably displayed the utmost fortitude, courage and devotion to duty.' His commanding officer was later to write:

> Flight Lieutenant Hamer has demonstrated his superior ability not only in the air but on the ground. As Squadron Bombing Leader since the formation of the squadron, his personal ability and instruction has consistently been of the highest order. Now on his second tour of operations, his many targets include Bremen, Frankfurt, Cologne, Berlin (three), Hamburg (four), Hanover and Mannheim, This officer's splendid record is most deserving of the award of the Distinguished Flying Cross.

On 9 February 1945 Ronald switched from an operational to an admin role with the special duties branch of the RAF. After leaving the Royal Air Force he was never to fly again.

Ronald and his wife Edith moved to Radnorshire, where for a few years they ran the New Inn at Llanbadarn Fynydd. They thought they had actually bought the New Inn on the agreement of a handshake from the owner, but later found out that he had gone back on his word. However, they liked the area so much that they decided to stay and raise their family in the county. Despite his slightly unpromising introduction to Radnorshire, Ronald was to spend the rest of his life in Llandrindod Wells, becoming a well-known figure. He married for a second time in 1973, and the couple ran a successful ladies and gents outfitters in the town. Ronald died in February 1989 aged 70.

At the beginning of this chapter the story was told of the loss of the Lancaster piloted by Butch Beaumont, as a result of which all the crew were listed as missing. It was 1947 before it was discovered exactly what had happened.

During the early years of the war it soon became obvious that the system set up to trace RAF aircrew who were missing, believed killed, was woefully inadequate. This led to the formation of the Missing Research Section in 1941 which would collect information from as many official and unofficial sources as possible in order to determine the fate of these missing men. As Europe became liberated the service was able to operate in France, Belgium and eventually Germany. By December 1944 the MRS was expanded and named the Missing Research and Enquiry Service (MRES). The task was enormous as there were 42,000 aircrew listed as missing and by July 1945 the Air Ministry took the decision to expanded the MRES to over 25 times its current size, the service being spilt into six sections each with its own geographical area. Almost all the members were volunteers from various sections of the RAF.

As the war ended Europe was in chaos. Prisoners of war were often being transferred hurriedly from place to place, whilst records were being burned by the Axis powers in case some incriminating piece of evidence was uncovered. As the teams moved into Germany they were trying to get information from the very people these airmen may have bombed just a short time before, and many faced open hostility.[2]

In Butch Beaumont's case the MRES received a report that the Burgermeister of the small village of Havert on the German/Dutch border had reported a loud explosion over the village on the night of 21/22 June 1944 and that there had been an aircraft crash the same night just outside the village. Although this was some miles away from where Butch had been flying to on the night he disappeared, it was along his route. The MRES visited the village and were shown a grave in the local cemetery. Men from the local Luftwaffe base had attended the crash site the night it happened and had cleared away the wreckage, while two local policemen, with the help of the farmer on whose land the plane had crashed and some Italian prisoners of war, conveyed the bodies to the church in Havert and had the aircrew buried. Five airmen were in one grave and another grave contained the body of a sixth airman, whilst the seventh crew member was never found. One of the burial party had imprinted on a metal strip the name rank and number of the five airmen in the one grave, but the airman in the single grave was not able to be identified. This led the team to list both F/Sgt Clark and W/O Hurley as missing with no known grave. They are remembered on the memorial wall at Runnymede.

The MRES conveyed all six bodies for reburial at the Rheinburg war cemetery. Five have inscribed headstones, and the sixth is listed as an unknown airman of the Royal Air Force.

Ronald Alfred William Beaumont was posthumously awarded the Distinguished Flying Cross.

Another family who benefited from the work of the MRES was that of James and Clara Morris of Llandrindod Wells, who found out what happened to their son, Ivor James. Ivor was born in 1923 and on leaving school drove a bread van for Cecil Lloyd in Crossgates before he joined the Royal Air Force Volunteer Reserve. He trained at No.1660 Conversion Unit before being posted on 18 July 1944 to 207 Squadron based at RAF Spilsby in Lincolnshire, where he was one of the two air gunners that formed part of a Lancaster crew.

Ivor's first sortie was on the night of 26/27 July, when they flew to Givors in France. On the night of 28/29 July, Flight Lieutenant Kenneth Marshall piloted Lancaster MkIII serial ND872 to Stuttgart as part of a force of 419 Lancasters led by two Mosquitos of the Pathfinder force on what was intended to be one of the last big raids on the town. There was a bright moon that night and the German night fighters intercepted the bombers before they had even got through France, shooting down 39 aircraft, of which Ivor's Lancaster was one. The aircraft was then near the village of Bebenhausen, approximately 40km from its target, and still had a full bombload on board. A local farmer, Mr Huber, witnessed some of what happened next. At about 10pm an aircraft flew low over the village in flames, crashing about 2km outside the village in a forested area, whereupon the plane exploded scattering wreckage over an area of approximately 500 square metres. The seven airmen were recovered from the aircraft by a work party from the nearby Etcherdigen airport, but the manner of the crash rendered individual identification almost impossible. The crew was buried in a mass grave near the village church without any ceremony.

After the war the crew became part of the caseload of the Missing Research and Enquiry Service (MRES), and on 25 January 1949 the unit was able to re-bury the men in the Durnbach War cemetery. Ivor James Morris is remembered on both the Llandrindod Wells War Memorial and Penybont War Memorial.

9　The Pathfinders

During early 1942 Bomber Command became increasingly aware that the accuracy of their bombing missions left much to be desired. The method developed to improve that accuracy – the use of Pathfinders – was largely down to one of Radnorshire's most famous airmen, Sydney Bufton.

The relatively prosperous and well-known Bufton family lived in Grosvenor Road, Llandrindod Wells, in an impressive Victorian house called The Links which commanded views of both the golf course and the boating lake. James Osborne Bufton was an alderman on Radnorshire County Council, and his elder brother had written *The Ramblers Illustrated Guide to Llandrindod Wells by a Native* in 1896, which James updated in 1906.

James and his wife Florence were the parents of five children – four boys and one girl – all of whom would become high achievers in later life. The eldest son, W.E. Bufton, graduated top of his law school in 1928, winning the £50 Sir Samuel Evans prize for the best honours paper of the year. He became a respected solicitor, serving as assistant solicitor to Radnorshire County Council for two years before becoming clerk of the peace to Pembrokeshire County Council. Next came Sydney Osborne, born in 1908, then in 1911 Mary, who became one of Wales' youngest female lawyers and worked for the census department during the Second World War. John Raymond was born in 1915 and the youngest son, Harry Emlyn (known as Hal), came along in 1916.

Tragedy struck the family on 25 June 1936 when a coach carrying Mrs Bufton, who was returning from a golf tournament in Aberystwyth, was struck by a lorry at approximately midnight on a nasty bend on the Rhayader road. Two ladies were killed instantly and Florence was seriously injured and trapped by metal that had been torn from the roof of the bus. One of the passengers rushed to a nearby farmhouse to get help whilst Mrs Bufton's friends assured her that they would soon have a doctor to help. She apparently replied, 'A doctor? I think I need an engineer!' It was the local doctor who arrived, and he and a policeman worked with hacksaws by the headlights of the doctor's car to free her, before rushing her to the local hospital. She did not survive the night.

Sydney, John and Harry (Hal) Bufton were all destined for the Royal Air Force. John's story was told in the previous chapter; this chapter starts with the stories of Sydney and Hal.

Sydney was educated first at Llandrindod Wells and then at Dean Close School in Cheltenham, where he excelled not only in the classroom but also at sports, particularly

RAF Hockey Team 1936-37.
Sydney is second from the left in the front row. (© Bufton family archive)

hockey. He was to be a Welsh international hockey player and also represent the RAF between the years 1931 and 1937. Sydney's real talent, however, was to emerge in the field of aviation and electronics. His masters tried to push him into the Royal Navy when he left school, but he thought that choice would seriously curtail his sporting activities. He objected to the army on the grounds that he didn't like their drab uniform. Despairing at this attitude, his alderman father called together a committee including the chief education officer for Radnorshire, the chief constable and Sydney's old headmaster. Seizing on a talent he had for electronics (he had made his own radio sets in school), they suggested that either the Marconi radio company or the Vickers engineering company might take him on to do an engineering degree. Sydney plumped for Vickers while also doing a night school course in the evening at Erith Technical College.

In the summer of 1927 Sydney began to wonder what he might do once he had qualified. A friend pointed out that with his qualifications and interests, the Royal Air Force would be almost certain to have him, and accordingly he took a short service commission in the RAF in December 1927, with the intention of keeping up his studies in engineering. Sydney trained at No.3 Flying Training School in Egypt and made his first solo flight in March 1928 at Abu Sueir.

In December 1928 he was posted to 100 Squadron in Bicester in Oxfordshire as a qualified pilot. Being judged as exceptional and having won the Clarkson trophy for

Sydney Bufton (on the right) with fellow pilot 'Creek' Larking at Baghdad en route for Tehran in August 1934. (© Bufton family archive)

aerobatics, 18 months later he was posted to No.5 Flying Training School as a qualified flying instructor.

At some point he obtained a permanent commission in the RAF, and was transferred to the Home Aircraft Depot to do an aircraft engineering course. Sydney would later be much teased by his peers, particularly his friend Barnes Wallis, for never finishing his aeronautical degree and would become the only Fellow of the Royal Society of Aeronautical Engineers (FRAeS) without a degree. Sydney's next stop was Iraq where he was posted to the Hinaidi aircraft depot.

In 1936 he returned to England. He had applied to join a flying boat squadron but instead found himself posted to the Directorate of Training where his main role was overseeing the setting up of the new training schools for the expanding RAF. His only flying was for leisure and to keep his hand in.

In 1937 he was made a squadron leader. It seems highly likely that people in high places were keeping an eye on Sydney for in January 1939 he was sent to the Royal Air Force Staff College. Here he was taught everything from organising formal receptions and letter writing to politics, tactics and communications, as well as intelligence and the organisation of ground, air and sea forces. During this time Sydney was attached to two operational squadrons – a bomber squadron flying Blenheims and two weeks with one of the first operational Spitfire squadrons; he found flying the Spitfire particularly exhilarating. Graduating with distinction from the RAF Staff College, he was now 31 and a staff officer.

A few short weeks later Hitler invaded Poland and Sydney was sent to France with the advanced strike force; he was a staff officer at the headquarters of the British air forces. During the Dunkirk evacuation he ensured that all personnel under his command had left safely before he and one other officer packed the last bits of sensitive equipment into a Blenheim and flew home from Nantes. He reached England at 8pm and after a smooth landing at Gatwick he went up to London. Enjoying a civilized drink after the chaos of the past few days Sydney reached a decision. His career in the RAF had so far been almost idyllic but now he had seen first hand the effects of war. An entry in his diary for 18 June 1940 reads:

> I have succeeded at last in getting a flying job. It was difficult to get, and I could easily have got myself a staff job or an engineering one. However I have basked so long in glory earned by the pilots and crews of the RAF – I must earn it for myself. I have lived through these years in the glamour of the service – the reputation for daring and devilry; I have been paid by the nation through all these years and I owe the nation all I can give.

Sydney was posted to a bomber squadron and determined from the beginning to lead from the front, not from his office like some other commanders. Whilst he earned a great deal of respect from his men for this style of leadership, it seems that his father was less than pleased. As Sydney wrote home to his father less than a month after taking the job:

> The job of Squadron commander is really grand. It is the finest in the RAF and is the most important one. You are wrong when you say the staff jobs I have held are more important. We in the Squadrons are the knife edge of the huge organisation behind us – the Station, the Group, the Air Ministry, Bomber Command, the Cabinet, the whole aircraft industry. We are the knife edge, and mine is the responsibility of keeping it sharp and gleaming and directing its blow aright ... So you see this is the most important job in the RAF.

Sydney's decision was vindicated when on 24 September 1940 a recommendation was put forward to award him the Distinguished Flying Cross, Arthur Coningham the commander of No.4 group writing that Sydney was:-

> A very capable Squadron Commander who has set an excellent example to the members of his Squadron. In spite of his multifarious Squadron duties he has himself, as Captain, recently carried out eight operational flights over enemy country in a period of six weeks. His calm confidence and cheerful demeanour invariably imbue an excellent offensive spirit in his flight crews. Strongly recommended for the DFC.

This must surely have pleased his father.

On 20 July Sydney took command of 10 Squadron at Leeming in North Yorkshire, then on 12 April 1941 he took command of the newly reformed 76 Bomber Squadron. The squadron was equipped with Halifaxes and would carry out its first bombing raid on 12 June, but by then Sydney had moved again, having been sent to command RAF Pocklington

Hal Bufton and Jeanne Greenland sit beside each other on the top diving board at the Metropole Hotel's swimming pool on 17 May 1937.

(© P. Davies)

in Yorkshire on 29 May. During this time he found it hard to get in any operational flying. Then on 1 November he was posted away from the operational scene altogether – he had been promoted to group captain and was made deputy director of Bomber Operations at the Air Ministry in London. Sydney was one of the youngest officers on the Air Ministry staff and one of the few to have flown on operations in the Second World War.

But what of Hal Bufton by this stage of the war? He had followed his brothers into Llandrindod Wells County School and then into the RAF, winning an open scholarship to Cranwell College. While at Cranwell he was offered the sword of honour, as the cadet who in the opinion of both his tutors and his peers had shown outstanding qualities as an officer. Hal declined this honour but took the principal science prize, a merit award that he had won fairly and squarely in open competition. He was commissioned as an officer in the RAF in December 1936 and his first posting was to 214 Squadron at Scampton in Lincolnshire to fly the new Handley Page Harrow bomber.

In 1940 Hal joined a select group working at Boscombe Down in Wiltshire as Flight Commander. It had been noted that the German Luftwaffe had a far more accurate night bombing system than did the RAF. The Knickebein (crooked leg system) was allowing the Luftwaffe to bomb British targets at night extremely effectively and Prime Minister Winston Churchill personally ordered and oversaw the setting up of the Blind Approach Technical and Development Unit (BATDU) at Boscombe Down. Officers like Hal who had a good scientific background were transferred from other duties in order to man this new unit. They would eventually become the Wireless Investigation and Development Unit (WIDU). No expense was spared and BATDU had top priority for receiving equipment and personnel.

Hal spent most of his time at Boscombe Down stooging around the night skies in old Anson and Whitley bombers, trying to prove his theories on blind flying. A critical turning point came on 21 June 1940. At this stage in what would become known as the battle of the beams, many British boffins were claiming that the sort of radio waves needed to direct an aeroplane could not be bent around the curvature of the earth, so it was useless looking for any such 'beam'. T.S. Eckersley of the Marconi radio company asserted that the beams could be bent and could be followed by an experienced operator right to a target in Britain. Winston Churchill got to hear of this and ordered BATDU to try to find the beams and jam or destroy them in some way. A flight was arranged with Hal as pilot and equipment set up by physicist Dr R.V. Jones, the premier government scientist involved in the project. Perhaps a little worried about disappointing the prime minister, T.S. Eckersley withdrew at the last minute and tried to cancel the flight, but Dr Jones persuaded him that Churchill would want to know who had overridden his authority by cancelling a specially ordered flight and to consider the consequences.

Hal and his crew took off, with no clear orders other than just to fly to and fro across country trying to pick up any unusual radio activity centred around the 30 MHz frequency. They stooged about in the dark for what seemed an interminable time when suddenly the radio operator picked up a signal. A steady beam on the 31.5 MHz frequency was being sent across the Channel. They subsequently located a cross beam, and the radio op and navigator between them were able to plot the course that the German bombers would be taking. They were headed straight for the Rolls Royce factory at Derby. At this point it was the only factory turning out Rolls Royce Merlin engines, the type that were fitted in Spitfires, Hurricanes and some bombers; if it had been destroyed it would have spelled disaster for the aircraft industry. The men aboard Hal's Anson used specially modified American amateur radio sets to disrupt the beam and give a confused picture to the German bombers, not one of which found the factory that night.

Despite seeing results such as these, Hal craved a more exciting career and early in 1941 got himself transferred to an operational squadron. In the spring of 1941 he married his long-term girlfriend Jeanne Greenland; they had known each other since 1937. Jeanne was both a British and Welsh swimming champion and in 1938 at the age of 18 represented Wales in the Commonwealth games held in Sydney, Australia. Coming second in the breaststroke, she gained the team's only silver medal of the games. Jeanne was picked to join the Olympic team but the 1940 games were cancelled.

Hal was posted to 9 Squadron which was based in Honington, Suffolk flying the Vickers Wellington, Barnes Wallis's geodetic wonder, affectionately christened the Wimpy by her crews. On the night of 26/27 August 1941 he took off in a Wellington Mk1C, serial number W5703. Their destination was Cologne. They had barely reached the target when Hal was aware of problems with the aircraft. They managed to drop their bombs on the target but one engine burst into flames on the return journey. Shortly after this the other engine seized and Hal gave the order to bail out.

All six crew members got out of the aircraft safely, but they became split up as they descended. Hal landed close to Catillon to the south-east of Cambrai in northern France and walked towards the first house he saw. He was given food and an overcoat, and a farmer then directed him to a nearby barn, where he met up with fellow crew member Sgt Bill Crampton. On landing Crampton had used his secret button compass in an effort to locate his fellow crew members. He was only partly successful in this, and just before reaching the farm where Sgt J.T. Stickles, Sgt S.R. Murray and Sgt D.A. Wright were hiding, he was directed to the barn where Hal found him. They were later to learn that they had had a very lucky escape, as the three crew members hiding in the original barn were all captured by the Germans later that day. Sgt Stickles, a Canadian, was taken to the infamous POW camp Stalag Luft 3 (scene of the Great Escape) and remained there until the camp was liberated in May 1945. It has not been possible to find out what happened to Murray or Wright, but the hope is that they were also taken to a camp and survived.

Harry Emlyn Bufton.
(© Bufton family archive)

Bufton and Crampton remained hidden for the remainder of the day. Later that evening another French farmer took them several miles south towards the village of Guise. Here the farmer hid them in a duck shooting hut for ten days. They were moved around and remained hidden until the 'Organisation' could be reached.

The French people, many of whom risked their lives to rescue downed allied airmen, had an excellent system for repatriation consisting of safe houses and transportation routes. Known simply as the Organisation, it saved countless allied lives, but did have some drawbacks. The system could be very slow and in order to work it needed the utmost secrecy, often leading to mistaken reports of death back in the UK. Alderman J.O. Bufton received news on a Saturday night while at a dinner that he had lost yet another son, his son John having been killed ten months previously.

Eventually Hal and Bill were taken to La Madeleine, now a suburb of Lille. Here they met up with the final member of their crew, Sgt Kenneth B. Read. Ken had landed further north than the others and had walked for some time before encountering any friendly locals. He learned about the capture of the other three crew members that night and decided to head even further north in the hope of escaping. In Orsinval he was befriended by a Belgian baker with whom he stayed for six weeks before the same Organisation which was helping Bufton and Crampton could be reached.

The three of them were issued with new clothing and new identity cards and spent the next three weeks hidden together. Eventually Hal made it to Gibraltar and from there by sea back to Britain on *HMS Manxsman*, arriving on 20 December 1941. Crampton and Read also made it back to the UK. Crampton was subsequently lost without trace on 31 May 1942 when taking part in the first thousand bomber raid that the RAF carried out; he is remembered on the Runnymede memorial.

On 10 July 1942 and now holding the rank of wing commander, Hal was appointed commander of 109 Squadron which had been formed at Boscombe Down and had taken over the work of BATDU/WIDU. No.109 was then based at Stradishall in Suffolk flying Wellingtons, but they moved to Wyton in Cambridgeshire that August. Later that month the first Mosquito aeroplanes arrived at the base and by December they were an entirely Mosquito squadron. It was this period that saw the two brothers engaged on the same broad project.

It was the previous November that Sydney had been appointed to the Air Ministry. His work there was far too extensive to be able to go into detail here, but he did begin to identify a recurring problem with night-time bombing missions over Germany and elsewhere on the Continent. It had been commonplace for the bombers to carry cameras with which to photograph the damage that had been caused in a given area, and analysis of these pictures showed that in 150 raids over a period of three months only 21 had actually hit their target area. Further analysis of eight raids on Essen between 8 March and 12 April 1942 showed that almost 90 percent of the aircraft dispatched had dropped their bombs between five and one hundred miles off target. Some crews got angry and disbelieved the evidence, one intelligence officer simply scrawling across the paper in red pencil 'I do not accept this report'. Others got depressed at how badly they had done.

Winston Churchill himself took the matter very seriously and wrote to Sir Charles Portal, Chief of the Air Staff and Sydney Bufton's boss: 'This is a very serious paper and seems to require your most urgent attention. I await your proposals for action.' Tasked by Portal to come up with a solution, Sydney's proposal was to have a dedicated force whose only job was to fly to the target and mark it either with flares or fire bombs. He suggested selecting the best crews from the currently available squadrons and forming them into an elite force. It was on this point that he first fell foul of Air Vice Marshal Arthur (Bomber) Harris.

Three weeks after Sydney had first put forward the idea, Arthur Harris called a meeting of all his top staff. Records held by the RAF Historical Society recount a slightly stormy meeting. Harris's opening gambit was to say, 'I need hardly tell you that I am totally and fundamentally opposed to the idea, but I wouldn't mind hearing your views.' Harris at one point suggested that if they were to take the best crews from every squadron, chances for promotion would be lost and this would weaken morale.

This was too much for Sydney who, in his own words recounted how, 'This shook me, having had two brothers who had been shot down and having been pretty well shot down myself. I banged on the table and said, "Sir, you will never win the war like that; these people don't know if they will be alive tomorrow and they couldn't care less about promotion."'

From his own experience Sydney knew in his heart that he was right in his plan, and he set about an informal consultation amongst squadron commanders. Almost everybody agreed that a dedicated squadron trained purely as target finders was not only desperately needed but long overdue. He wrote repeatedly to Harris but in vain. Then Sydney had a lucky break. He was standing in for his director and was due to go to a meeting with Air Chief Marshal Sir Charles Portal, but Sir Charles was called away at the last moment so Sydney met with his deputy, Sir Wilfrid Freeman, a man Sydney knew personally.

'Morning Bufton, any problems?' were the first words Freeman uttered and Sydney took it upon himself to mention that he was getting nowhere with the target-finding force. Sir Wilfrid asked for any paperwork or letters Sydney had on the subject, said he would read them and then ring Sydney back.

An hour later Sir Wilfrid was on the phone. He asked if Sydney had received a reply to a letter he had sent to Arthur Harris setting out exactly why the target-finding force was needed in very clear and concise terms.

'No, Sir'.

'Do you know why?' continued Sir Wilfrid. Again Sydney replied in the negative.

'Because there isn't a reply. You've beaten Harris at his own game. The Chief will be in on Monday. We have got to have that force. I will talk it over with him.'

Sir Charles Portal telephoned Sydney on Monday morning to apologise, maintaining that he had not had the proper information on the subject or he would have agreed with Sydney earlier. He also said he was calling Arthur Harris in to meet with him, and asked Sydney to get a plan together on the setting up of the force.

Air Ministry legend has it that Harris arrived in Sir Charles Portal's office the next morning and almost the first words out of his mouth when the target-finding force was mentioned were 'Over my dead body'. Only Sir Charles Portal, backed up by Sir Wilfrid Freeman, could have forced the decision on Arthur Harris, but it was something that Harris resented throughout the rest of the war. Although the force was here to stay, Harris was determined to put his own stamp on it while at the same time keeping his distance.

Harris insisted on christening the new force 'the Pathfinders', a name Sydney and others in his department didn't feel summed up their role at all. He also designed their badge. He then told Donald Bennett (the man Harris himself chose to run the force) that he had fought tooth and nail against it and wasn't going to waste any time on it. Lastly but certainly not least, he increased the number of missions crews were asked to fly. He reasoned that if this force had the best crews the RAF had to offer, then the RAF ought to get its money's worth. He doubled the number of sorties, so while ordinary crews flew 30, the Pathfinders were to fly 60. He freely admitted that this severely cut a crew's chance of survival, but he felt the force warranted it. It was suggested he did this to make the force unpopular with crews, and a compromise was eventually reached at a figure of 45 missions.

Meanwhile the work assembling and organising the Pathfinder force was put in hand. This was where Hal's previous work with radar and wireless was put to good use, and he was

Sydney Bufton, in the centre of the seated row, when Director of Bombing Operations at the Air Ministry. (© Bufton family archive)

instrumental in perfecting the new Oboe system of blind/night flying. Using a system of radio markers, Oboe would lay a path approximately 35 yards wide from a base in England to a target in Germany. A Mosquito, or sometimes a Lancaster, carrying the Oboe equipment would fly to the target laying down the signal. An operator in England would then be able to tell the pilot of the bomber if he was keeping within the signal corridor. The main drawback was that only one aircraft at a time could use the signal, but if small numbers of aircraft using the signal could then drop flares accurately leading to and over the target for the following aircraft to use, and their bombs fell accurately, the next wave of bombers would have a large area of fire created by the previous bombs at which to aim. That, in brief, was the theory.

On the night of 5/6 March 1943, after numerous smaller trials, Oboe was given its first major test. The chosen target was Essen, and 442 heavy bombers were to take off behind the eight Mosquito Pathfinders led by Hal Bufton. Three of the Mosquitos (including very much to Hal's dismay his own) were to suffer from equipment failure, a fourth for reasons unexplained placed his red markers almost two miles off course. The remaining four placed their markers perfectly, enabling the majority of the following bomber force to drop their bombs right on target.

This not only set the pattern for future bombing raids, vindicating the many hours of hard work that Hal and his fellow pilots had gone through, but also ensured that Sydney's Pathfinder force was here to stay.

In the early part of 1943 Hal Bufton was to receive both the Air Force Cross (AFC) and Distinguished Flying Cross (DFC) within a matter of weeks of each other. He was

Pathfinders dinner, 15 August 1944. Sydney is standing just to the left of the easel and Hal is the central figure in the three faces framed by the easel. (© Bufton family archive)

subsequently awarded a Distinguished Service Order (DSO) for outstanding leadership in past operations and the Order of the British Empire (OBE) (Military).

It must not be thought that Sydney's life during this period was all work and no play. On 1 January 1943 he married his fiancée Susan Browne. They had first met at a dance in the Grosvenor House Hotel in December 1940. The pair set up a regular correspondence although, as Susan was working at Bletchley Park, neither could tell the other much about what they did.

In March 1943 Sydney Bufton was promoted again, this time to become Director of Bombing Operations, and he remained in the top echelons of command throughout the rest of the war. He was present when some of history's most momentous decisions were made, and pushed for the bombing of the oil refineries and ball bearing factories to slow down Germany's industry. He also watched with interest the formation of 617 squadron, better known as the Dam Busters, an elite group set up and nurtured by Arthur Harris himself, the man so much opposed to elite groups.

In January 1945 he was made a Companion of the Order of the Bath (Military). He had worked closely with the American forces in the latter part of the war and they honoured Sydney by making him a Commander of the Legion of Merit in October of the same year, the highest award a non-American could be given. His career after the end of the war is told in Chapter 15, along with that of his brother.

Two other airmen from Radnorshire – Douglas Hayden Harper and Richard Frank Batram Powell – were to fly in the Pathfinder force which the Bufton brothers had helped establish.

The son of William and Edith Harper, Douglas was born in Llandrindod Wells in 1911. He joined the RAFVR, trained as a wireless operator and was posted to 83 Squadron, an elite squadron of Lancaster Pathfinders, based in Wyton near St Ives in Cambridegshire.

Douglas made his first flight with the squadron on the night of 22/23 March 1943. His pilot was South Rhodesian Flying Officer N.C. Johnson, and also on board were Sgt G.T. Still, F/O W.F. Coldwell, Sgt G.B. McFarlane, F/S A.H. Penner (RCAF) and Sgt R.O. McCullagh, also of the RCAF. Their mission that night was to bomb St Nazaire, site of a major U-boat base at the mouth of the Loire. There was very good visibility, they dropped both their markers and their bombs right on target, and the mission was deemed a complete success.

A few nights later, on 27/28 March, the crew set off again, this time to bomb Berlin. There was thin cloud over the target with a smoke haze from fires already started, and the crews used the glow from the fires as an aiming point. One of their 4,000lb bombs was seen to explode, but then it was discovered that one of the 1,000lb bombs was frozen to its carrier and would not release. Whilst the pilot took frantic action to avoid German night fighters, the navigator kept plotting the course and the bomb aimer, working without his oxygen mask at 20,000 feet in the open bomb bay to free the bomb. After 40 minutes' work he succeeded and the bomb was able to be jettisoned.

Their third trip, on 30 March, was also to Berlin, in Lancaster Bomber serial number R5754 OL-X. At 11.33pm Douglas sent a message indicating that the aircraft was turning back due to severe weather conditions. A bearing taken at that time fixed the aircraft at a position 5402 N – 0442 E. Nothing more was ever heard from the plane. The wing

Sergeant Doug Harper photographed on 10 March 1943. (© P. Davies)

commander of 83 Squadron wrote to the under-secretary of state at the Air Ministry confirming that nothing had been heard since that radio message, and that although the crew were relatively new to operations (the pilot was on his seventh sortie and the rest of the crew were on their third), they were an efficient and steady crew who could be relied upon to take the correct action when faced with any emergency. He further added that other crews on the same mission had reported that there were mild icing conditions. Ice was a considerable hazard to air crew, as the control surfaces could become jammed, rendering the aircraft uncontrollable. Nobody on the raid reported an aircraft going down and no fires were reported in the area where the plane was last known to have been. Aircraft flying in the area the next day were asked to keep a look out, but no trace was ever found of the crash. Douglas Harper and all the crew members are remembered on the Runnymede memorial for those who have no known grave.

Richard Powell, known as Dick, was born in Buckinghamshire in 1920. Very little is known about his early life, but some time between September 1939 and August 1940 he applied to join the Royal Air Force. He followed the usual training route before being selected to train as a navigator. On 23 April 1942 he was commissioned as a pilot officer on probation and six months later, on 23 October, he was promoted again to the rank of flying officer. As he trained at RAF Upwood, which was the home of the Pathfinder Force Navigational Training Unit, his navigational skills were probably higher than average and he would be destined to join one of the elite Pathfinder squadrons. Thus, in December 1943 he was posted to RAF Oakington in Cambridgeshire to join 7 Squadron flying Lancaster bombers with the Pathfinder force.

Dick's first raid was on the night of 5/6 January 1944, the target being Stettin (Szczecin), an industrial town on the German/Polish border which was a centre of weapons production and would be the focus of very many of Bomber Command's raids. After a short break Dick was next airborne at the end of January when for three consecutive nights he headed to Berlin. Berlin was once again Dick's destination on the night of 15/16 February, when a force of 891 bombers (comprising at least 500 Lancasters and over 300 Halifaxes) was despatched, the largest total ever sent against Berlin. Three nights later, on 19 February, Dick Powell and the crew of Lancaster JB468 were reported missing. They had been heading for Leipzig and did not return, one of 79 aircraft out of 823 sent that was shot down, Bomber Command's heaviest losses yet. Dick's aircraft had been attacked while over Wittenberg about 50 miles from Leipzig by a German night fighter. He and Flying Officer Frank Stephenson had been working around the navigator's table when without warning it exploded in front of them. The surprise attack had come from a German weapons system

Squadron Leader K. Davies with his crew, RAF Oakington, December 1943.
Dick Powell is second from the left. (© D. Cheetham, 7 Squadron Association)

known as Schrage Musik – strange music – which used an upward firing auto-cannon mounted in the canopy of a night fighter, the German pilot flying behind and below the bomber to make use of a blind spot on the Lancaster. The first sign that the Lancaster crew had that anything was wrong was the strange and almost musical drumming as cannon shells rattled into the fuselage.

Five of the crew managed to bail out. Dick Powell, Sgt Woolston the flight engineer, F/O F. Stephenson the air bomber and Sgt R. Childs the mid upper gunner, all managed to land safely, whilst F/Sgt A. Grange, the rear gunner, had been seen to bail out but did not land near the others. The pilot Sqn/Ldr K.G. Davis and the wireless operator F/O K. Marriott went down with the aircraft; Marriott had been injured and it seemed that Davis was attempting to make a forced landing, but the Lancaster crashed and both men were killed. F/Sgt Grange was listed as missing but Dick and his three friends were apprehended by the Germans. First the men were taken for interrogation to the Durchgangslanger Der Luftwaffe (Dulag Luft), and Stephenson was rather taken aback when the Luftwaffe interrogating officer slapped a photograph on the desk of the entire crew and the rest of his squadron lined up in front of a Lancaster on the runway at Oakington; as Stephenson put it, 'So much for security'. Dick was next sent to the infamous Stalag Luft III prison camp at Sagan about 100 miles south-east of Berlin and scene of 'the Great Escape', when 76 men escaped through a tunnel on the night of 24/25 March 1944.

For ten months Dick and his friends were held at Sagan until on 27 January 1945, in one of the harshest winters of the century, they were told they were going to have to march to an unspecified destination. Some months before, Hitler had started what were to become known as the long marches. Fully aware that the Allies were closing in on one side and the Soviets on the other Hitler was trying to slow down the liberation of POWs and add to

7 Pathfinder Force Squadron in January 1944; 90% of these men would be either killed or taken prisoner of war. (© D. Cheetham, 7 Squadron Association)

the chaos that was sweeping Europe. Men were herded out of the camps, separated into groups of about three hundred and forced to march across various routes, either further into Germany or towards Poland or Czechoslovakia. Men were often split up or grouped with prisoners from different camps to add to the confusion. Some of the guards were harsh and would think nothing of shooting a prisoner who was too ill to carry on or who tried to escape; other guards were lenient, aware that soon they were all going to be in the same boat as there was little in the way of supplies or shelter. The men could only take what they could carry; some didn't even have boots on their feet or coats on their backs. There was no order and no explanation of where they were going. In some towns people would share what little food they had with the prisoners, at others they would throw stones and sticks – anything to keep away both the prisoners and the guards as there was no food for extra mouths.

Over the days following the start of their march towards the rail head at Spremberg 62 miles away, hundreds of prisoners died; the snow was nearly a foot thick and in the night the temperature would drop to minus 25. All the time the prisoners had no idea about what was going to happen to them when they reached their destination. At one point, unaware of the nature of the lines of moving men, an RAF plane straffed the column. At some point Dick was reached by advancing allied troops and taken to a centre where there was food, warmth, medical attention and clothes. He would be ferried back to the UK by the RAF in what became known as Operation Exodus. His further career is told in Chapter 15.

10   Of U-boats, Ferry Command, Arctic Convoys and Barrage Balloons

Bert Grimshaw, the son of Albert Lofthouse Grimshaw and Elizabeth Hannah Grimshaw, was born in Newton-le-Willows in Lancashire in 1917. He was educated at Blackpool Grammar School and then attended Loughborough College to do an engineering course where he obtained a BSc. Bert married Sheila Mabel Inskip, who had also obtained a BSc, and moved to his wife's home town of Llandrindod Wells, the couple living at Oxford House in the High Street.

On the outbreak of the Second World War, Bert joined No.142 Officer Cadet Training Unit. On 23 November 1940 he became a second lieutenant in the Royal Engineers and the following September transferred to the Royal Air Force, who were desperate for air crew. By 30 September Bert had become a pilot officer on probation, and he had qualified as a pilot by the end of the year. In 1941 he reached the rank of flying officer, and he became a flight lieutenant on 30 September 1943.

Bert trained initially on Hudsons at No.6 Coastal OTU in Thornaby on Teesside. On 28 January 1942 he overshot the runway on landing and ran his Hudson, serial number T9368, into a ditch. The aircraft was a write off but fortunately none of the crew were badly injured. He then moved to Wick, where he flew Hudsons of 220 Squadron, carrying out strikes against shipping as far as the Norwegian coast.

He was then posted to Pembroke Dock, where he spent some months flying coastal command operations in Sunderland flying boats of 228 Squadron. On 1 December 1943 Bert and his crew were on an anti-submarine patrol when they were attacked by eight Ju88s over the Bay of Biscay. There followed a 30-minute dogfight during which the Sunderland shot down two of the German aircraft before managing to reach cloud cover and escape. During the combat the aircraft had been peppered by small calibre ammunition, and wireless operator Mussert had been hit in the arm.

On Christmas Day 1943 the crew were on another anti-submarine patrol when a radio call came in directing them to look for possible survivors of another 228 Squadron Sunderland. They spent most of the day flying over the sea at about 3,000 feet, but sighted no wreckage. On New Year's Eve another Sunderland reported seeing a dinghy and survivors in the water and Bert's crew took off with supplies on board and headed for the position they had been given. The dinghy had drifted somewhat, but after nearly two hours of flying they spotted the men, and were able to drop food and supplies to keep them going until they were picked up by a ship.

In February 1944 Bert and his crew took off on another anti-submarine patrol, but about 40 minutes into the flight the starboard inner engine developed an abnormal knocking sound, shortly after which the engine burst into flames. At 6.12am Bert ditched the aircraft into the cold dark sea. One of the other Sunderland flying boats in the area spotted the fire and as Bert and the crew were scrambling into the dinghies the other Sunderland circled overhead and directed three high speed launches (HSLs) and one minesweeper to the area to rescue the crew. All ten crew members were picked up at 9.20 and were landed back at Tenby at 11.55 just in time for lunch. The aircraft (JM708) kept burning all the time they were in the lifeboats and had sunk by the time they were rescued. In March 1944 Bert was awarded the Distinguished Flying Cross.

Bert Grimshaw.
(© H. Grimshaw via E. Doylerush)

Bert was next posted to the Central Navigation School, flying Wellington bombers. The Central Navigation School had several functions, ranging from screening pilots to testing new or advanced types of navigation. On the night of 21/22 August 1944 Bert was flying in Wellington serial number HZ699. The pilot was Flight Sergeant J. Firth and also on board was 34-year-old South African navigator Flight Officer William Auld DFC and 23-year-old Liverpudlian wireless operator / air gunner Ronald Neal Ericksen. The crew were to make a wide sweeping flight out over the Irish Sea as part of a navigation exercise, before returning back over Wales and home to Shawbury. But the plane crashed when it struck high ground at Tower Hill on the fringes of Ruabon Mountain about 3 miles east-north-east of Llangollen in north Wales. Some senior school boys from Bingley Grammar School were camping with two of their schoolmasters at the nearby farm of Rhos Pengwern and were roused at 3.15am by Mr P. Edwards, the farmer. They could see several fires on the mountain above them and Mr Edwards said that he thought there had been an air crash. Two boys were sent to get help from the police in the next village, whilst the remainder climbed the mountain towards the scene of devastation.

Flight Sergeant Firth survived the crash but was very badly injured; a nurse arrived from the local village and set about bandaging him up before an ambulance arrived from Wrexham. Ronald Erickson was also very badly wounded, and under direction from the nurse the boys tried to keep him warm and made splints for his legs before trying to get him to the waiting ambulance. It was unfortunately to no avail and Ronald died before reaching the hospital. Bert Grimshaw and William Auld had been killed outright. F/Sgt Firth had no memory of the crash and was unable to tell the court of inquiry anything about what had happened. At the time the aircraft crashed it was twelve miles off course, but the inquiry concluded that the pilot was not aware of this.

Bert Grimshaw is buried in his family's grave at Carleton cemetery in Blackpool.

Another Radnorshire airman who was to become involved in anti-submarine patrols was Thomas Harold Matthew Instone. Tommy, as he was known, was born on 15 January 1921 in Llandrindod Wells where his parents, Harold and Fanny Instone, ran a local butcher's shop on Temple Street (the shop is still a butcher's but is now in the hands of the Williams family). Tommy and his younger brother Fred were bright, fun-loving lads. Tommy loved music, especially the new dance bands, and could play several instruments. His favourite was the accordion, but he liked nothing better than gathering his friends around the public house piano for a sing song. Before he joined up he would play at dances in the Rock Park.

Throughout the 1930s, as recounted in Chapter 4, air pageants were a regular feature at the Ddole airfield. Fred recalled how his brother jumped at the chance to take a flight during one such air display, and from then on Tommy was determined to join the RAF. Tommy attended the Llandrindod Wells County School in Alexandria Road (now demolished). He had a talent for languages and an ability to fix all manner of mechanical and electrical items.

On 29 August 1941, 20-year-old Tommy presented himself to the RAF and was initially sent to No.1 Recruitment Centre in Penarth in south Wales. Four months later he was posted to No.3 RC (reception centre) at Padgate near Warrington in Cheshire, and then to No.10 RC at Blackpool on 5 December. It is not clear whether he wanted to be a pilot, but in any event the RAF had other ideas and Tommy was enrolled on a radio operator's course. After four months he was on the move again, this time to the No.2 Signal School at Yatesbury in Wiltshire. Here he would finally be testing his skills in the air.

Very little is known about his time in the RAF during 1942 and 1943. One mystery is what happened to him on 20 November 1942. His service record for that date shows an admission to the Cheltenham Emergency Hospital, from where he was transferred almost immediately to the Royal Victoria Hospital at Netley on the south coast in Hampshire. At the time this was the biggest military hospital in the world and was run along the lines of a small town. Tommy was discharged from there on 20 January 1943, having spent two months in hospital. He was obviously judged fit enough to complete his training and on 23 March 1943 he was at the air crew reception centre in Regents Park. On 10 April 1943 Tommy went to No.18 Initial Training Wing in Bridgnorth before being sent to No.4 Radio School at RAF Madley in Herefordshire where he stayed between June and September. The next stop for Tommy was No.10 Air Gunnery School at Walney. It was here that he would learn the other half of his trade, for many radio operators doubled up as air gunners and Tommy was to be no exception.

On completion of this course in December, he was finally ready to be posted to an operational training unit. Having spent eleven days at the No.2 Personnel Distribution Centre in Wilmslow he was sent to No.111 Operational Training Unit (OTU) (Coastal) in the Bahamas. This unit had been formed to train general reconnaissance crews on American-built aircraft. Here Tommy enjoyed an interesting Christmas, for with his musical talents he entertained not only the airmen, but also the island's governor the Duke of Windsor, the man who as Edward VIII had briefly been king seven years previously.

Tommy enjoyed five months of sunshine before being told he would be returning to England. In May 1944 he was assigned to No.45 Atlantic Transport Group, and headed to Canada in order to pick up an aircraft to ferry home. Tommy and his crew arrived in Canada on 25 May and were back in the UK the next day. In the early part of June he was allocated to No.1674 Heavy Conversion Unit (HCU). This was a unit based at Aldergrove in Northern Ireland that provided conversion training for crews intended for long range patrol squadrons within Coastal Command.

After another month of training he was finally deemed ready for operational missions and on 2 July 1944 he was sent to join 59 Squadron. This squadron flew Liberators out of Ballykelly in Northern Ireland, primarily tracking and hopefully sinking German U-boats. They also sent Liberators over to France to help with the invasion. In June, the month before Tommy arrived, the squadron had sent out a record number of 98 sorties, quite a few of them in bad visibility, and there had been three crashes resulting in fatalities.

Sergeant Tommy Instone was not the only new boy to arrive at No.59 that July. Pilot Officer J.O. Lloyd from New Zealand and two Canadian Pilot officers C.R. Siegler and R.H. LeGrow also arrived that month, and they all joined the same crew. A Liberator usually carried a crew of nine, but because of the length of patrols it was common to carry extra wireless operators, navigators or pilots. It was a crew of ten that Tommy first flew with on 9 July 1944. His pilot was Flying Officer J.O. Lloyd, the second pilot was P/O R.H. LeGrow. Sgt Tommy Instone was one of the four wireless operators and F/O C.R. Siegler and Sgt H. Newell were the navigators. Flight Sergeant Mclay was also on board and Sergeants Lowe, Pratt, Grill and Christie made up the rest of the crew. Their first sortie was a U-boat patrol and after seven and half hours in the air the crew was recalled to base, the squadron diary recording the sortie as uneventful. Another uneventful sortie by the same crew was made on 13 July.

There is no other listing for this crew until 17 August. The aircraft took off just after 11.30pm on another U-boat patrol. The patrol was again relatively uneventful and the aircraft was ordered to return to base. Shortly after they started back, however, they received a radio signal to divert to RAF Tain on the east coast of Scotland, probably due to weather conditions back at the base in Ireland. This the aircraft duly did, flying at the prescribed height of 6,000 feet. They

Tommy Instone in the Bahamas in early 1944. (© Fred Instone)

Tommy Instone. (© Fred Instone)

thought they had crossed the west coast of Scotland close to Tiree, but it was at about this time that something started to go wrong. There was a series of confused radio signals and the pilot reported an unclear homing beacon from Tain. The aircraft eventually arrived over Skitten Airfield, but the pilot took it to be the nearby Wick Airfield as they had received a signal from the Wick responder beacon. After verifying his position and obtaining a course to steer and the distance to Tain, he set course for Tain Airfield. The Liberator had been flying for 17 hours, but it was possible for a Liberator with a full tank to fly for 19 or even 20 hours. While the wireless operators still struggled with the faint signal beacons, one of the engines started giving trouble. Fluctuating and spluttering, it appeared to be running out of fuel, and it stopped working altogether just as a second engine followed suit, shortly after which the aircraft crashed into a mountainside at about 1,300ft about three miles outside the village of Helmsdale. The resulting investigation stated that the primary cause of the accident was loss of power on No.4 engine followed by loss of power on No.3 engine due to fuel starvation. This had caused the aircraft to lose height and crash into the high ground over which it was flying.

The only crew member to survive the crash, although severely injured, was the captain, F/O Lloyd. Although he was a very experienced pilot, the official report concluded that he had not handled his navigator, wireless operator or flight engineer as might be expected of a captain of this type of aircraft. Because of his injuries, it was considered that taking any action against F/O Lloyd would prejudice his recovery. Thomas Instone was 24 years old and had been killed on his third operational flight.

Tommy Instone and four of the crew members were buried in Wick cemetery, his family travelling from Llandrindod Wells to attend the service. Other crew members were returned to their home towns for burial.

Tommy Instone's grave in
Wick Cemetery, Caithness.
(© Fred Instone)

Tommy Instone's flight from Canada to the UK in 1944 was organised by RAF Ferry Command, which had been formed on 20 July 1941 (to be subsumed into Transport Command on 25 March 1943) to coordinate the flying of aircraft from their place of manufacture in Canada or the US to bases in Britain. Another Radnorshire-born airman was also headed for Ferry Command. Chapter 7 recounts the story of the youngest son of the Peirson Jones family, Chris, who became a fighter pilot. His elder brothers Humphrey and Martin had emigrated, first trying Canada, then New Zealand, before finally settling in Australia. Martin became a building contractor in the state of Victoria, and it seems that he would have been quite content to stay in Australia if it hadn't been for the Second World War. Although in the early days of the war Australia was remote from any direct threat (it would be over a year before that from Japan became manifest), as part of the British Empire, Australia and her people were soon keen to 'do their bit'.

The Peirson Jones boys were no exception. Humphrey joined the 2nd Australian Infantry Force and on 23 May 1941 32-year-old Martin headed to Melbourne and enlisted in the Royal Australian Air Force (RAAF). He hoped to become a member of the air crew and was given the initial rank of aircraftsman second class. He had been promoted to leading aircraftsman by the time he reached No.2 Initial Training School in August, where he discovered he was going to be trained as an air observer, a role that would eventually morph into that of navigator. Under the Empire Air Training Scheme many men from all over the world were sent to Canada to complete their air crew training, and it was to Canada that Martin was sent next.

On his arrival on 16 October 1941 he was attached to the Royal Canadian Air Force (RCAF) and started his training at No.1 Air Observers School at Malton in Ontario. From there he moved to No.3 Bomb and Gunnery School at RCAF MacDonald, close to Lake Manitoba, to learn about bomb aiming and gunnery techniques, and then to Rivers, Manitoba, to the No.1 Air Navigation School. As aircraft grew in size and required a larger crew to fly them, the original role of observer was changing and many of those who had started training as observers were now having extra training as either navigators or air gunners. Martin fell into the former category and embarked on a course of aerial navigation. After a month he was sent to No.1 'Y' Depot in Halifax, Nova Scotia on 29 April 1942. The 'Y' stations were usually the last port of call before going overseas, and men enjoyed a period of embarkation leave while here. Martin, however, was initially posted to Dorval near Montreal in Quebec, where he was attached to 321 Squadron RAF Ferry Command (RAFFC); their primary function was to keep the beleaguered RAF supplied with new aircraft from the factories in Canada. It was at Dorval on 29 June 1942 that Martin took his first operational flight. Just over a week later, on 7 July, he navigated his first RAFFC flight from Dorval to Accra in Ghana, a distance of over 5,000 miles.

Although they weren't flying in the main operational theatres, it wasn't all plain sailing for Ferry Command. Only a short while before the Second World War, crossing the Atlantic

Martin Peirson Jones is on the far left in the back row of this picture taken at Rivers in Manitoba, Canada, in 1942. (© P. Eckley)

by air would have been worldwide news. Now, night after night pilots took off in darkness to cross thousands of miles of sea. Countless things could have gone wrong anywhere along the route and they would have little or no hope of being found in thousands of square miles of open ocean. Then as they approached land they would have the same chance as any other aircraft of being shot down by an enemy raider looking for weary crews. Between his first flight in June 1942 and his last flight with Ferry Command on 26 September 1944, Martin spent 2,300 hours in the air. He had risen through the ranks from aircraftsman second class to sergeant, had become a pilot officer in May 1943 and a flying officer in July 1944. Martin's flying log illustrates the extent of journeys that Ferry Command pilots undertook. Having crossed the Atlantic to Accra, Martin's next stop was Cairo; from there it was to Bathurst (Gambia) then on to Gibraltar en route for the UK. The journey took 19 days. During the next two years Martin would help ferry planes from Dorval to Accra 21 times; he would also fly to India, Gander in Newfoundland, Gibraltar, the Azores, Italy, Rabat in Morocco and seven times to the UK, finishing his flying here in September 1944. He was admitted to the Queen Elizabeth Hospital in Birmingham on 24 November 1944 for reasons unknown and remained there until 19 December. He gained further promotion when he became a flight lieutenant on 21 January 1945, but his operational flying days seem to have been over. He returned to Dorval and served at the headquarters of No.45 group.

He returned to Australia in February 1946 and was demobbed from the service on 8 August that year. On 13 April 1950 at the age of 41 he died from an unspecified disease, leaving a wife, Iris, whom he had married after the war and a son, Martin. His family erected a sundial in his memory in the churchyard at Nantmel.

Another Radnorshire airman was to find himself protecting Arctic convoys ferrying supplies to the Soviet Union. Ian Leslie Thomas Miller, son of Lt-Colonel William and Constance Miller of Llandrindod Wells, was born in 1924. Although Ian's father was an army man, Ian decided to join the Royal Navy Volunteer Reserve, where he became a sub-lieutenant. As far as we know, he is the only Fleet Air Arm pilot to have come from Radnorshire.

Ian had flown the Hawker Hurricane with two squadrons based at Yeovilton before being attached to *HMS Nairana* flying Wildcats of 835 Squadron. The *Nairana* had been operating between Scotland and Murmansk in Russia. On 12 December 1944 the *Nairana* was returning in convoy from Murmansk to Loch Ewe in Scotland when she was attacked by torpedo-equipped German Ju88s. Ian was among the pilots that took off from the deck of the *Nairana* to protect both the aircraft carrier and the rest of the convoy.

Flying a Wildcat MkVI serial number JV644, Ian quickly shot down one of the Ju88s and was seen to chase a second one out of sight, but failed to return to the carrier. No trace of Ian or his plane was found. The action earned him a posthumous 'Mentioned in Dispatches' which appeared in the *London Gazette* on 20 March 1945. He is remembered on the Lee-on-Solent memorial in Hampshire which lists the 1,925 members of the Fleet Air Arm who have no known grave, most of them having been lost at sea, and also on his parent's grave in Llandrindod Wells cemetery.

Ralph Speake, who attended primary school in Newbridge-on-Wye, was to find himself working with barrage balloons, probably not what he envisaged when he joined the RAF shortly after the outbreak of the Second World War. Following an initial eight weeks of 'square bashing' at Bridlington north of Hull, he was sent to the No.12 School of Technical Training at Melksham in Wiltshire. His initial trade training was that of bomb armourer, but it soon included weaponry, enabling him to become a general armourer.

Leading Aircraftsman Ralph Speake's first posting was to 12 Squadron at Binbrook in Lincolnshire, a squadron that flew Wellingtons. Ralph's job would have been to see that everything from the bombload to the machine guns to the flare pistol were in perfect working order. In March 1942 he was sent to join the newly formed 980 Balloon Squadron, which operated barrage balloons to guard places that were considered a major target from the air. Although there are many famous pictures of barrage balloons around London during the war, this was not the only place they guarded, and soon Ralph and 980 Squadron were aboard ship and bound for Rangoon.

Between their travel orders arriving and the squadron reaching Liverpool by train, Rangoon had fallen, so they sailed to Freetown and then Capetown in South Africa; from there they headed to Bombay in India. The squadron would eventually end up in Iran guarding oil refineries. The huge gas-filled barrage balloons would be attached to wires which could be raised or lowered to different heights around the area to be protected. The wires were attached to portable winding gear so that they could easily be moved, not allowing enemy aircraft to become too familiar with where each balloon was placed. The balloons were painted silver, a colour which made them hard to see when in the air, whilst the wires securing them to the ground were practically invisible, the idea being that enemy aircraft would fly into the wires and crash. Occasionally a pilot would take pot shots at a balloon but the resulting explosion from the huge bag of gas could quite easily have brought a plane down.

Between March 1942 and March 1944 Ralph travelled to India, the Persian Gulf, Iraq, the Suez Canal and Sicily before arriving back in the UK and heading for the Photo

Ralph Speake. (© R. Speake)

Reconnaissance Unit (PRU) at RAF Benson in Oxfordshire. This was home to two reconnaissance squadrons (540 and 544) and part of Ralph's duties was to change the colour cartridges in the identifying flares to ensure the right colour for the day. (Aircraft were equipped with a flare chute just behind the cockpit from which a coloured flare would be fired if you were approaching an Allied installation or convoy to identify that you were a friendly aircraft; the colour was changed on a daily basis to stop the Germans using the same trick.) Ralph's next posting was to 280 Squadron which flew air sea rescue missions in Warwicks, a long range variant of the Wellington that was equipped with a special airborne lifeboat that could be dropped to downed airmen in the water. Ralph serviced not only the lifeboat but all the equipment that went with it. Ralph ended his RAF service with 280 Squadron at Beccles in Suffolk before returning to Radnorshire and settling in Llandrindod Wells.

11   The Mediterranean and Middle East

A number of Radnorshire airmen saw service during the Second World War in the Middle East, notably in North Africa. Kenneth George Charles Davies, the son of Mr and Mrs George R. Davies of Llowes, attended Llandrindod Wells County School and became an international schoolboy rugby player. On 1 July 1939 he joined a territorial unit of the Royal Artillery and became a second lieutenant. Just over a year later, on 7 September 1940, he transferred to the RAF, being given a temporary commission as a pilot officer. Having gained his wings, he married Joyce Mayall in St Mary's Church in Hay-on-Wye in September 1941, then was sent as a Hurricane fighter pilot to Air Headquarters Western Desert (AHQWD). Shortly after arrival he was posted to 208 Squadron, who were conducting photo reconnaissance duties from Tmimi, about 100 miles from Tobruk in Libya, where he joined 'E' flight. His first recorded sortie on 17 January 1942 was relatively uneventful, as was his tactical reconnaissance patrol on 28 January. Three days

Kenneth Davies.
(© Radnorshire Museum)

later he took off for a reconnaissance flight to Trig El Ard, flying Hurricane serial number Z4348. During the flight he was attacked by two Me109 German fighters. In the ensuing dog fight Ken flew low in order to escape and in doing so disturbed large quantities of desert sand which created a dust storm, allowing him to evade his pursuers. Unfortunately the Hurricane had been hit in the oil tank and was suffering severe engine trouble and Ken crash-landed the aircraft about 20 miles south-west of Tengeder. Ken was uninjured and was fortunately found by a unit of the Green Howards who were able to arrange a car which got him back to base the next morning. Ken arrived to find that the squadron was on the move to Acroma airbase approximately 20 miles from Tobruk.

Undeterred by his crash in the desert, Ken was flying again on 3 February carrying out tactical and reconnaissance missions. More sorties on 4 and 7 February saw him taking his Hurricane on long range dessert missions.

Then on 9 February, flying Hurricane V7836, Ken took off for a tactical reconnaissance mission of the Jobel area east of El-Faida. Nothing more was heard from him and his Hurricane was never found. He is remembered on the Alamein Memorial and on the Llandrindod Wells County School Memorial.

Alan Cecil Colin Lloyd's service in North Africa was as part of the ground crew. The son of Arthur and Emily Lloyd of Rhayader, Alan attended the County School in Llandrindod Wells and on leaving joined the Royal Air Force as a ground wireless and electrical mechanic. He started his training as an apprentice at RAF Cranwell, attending the No.1 Electrical and Wireless School. Alan was part of the 41st intake whose course started in March 1940 when he would have been only 17; the apprentices could start training before their 18th birthdays as they were in technical and not combat roles. The apprentices were housed in large dormitory blocks containing hard wooden beds, each with a bedside cabinet and a metal locker fixed to the wall. The dormitories themselves were set out in blocks of eight with a set of bathing facilities in the middle of each block. The dining hall was just as basic, with long wooden benches and bare wood trestle tables, and the food was not exactly gourmet, but it was usually hot and plentiful. The day would start early and although the boys were not regular servicemen they were expected to do all the same drill, marching, PT and parades. For all this they were paid one shilling a day with 5d being kept back and paid at times of leave. Although they were worked hard they also played hard. A contemporary of Alan's recalled how one young man decided to see what would happen if he dropped a live round of .303 ammunition into the top of the lit stove in one of the classrooms. For a few moments nothing happened, then all of a sudden the round metal hot plate on top of the stove shot up nearly to ceiling height and the grill collapsed, showering hot coals over all the lads warming their feet.

For some reason Alan was listed as not finishing his full two-year course. This could have been for any number of reasons, but probably not because he had in any way failed, as he did join the RAF, being posted to 108 Squadron. This squadron had been based at Kubrit in Egypt since August 1941. Primarily flying Wellington bombers, they were conducting mostly night-time raids when Alan arrived.

On 24 July he was either close to or part of the ground crew 'bombing up' a Wellington – loading it with its bombs prior to its sortie – when a 40lb incendiary bomb exploded and started a fire. The explosion was enough to completely write off the Wellington they were working on, and shrapnel damaged at least one other Wellington parked nearby. A list was made in the squadron records of those who had died in the accident, but there is no mention of Alan's name. There was, however, mention of several other personnel on the base being injured and as Alan is listed as dying four days later, and as no other incident is mentioned involving loss of life at the base between the accident and the time that Alan died, it seems that he was one of those injured. He was buried in the Heliopolis War Cemetery in Egypt and is also commemorated on the war memorial in his home town of Rhayader and on the Llandrindod Wells County School memorial. The year that Alan joined Cranwell he was part of a group of 192 boys who would go on to serve in the RAF, of whom 17 were killed during the Second World War.

Apart from enemy action and accidents, disease could also be the cause of death. Alfred John Vaughan was born in 1919 to George and Annie Vaughan of Builth Road near Builth

Wells and became a pupil at the County School in Llandrindod Wells. During the war he served as a corporal with the RAF in Egypt where he developed typhoid and died in the Royal Naval hospital in Alexandria; four other airmen died of the disease around the same time. Alfred was buried in the Chatby Military and War Memorial Cemetery in Alexandria, and is remembered on the Llandrindod Wells County School Memorial and on a plaque in the church at Cwm Bach Llechryd. Alfred was married to Lillian Vera Vaughan.

Harold Alford's posting was to Malta. The son of Harold J.L. and Helen D. Alford, Harold junior was born in Rhayader in March 1920, shortly before the family moved to Newbridge-on-Wye, where the Alford family had owned the Cambrian Steam Bakery since 1912. Harold joined the RAFVR between February and March 1940 and had reached the rank of sergeant when he was posted to 221 Squadron based at RAF Luqa on the island of Malta, which flew Wellington bombers. The squadron was engaged in anti-submarine duties, as well as finding and illuminating Axis convoys with powerful searchlights to aid attacking aircraft. Some of the Wellingtons were also equipped with torpedoes for night bombing raids. No record has come to light as to when Harold joined the squadron, but he must have been in the UK in June 1941, for that is when he married Winifred Mary Weale.

On 4 April 1943, Harold, along with Sergeants L.T. Harris and A.F. Jolicouer (who were both listed as pilots), took off in a MkVIII Wellington, Serial No. HF 910, to conduct a test. The fact that they did not have a full crew on board and that it was marked down as a test flight suggests that the aircraft may have being undergoing some form of maintenance or repair. They were only about two miles from the coast when the fabric started to strip off the wings of the Wellington (which was a completely fabric covered aircraft). Although a Wellington could still fly with severe damage to its fabric, the amount of fabric they were losing from the wings and the aileron control surfaces was making the aircraft unmanageable. As they were quite close to the coast of Malta, the pilot took the decision to ditch the plane even though the crew were not wearing any life jackets. As the aircraft ditched an attempt was made to launch the lifeboat, but it was quickly discovered that the lifeboat launch mechanism was faulty and the boat could not be freed. Presumably the crew had managed to send a radio message telling of their plight, for a rescue mission was soon mounted and Sergeant Jolicouer was rescued unharmed, Sergeant Harris was injured but survived, but Harold Alford had been killed. The aircraft sank without trace, and the official report stated that no blame for the accident could be put on the pilot.

Harold was listed as lost at sea and is remembered on the Malta War Memorial. He is also remembered on the memorial at All Saints Church in Newbridge-on-Wye.

As the war turned in the Allies' favour, bases in North Africa began to be used in attacks on the Italian mainland. One of those to be a member of the crew on such missions was David Colville Price. David was born on 14 January 1924 at Dolafallen farm just outside Cwmdauddwr, near Rhayader. There is some dispute as to whether David and his elder brother Gerwyn Claude Tasker Price (born on 16 May 1922) were born on the Breconshire or the Radnorshire side of the county boundary, but they are included here not just because they joined the RAF but because of their connection with another Radnorshire pilot, Cyril Evan Robinson, who was killed whilst flying with the Royal Flying Corps in France in the First World War.

David was just 16 years old when war broke out and decided that when the time came he would like to try for the Royal Air Force. In July 1941 at the age of 17 he was asked to attend for the first stages of his recruitment and took a series of exams and tests. As a result of these, which showed he had exceptional hearing, the RAF decided he would be a radio operator /air gunner on bombers, not the pilot he had hoped to become. For the time being, however, he went back to school. It was the middle of 1942 before the now 18-year-old David was called upon to join the RAFVR. He was presented with his RAF uniform and a travel card and told to report to Blackpool for his first stage of radio operator training. David was to spend a year at Blackpool, for as well as Morse code radio operators also needed to learn how to fix or even rebuild a radio mid-flight from a limited range of spares. By the time he had completed his course David could transmit and receive 25 words a minute in Morse code in the quiet, steady atmosphere of a classroom. The trainees then had another two months learning how to operate under actual flying conditions in a noisy bumpy aeroplane at RAF Madley in Herefordshire, and with radios that required retuning every few miles.

David was also put through a course of parachute training in case the aircraft was hit and he needed to bail out, and he was given gunnery training because the wireless operator on many of the heavy bombers was expected to use a machine gun if there was heavy enemy action. This training took nearly another year. Then in early July 1943 David was sent to No.21 Operational Training Unit at Moreton-in-the-Marsh, Gloucestershire. David's first operational trip was while serving on this unit when he and his crew took Wellington Bomber serial no. X9606 to bomb an ammunition dump at Fôret de Mormal in France on 2 September 1943.

In October that year David, along with a hundred other crewmen, was sent to join 104 Squadron in North Africa, sailing from Liverpool. The squadron was carrying out bombing

David Price is the right-hand member of this group of trainees at Blackpool in October 1942.
(© Diane Fellowes-Freeman)

No.21 OTU at Moreton-in-the-Marsh. David Price is second from the left in the middle row in the left-hand block. (© Diane Fellowes-Freeman)

David Price (left) in Tunis. (© Diane Fellowes-Freeman)

raids on Italy and on the night of 1/2 December his aircraft was sent to bomb the railway station at Pontassieve. David and this crew had been together all through basic training. His pilot was Flying Officer R.W. Johnson; also on board that night were Sgt Cockram, Australian Flight Sergeant C.G. French and Canadian Flying Officer D.J. Whiting. They successfully bombed their target, but an engine was shot out and the pilot flew home on just one engine. They had just made it back to North Africa when the aeroplane burst into flames and the pilot ordered everyone to bail out. David duly did so, counted as he had been taught so as to be away from the slipstream of the aircraft, then pulled the handle on the harness to find that it came away in his hand. He had not been told that this would happen and for a moment thought that he had 'had it'. Then the parachute opened and he landed in a riverbed near Ferryville (since renamed Menzel Bourguiba) in Tunisia. He had kept hold of the parachute handle in those heart-stopping moments before his chute opened, and found he still had hold of it. It was to hang on his mother's dresser in Cwmdauddwr for many years.

David walked for over five hours through the desert and eventually crawled into an American hospital with blistered and bleeding feet. The pilot, Flying Officer Robert Winn Johnson, a 21-year-old Liverpudlian, and the plane were never seen again; it was his second operational trip.

On Christmas Day 1943, the squadron received the order to move out and as David had not been reassigned to another crew, he and four other airmen were instructed to load up the remaining squadron equipment in four lorries and head for Italy. They teamed up with a convoy of Americans and sailed over to Naples in an American landing craft. They then made their way over to Foggia, a large allied air force base.

It would be January 1944 before David was reassigned to another crew, and 16/17 January saw David involved in a hairy landing. Again they had bombed the target and were on their way home when the pilot realised that the hydraulic system was malfunctioning, causing the flaps (vital for landing the plane) to stop working. The radio gave up next, but luckily they had a skilful pilot who was able to put her down safely back at base.

On 2/3 March they were hit by flak, but nobody was injured and they returned home safely with five holes in the wing. On 21 May their plane crashed on landing but again there was no serious injury. After he had flown 38 operational sorties, on 23 February 1945 David was taken off flying duties due to the effects of a duodenal ulcer. He did not leave the RAF but used his radio operator skills at various 'Y' stations throughout Britain, stations that collected information for all branches of the services as well as MI5 and MI6. They also acted as direction finding stations locating enemy activity.

In 1946 David married his sweetheart, Zena Hedges of Ithon Villa, Llanelwedd. This was her mother's house and the house that her uncle, Cyril Robinson, had left to join the

A photograph taken by David Price in Foggia, 1944. (© Diane Fellowes-Freeman)

Gerwyn Tasker Price,
(© Diane Fellowes-Freeman)

Royal Flying Corps in 1917. David was discharged with a war pension in the 1950s. He died on 10 May 2015.

His older brother, Gerwyn, had also enlisted in the RAF but had no intention of flying, instead joining as an apprentice clerk. He married a WAAF plotter in 1941, but the marriage failed and he went on to marry another plotter, a marriage that lasted until Gerwyn's death.

In the period of the phoney war Gerwyn was sent to France to help build airfields and set up bases. When the mad scramble towards the Dunkirk beaches was under way, Gerwyn initially could not get on board a ship. Two weeks after most of the forces had left, Gerwyn made it to the port of St Nazaire and managed to get on board the *Lancastria*. Seeing that the ship was already overcrowded, he disobeyed an order to get below decks. This disobedience helped to save his life when the ship suffered three direct hits from a Ju88 and sank with the loss of over 4,000 lives, the largest loss of life in British maritime history. After such a bad start perhaps Gerwyn was quite happy to become an unadventurous adjutant in East Africa, a post he retained for the rest of the war.

Another Radnorshire airman who was to become involved in bombing targets in Italy was Peter Davies. His father Gwilym Davies was a prominent councillor in Llandrindod Wells and his mother was a keen golfer. The family were friendly with the Buftons of The Links (see pages 127 and 153) and Peter's mother was on the coach the night that Florence Bufton was killed returning from a golf tournament (see page 153). Although Peter was a lot younger than the Bufton boys he was friendly with them growing up and Hal Bufton's girlfriend, the champion swimmer Jeanne Greenland, taught Peter to swim in the outdoor swimming pool at the Metropole Hotel.

As Peter was growing up he showed a keen interest in aviation. When a DH60 Moth crashed into the front of Rhydllanddu farmhouse on 27 August 1932, there in a photograph of the crowd of onlookers is a small boy in short trousers peering excitedly at the aircraft (see page 70). It was Peter, gaining his first close up look at an aircraft. Some time later Peter was among the schoolchildren who took to the air in the 'Youth of Britain' piloted by Alan Cobham and flown from the Ddole airstrip just over half a mile from where the Moth had crashed.

Peter was educated at the Llandrindod Wells County School and when the Second World War began he joined No.579 Air Training Corps County School flight (see pages 91-93); it would be early 1943 before Peter was able to enlist in the Royal Air Force. He commenced his training at New Quay in Cornwall followed by four weeks at the No.1 Radio School at RAF Locking in Weston-Super-Mare. Here Peter finally made it into an aeroplane, logging

Cadets of Llandrindod Wells County School Flight 579. Peter Davies is on the right. (© Peter Davies)

20 hours in an Anson, but not as a pilot, as he was destined to become a flight engineer. In June 1944 he was posted to St Athan in south Wales, where he embarked on an intensive flight engineering course which took him until Christmas, a period of leave then seeing him back in Llandrindod Wells.

His next stop was Greenock, where he boarded a boat to Italy, arriving in January 1945 to serve with 104 Squadron. This had originally been a Wellington bomber squadron, but was converting to flying Liberators. The Wellington had a crew of five, but the Liberator a crew of seven, so two new members were needed. So it was that Sgt Peter Davies and Sgt C. Williams joined the already experienced crew of Sgt D.G. Knight, Sgt C.A. Hoskins, Sgt R.A. McCabe, Sgt H.R. Calder and Sgt D.S. Gibbs. Their first operational sortie as a complete crew was when they flew in Liberator KL 382 to bomb a railway bridge at Verona Parona on 11 March 1945, a successful mission as they saw the bridge in flames. The next day they were off again, this time to the marshalling yards at Padua, though they were unsure of their success. March 19 saw them take a different Liberator, KH403, to the marshalling yards at Pragersko in Yugoslavia; again they spotted the target markers and reported that in general the raid had been successful. Railway yards were becoming a bit of a speciality for this crew, and on 22 March they bombed Villach North marshalling yard. A week later yet another marshalling yard, this time at Graz, succumbed to the crew's attentions.

Peter's crew bombed Trento marshalling yards on 2 April. It would not be till 19 April that the crew took off again, this time to bomb Malalberco. The next night they were back at the scene of their first bombing raid as they once more took a crack at Verona Parona bridge; they had apparently only damaged it the first time. For their last operational sortie the crew were once more back to bombing railways as they headed for the Freilassing marshalling yards; they did not see their bombs burst but reported a great deal of smoke over the target.

As the war in Europe drew to a close, Peter and his crew were involved in more pleasant trips, their Liberator becoming a welcome sight as they flew missions ferrying supplies to allied troops. Between 8 and 23 May 1945 they flew back and forth across Italy taking everything from petrol to Compo rations and biscuits to the allied troops, who were now occupying every part of the country. In August, 104 Squadron joined Operation Exodus, the mass repatriation of allied prisoners of war. As Germany was defeated and prisoner of war camps were liberated it became obvious that a swift method of transferring the ill, the wounded and the displaced was needed. The RAF stepped in offering the services of hundreds of its bombers, Peter's Liberator among them. Between 4 August and 28 September 1945 the squadron as a whole flew 47 Operation Exodus sorties.

Peter had already been sent to a Lancaster bomber conversion unit, for eventual posting to the Tiger Force that would be active in the Far East. Although the war in the Far East had ended in August 1945, Peter didn't finish his conversion course until October, when he was posted to Abu Sueir in Egypt. There he joined another crew on 104 Squadron on 10 January 1946 with 'A' Flight commander F/Lt Honeybourne in the pilot's seat. Peter had his last flight in an RAF aircraft on 1 May 1946.

Later that month Peter left 104 Squadron and joined the permanent staff of No.22 Personnel Transit Centre at Almaza. On 23 December he boarded a ship at Port Said bound for Toulon, and from there he travelled by train to Boulogne to begin a period of 47 days leave. He was then posted to the HQ of No.91 group in Abingdon where he spent the remainder of his time with the RAF before leaving the service on 15 May 1947, returning to the peace of Llandrindod Wells, where he set up an electrical shop. He married, and with his wife and four children Jonathan, Sarah, Jane and Emma eventually moved to Upton on Severn near Malvern, where they owned and ran the Swan Inn. A regular visitor to their pub was none other than Sir Alan Cobham, with whom Peter had flown in the 1930s. Peter is still living in a cottage next to his old pub.

As the war moved north through Italy and the Balkans, the RAF's bases in Egypt became more orientated to training rather than taking

Sergeant Peter Davies is Italy in March 1945 (top) and in Egypt in June 1945 (bottom), where he is second on the left in the back row. (© Peter Davies)

part in active operations. It was during this period that Sgt Denis James Thomas Watts, son of Ernest and Lillian Watts of Lower Cwm in Knighton was posted to No.70 Operational Training Unit, which was then based alongside the Great Bitter Lake. Denis, an air gunner, was still under training. On 17 August 1944, as part of the crew of a Martin Baltimore light bomber, an American built aircraft, he took off on a night bombing exercise, but minutes later the aircraft crashed into the lake. All the crew were killed and were buried in the Fayid War Cemetery.

A report into the accident heard that shortly after the plane had taken off, the pilot landed it again after one of the crew members expressed concern about something (the report was not specific as to what), but almost immediately took off once more. Very shortly after this second takeoff the aircraft was seen to dip and fly into the lake. It took four days for the aircraft to be recovered but no clear cause of the crash was ascertained. One suggestion was that the pilot had taken off the second time with the gyro 'caged' (not reset for flying) and once he realised his mistake leaned forward to correct it, but in doing so pushed the stick forward accidently, so dipping the nose of the aircraft, and at this point the aircraft was too low for him to correct the manoeuvre. There was also a suggestion that the artificial horizon on the Baltimore aircraft could be sluggish until the aircraft had been in the air for a few minutes. The report concluded that the pilot was proficient on the aircraft type, on the instruments and night flying, and it had just been a tragic accident resulting in the loss of four young lives.

Denis is remembered on the Knighton War Memorial.

Another Radnorshire airman was to have connections with the Middle East both during and after the war. William Allcock Griffiths was born in Darlaston in the Black Country on 14 May 1918. A year before he was born his mother, Sarah, had lost her brother William Thomas Lloyd Allcock of Knighton, who had been killed flying in France with the Royal Flying Corps at the age of 19 (see pages 19-23). Sarah named her son after his uncle.

The Allcock family had a thriving grocery business in Knighton but William's parents had moved away to the Black Country after they had married. Their young son was of fragile health, however, so they decided to move back to the country. Initially they settled in Bucknell in Shropshire, just over the border from Knighton, and William thrived in the country air. A bright lad, he won a scholarship to Llandrindod Wells County School and on leaving went to Knighton to join the family grocery business. However William shared not only his uncle's name but also his passion for flying. His uncle had kept an extensive diary of his time in the Royal Flying Corps which had been preserved by his family and young William may have had the chance to read it. In 1937 William decided to join the RAF Volunteer Reserve and on 23 September he reported to No. 4 Elementary and Reserve Flying Training School at Brough in Yorkshire.

On 24 November, now commissioned as an acting pilot officer, he was posted to No.1 RAF Depot at Uxbridge in Middlesex. On 11 December, along with 44 fellow trainee officers, he joined Course 8 at the No.8 Flying School in Montrose. William finished the course on 9 July 1938 and, having decided not to go back to the family grocery business, applied for a short service commission in the RAF. His application was successful and on 23 August, holding the rank of pilot officer, he joined 207 Bomber Training Squadron at

Cottesmore in Rutland. Here he learnt to fly the Fairey Battle and Avro Anson. In late August 1939 the squadron moved to Cranfield in Bedfordshire. Still a training squadron, they came under the wing of No.6 Training Group Bomber Command on 2 September. War was declared the next day, the training was stepped up and 207 were soon training 30 men in every six week period to replace the crews of Nos. 15 and 40 Squadrons that were already based in France.

William Griffiths remained with 207 Squadron until 27 March 1940. Quite often steady, capable pilots were kept back to be instructors and it seems that William fell into this category, as his next posting was to a newly formed Polish training school at Hucknell in Nottinghamshire. Its primary aim was to provide crews for the Polish squadrons that were due to be formed that June. The squadron became an operational flying unit on 15 June and William was promoted to the rank of flying officer just over a week later. In October the squadron began to convert to Wellington bombers and moved to Bramcote in Warwickshire.

On 1 January 1941 the *London Gazette* announced that William Griffiths had been awarded a mention in dispatches. Unfortunately it is not known what the citation said, but it may have been in recognition of his work in assisting the setting up of the Polish squadrons. On 23 June 1941 William was promoted again, this time to the rank of flight lieutenant.

In September he transferred to an operational squadron based at Snaith in Yorkshire. 150 Bomber Squadron was also flying Wellingtons and the day after his arrival William took off on a test flight as second pilot to Pilot Officer Simpson. Also on board were Sergeants Wilkinson, McNab and Sutton. After a successful test flight, the crew took off that night for an operational sortie, joining 196 bombers to attack Berlin. They were picked out by searchlights, allowing the flak guns to fire at them, their front turret was damaged and they diverted to their secondary target. They bombed this successfully but were attacked by a German night fighter on the way home. Despite these incidents William Griffiths and his crew returned to base safely.

On 30 September 1941 William made his debut as first pilot on an operational mission as part of a force of 41 'Fresh Pilots' (pilots with no operational experience) that attacked Cherbourg. His next posting was on 26 October to Mildenhall in Norfolk where, along with the rest of his crew, he was to be part of a blind approach course with No.3 Flight. They completed the course by 7 November and then it was back to Snaith to take part in operational sorties once more and to find that 150 Squadron was about to be equipped with American Liberator aircraft, provided to the RAF under the lend lease system. William first took a Liberator up under dual instruction on 5 December 1941. December was then spent flying operational missions in the Wellington and continuing his training in the Liberator.

On 12 January 1942 William was posted to Polebrook in Northamptonshire to be commanding officer of No.1653 Conversion Unit, a posting that carried with it promotion to the rank of acting squadron leader. The unit was converting crews to flying Liberators which were going to be used in the Middle East, and on 9 March William Griffiths and his crew along with two other Liberators took off for Egypt. Once there, the aircraft were attached to 108 Squadron and were used to drop supplies over the Balkans. Apart from the supply drops, some members of the squadron were engaged in 'special duties'. On the night of 4/5 April William Griffiths and Flight Lieutenant Rolph-Smith flew separate missions over Yugoslavia, attempting to drop two army officers and three agents into the country. Both pilots had to bring their passengers home as the weather was considered too bad for the drop, as was the case on the following two nights, but they did manage to drop supplies and equipment.

On many nights William would be joined by inexperienced pilots on his special duties missions, for now his missions were almost solely for the Special Operation Executive (SOE). In recognition of this and of his work in training pilots, he was awarded the DFC on 17 September and on 20 October, along with Flight Lieutenant Rolph-Smith and Pilot

Photographs of 108 Squadron in the Middle East.
Above: Liberator line up and crew briefing;
Opposite: A Liberator crew boarding an aircraft for another supply dropping sortie
and waist gunners positions in a Liberator. (© Guy Griffiths)

186

Officers Austin-Smith and Madill, he was awarded the Order of the White Eagle by the exiled Yugoslavian government.

On 16 December 1942 he relinquished command of the squadron, having been posted back to the UK as flight commander of No.12 Operational Training Unit, where he remained until May 1943 when he went to the RAF Staff College. On passing out from the college he joined the headquarters staff of No.92 Group. He transferred to the Air Ministry on 16 March 1944, the year in which he married WAAF Jean Orton.

In November 1945 he returned to the Middle East, this time as chairman of the Middle East Establishments Committee. He was promoted to squadron leader in October and enrolled in the Royal Navy Staff College at Greenwich. February 1948 saw him on the directing staff of the combined ops school in north Devon. In May 1950 he went on a flying refresher course, this time flying Mosquitos, and also attended a night fighter training course. He became officer

Group Captain W.A. Griffiths, DFC.
(© Guy Griffiths)

commanding No.85 Mosquito Squadron in September 1950. Made a wing commander in 1952, he was put in charge of a Meteor Squadron at Leeming in Yorkshire before, in 1957, becoming base commander at RAF Butzweilerhof in Germany. He remained at Butzweilerhof until 1960 and was then posted to the British embassy in Budapest, after which, with the rank of group captain, he spent four months at RAF Henlow in the UK before being posted to Zambia. Here he became the senior British officer attached to the Zambian air force. In 1965 he was awarded the Grand Star of Ethiopia. In 1967 he became the permanent chairman of the Air Board and the United Kingdom representative for Nato in Brussels. Awarded the CBE in 1968, he became the senior RAF officer and director of plans and operations at the Allied Forces Southern Europe HQ in Naples. On 14 May 1973 he retired from the RAF and spent the next ten years working for the accountancy firm Deloittes.

In 1983 he retired to the New Forest, where he painted flowers and gardened. He died in January 1998.

12   The Far East

A handful of Radnorshire's airmen was sent to serve in the Far East, where disease could be as much of an issue as enemy action, and for two men this might have been the cause of their death, though there is little information to go on.

Thomas Frederick Rumsey was born in Presteigne to Percy and Anne Rumsey in 1914. He joined the Royal Air Force sometime between March 1938 and October 1939 and is listed as an aircraft hand which means that he would have been performing some sort of ground crew duties. He was also a class F reservist, showing that he had had at least some service experience before the outbreak of war. Thomas reached the rank of sergeant and served at the Air Headquarters in Delhi, which had a large staff of over 2,000 RAF servicemen, ranging from air crew and ground crew to members of the newly formed RAF regiment. It was here that he died on 14 October 1942. There are no details of the cause of Thomas's death. He was buried in the Delhi War Cemetery and is also remembered on the war memorial in his home town of Presteigne.

Reginald Jenkins Baker was the foster-son of Mrs M.A Hughes of Knighton and was 33 when war broke out. It hasn't been possible to ascertain what his peacetime occupation was and one can also only speculate on his role in the RAF. It seems likely, given his age and his rank of leading aircraftsman (LAC), that he served in the ground crew, servicing and repairing aircraft as well as keeping all the base vehicles operational, but he would have been called on to do all kinds of other jobs, such as fixing the radio in the mess and putting the ribbons in the adjutant's typewriter.

Reginald enlisted sometime after November 1941 and we know that he was in India in the summer of 1944, serving with No.359 Maintenance Unit. The Burma campaign was in full swing and the maintenance units were at full stretch keeping the aircraft in tip-top flying condition through extremes of weather that veered from baking heat to monsoon. No.359 MU, however, was primarily a motor transport unit keeping vehicles as opposed to aircraft running and had only recently come into being, having been formed at Colombo on 22 May 1944.

Reginald died in India on 13 August 1944. It is not known why he was there – perhaps some of the unit had been sent there or maybe he was on leave – nor what were the circumstances of his death. He is buried in the Ranchi War Cemetery in India and is also remembered on the war memorial in Knighton, the home of his foster-mother. It is not known if he had any other family. He was 38 years old.

The fate of Peter Ablitt, however, is known. The second son of Ernest and Blodwen Ablitt (née Jones), Peter was born in St Pancras, London in September 1918. Ernest, who had served in the RAMC during the First World War, was a qualified accountant and farm bailiff and it was the latter occupation that brought him and his young family to Radnorshire. They settled in a modest house, Llwynderw in Howey, just outside Llandrindod Wells in the parish of Disserth and Trecoed.

Peter joined the RAFVR sometime between August 1940 and March 1941 and by late 1943 he had reached the rank of warrant officer. He eventually became a pilot and on 28 January 1944, now holding the rank of flight sergeant, was posted to 17 Squadron, which had recently arrived in Ceylon. The squadron had seen action in Burma with the Hurricane fighter aircraft and was in the process of converting to the faster Spitfire. It was also engaged in cross service co-operation duties which included helping in military exercises and staging mock attacks such as that recorded in the squadron records of 13 March 1944 when Peter,

Peter Ablitt. (© Nancy Davies)

along with Flying Officer Miller, 'beat up' some destroyers in Trincomalee Harbour. The squadron records show that on 18 August 1944 Peter spent the afternoon performing aerobatics in his Spitfire MkVIII. The MkVIII had initially entered service in 1942, and with its supercharged Merlin engine was an extremely popular version of this iconic fighter. During his time in Ceylon, Peter had not flown one offensive mission. Then on 28 September, flying Spitfire MkVIII serial number JG532, he was returning to Vivuniya RAF base on the island when, for some unknown reason, the plane suddenly spun in from a height of about 700 feet. The Spitfire burst into flames as it hit the ground. Peter's body was taken to Colombo where he was buried in Liveramentu Cemetery. He is also remembered on the war memorial in Llandrindod Wells.

Although Peter Ablitt had not flown one offensive mission, Lionel Robinson was to have an even quieter war – and though being posted to the Far East, never quite made it. Born in 1921 at Ithon Villa, Llanelwedd, Lionel was the much younger brother of Cyril Evan Robinson, who he never knew; Cyril has been born in 1899, had joined the Royal Flying Corps and been killed during the First World War (see pages 29-30). Perhaps it was a photograph of his elder brother, or stories of his life that encouraged Lionel to join the RAF in March 1939, or even the displays by Alan Cobham and his Flying Circus held in Builth in May 1933, which he could not have failed to see from the garden of Ithon Villa.

After his assessment he was sent on an engine maintenance course. Coming out top of the course, he was given a pay rise and posted to Pembroke Dock in south-west Wales.

*210 Squadron Sunderland photographed by Lionel Robinson in 1940 while in formation.
(© Cathy Evans)*

Pembroke Dock was a Sunderland flying boat base and in January 1940 Lionel joined a crew as flight engineer. He had one alarming moment when he and the other flight engineer crawled out on to the wing of a taxiing plane in order to start a faulty engine. This they did but due to a heavy cross wind the pilot put on full power almost immediately. Lionel and his colleague were left clinging to the wing for dear life, digging their fingertips under the rivets and battered by the slipstream until the pilot realised what was happening and slowed enough for them to scramble back into the plane. After six months Lionel went to RAF Cosford in Shropshire for more technical training. From there he went on to Shrewsbury, where he was kept busy dismantling aircraft at a maintenance unit.

Flight Engineer Lionel Robinson (second from the left) and Sunderland crew at Pembroke Dock. (© Cathy Evans)

In January 1941 Lionel made it to the rank of corporal and was posted to Devon, where he met a WAAF called Eileen Bond, whom he was to marry in 1944. In 1942 Lionel applied for and was accepted onto a pilot's training course. Although he had many hours' experience in the air, he had to go back to the beginning and join the raw recruits straight from civvy street. He did however have the advantage of being used to service life.

In October 1942 he was training near the Solway Firth when one of the trainee pilots crashed and was killed. The commanding officer sent the rest of the recruits to the crash site to 'clean up', telling them it would be a good lesson in taking flying seriously.

Lionel was promoted to the rank of sergeant and was then sent to Canada to complete his flying training. While there, on 17 September

A group photo of those on the course at Charlottetown on Prince Edward Island. Lionel Robinson is the fourth from the right in the front row. (© Cathy Evans)

1943 he was commissioned and given the rank of pilot officer on probation. In October he obtained his wings and was sent to Prince Edward Island to learn the open sea navigation required for flying with Coastal Command. He became a fully fledged flying officer on 17 March 1944 and on 1 April returned to England.

In September he was posted to the Far East, but while he was on a ship in the Mediterranean he became unwell with what he thought was flu, but was soon in quarantine and on arrival in Port Said was sent immediately to a desert field hospital. He had caught tuberculosis and was sent to an army hospital near Johannesburg, where he was successfully treated. He returned home in March 1946, and relinquished his commission in the RAF on medical grounds on 22 July 1946.

He was to write the following to his granddaughter Beccy many years later:

Lionel Robinson at the controls of an Anson of No.33 Service Flying Training School, Carberry, Manitoba in 1943. (© Cathy Evans)

Well I never killed anyone and nobody killed me, for which I have since been rather glad; Grandmother I think contributed much more to winning the war than I did.

Lionel Robinson's wedding to Eileen Bond in 1944. (© Cathy Evans)

Another member of RAF ground crews was Wilfred Charles Evans, who was born on 23 October 1918 in Knighton. On leaving school he went to work for the local grocery business run by the Hamars, a prominent local family who lost two family members serving with the Royal Flying Corps in the First World War and who were to lose a third in the Second World War (see Chapters 3 and 7).

The mid 1930s was a time of expansion in the Royal Air Force and there were suddenly openings for young men of all abilities to train in trades they had hitherto thought out of reach, and to see the world into the bargain. Wanting to make more of his life, Wilfred applied to join up just after his 17th birthday and began his initial training on 13 November 1935. On 31 January 1936, with the rank of aircraftsman first class, he was sent to an air armament school to train as an armourer, learning about all aspects of the RAF's weaponry. On 11 September he was posted to 103 Bomber Squadron, then based in Andover, and spent the next three years with the squadron at various bases in Britain.

The squadron was earmarked as one of the advanced strike force squadrons and Wilfred found himself on the way to France on the day before the Second World War was officially declared. On 23 October 1939 he was awarded a good conduct stripe, entitling him to wear a chevron on his uniform sleeve denoting the award, and in December he was promoted to leading aircraftsman (LAC). In the early days of the war, 103 flew mainly reconnaissance missions. By May 1940, as the Germans advanced, the squadron was forced back into central France and on 21 May 1940 it began to withdraw completely. What was left of the pilots and planes headed back straight away, while Wilfred and the ground crew were sent to Brittany and evacuated via Brest, Wilfred arriving in the UK on 17 June. In the confusion of the withdrawal from France, 103 Squadron were sent to three different bases in England during June, Wilfred being initially sent to Honington in Suffolk before the squadron reassembled at RAF Newton in Nottinghamshire on 3 July. On New Year's Eve Wilfred was promoted to the rank of temporary corporal.

His next posting was to one of the newly formed Polish squadrons. No.315 was formed on New Year's Day 1941 and Wilfred arrived there on 29 January, but only stayed with them until March. In June he headed to No.2 Ground Armament School (GAS), perhaps learning about some new type of weaponry or systems. Two months later on 12 August he joined 452 Squadron of the Royal Australian Air Force which were based at Andreas on the Isle of Man flying Spitfires. Wilfred spent a year at Andreas, during which time he was promoted to the rank of sergeant. His next stop was the Personnel Despatch Centre at Blackpool pending an overseas posting and on 14 December 1942 he headed for India.

By 20 March 1943 Wilfred was based at RAF Cholavarum, and on 27 May he was transferred to RAF Vizagapatam, also in India, While here Wilfred had a brief spell in hospital, probably because of some form of illness. He returned to RAF Vizagapatam and served with a number of units including No.17 Care and Maintenance Unit. These C&M units, as they were known, were usually used to decommission airfields. In September 1944 he was posted to 34 Squadron, which was converting to Hurricanes and carrying out fighter bomber operations against Japanese bases in Burma. On 20 October he was posted to No.7034 Servicing Echelon. Servicing echelons had been formed on 14 November 1941 as separate units to their parent squadrons, for which they would carry out all the required maintenance. On 23 October 1944 another good conduct stripe was added to his uniform sleeve. On 1 June 1945, having accrued 35 days' leave, he left India for the UK, but at the end of his leave it was decided not to send him back to India. He spent the remainder of the war in the UK, was sent home on 1 September 1945, and remained on the reserve list until being released on 20 March 1946. On returning home to Knighton, Wilfred became a painter and decorator and in June 1948 he married Mabel Davies. He died on 11 April 1956, at the age of 38.

Wilfred Evans with his brothers whilst on leave. (© Malcolm Evans)

13   The Bombing of Radnorshire

Radnorshire was sending its fair share of sons to war but the civilian folk of the county were somewhat sheltered from the aerial bombardment that the larger cities faced. Radnorshire would, however, be bombed some 27 times. For some residents the bombing added a sense of importance to their tucked-away corner of the UK, and speculation would be rife as to what the intended targets were.

High on the list was the Elan valley, site of several water reservoirs that supplied water to the local area and also, more importantly in terms of military strategy, the large industrial centre of Birmingham; the dams or the pipeline must surely have been a target.

Next in order of speculation was H.M. Hobson, a company which made aircraft and motor components. Hobsons, originally based in Acton, London had a contract with the Air Ministry to make aircraft components vital to the war effort. The Air Ministry had a policy of spreading production about the country so that enemy bombing raids would not be able to halt production of aircraft for very long. A War Department land agent was tasked with finding suitable property and negotiating the terms of use for the duration of the war, and Hobsons soon headed to Radnorshire to a brand new shiny building that had only just been completed – it had been built as the new county school for Knighton. There was some grumbling from certain quarters as the new school had been long awaited, but the townspeople were persuaded that the ministry's need was greater than theirs. Whether or not the Germans ever knew that there was an aircraft factory tucked away in the town, or that a major water supply line ran through the county, we will never know, but Knighton became the first place in Radnorshire to be bombed when on 1 July 1940 the Luftwaffe dropped bombs on Gwernaffel just outside the town.

The incident happened at approximately 11.50pm. An aircraft was heard to circle the area, and then there were apparently six bursts of cannon fire followed by the dropping of twenty bombs. One failed to explode but the others left large craters between 12 and 14 feet in diameter and four to five feet deep. The bombs had fallen a mere 400 yards from the main water supply running from the Elan valley to Birmingham – the pipeline survived but two greenhouses were damaged. Whether this was a real attempt at bombing the pipeline or just an almost lucky hit will never be known.

The Luftwaffe were back over Radnorshire again at 9.30pm on 31 July. This time nine high explosive bombs were dropped at Penyclwadd farm on Weston Hill, Llangunllo. Seven of these dropped harmlessly on the mountainside, but two landed about 300 yards from the farm, causing damage to outbuildings.

The next night (1 August) saw the Luftwaffe target the Elan valley directly, but the dams were in no danger of being breached for the bombload mainly comprised of bales of leaflets. These propaganda leaflets were printed copies of a speech Hitler had given to the Reichstag on 19 July 1940 entitled a 'last appeal to reason', and were supposed to convince the British population how reasonable Hitler was. Apparently British Prime Minister Winston Churchill's reply to the appeal was brief and to the point: 'I do not propose to say anything in reply to Herr Hitler's speech, not being on speaking terms with him.' The leaflets blew across the Radnorshire hillside in their thousands and there are even some still in existence today.

On the night of 15/16 August, St Harmon near Rhayader was bombed, when twenty high explosive bombs fell in the Garn and Lygyn hills. One sheep was killed and one of the bombs failed to explode. But this was indicative of an emerging danger, that of the unexploded bomb. The raids were at night and often it would be hard to work out after ten or twenty loud thumps whether all the bombs that had dropped had in fact gone off; this, combined with the terrain and rural nature of the area, makes it not too surprising that one unexploded 500lb bomb that had fallen on Llaithddu during the war wasn't found until 1962.

The night of 29/30 August saw a change in the bombing pattern as the first incendiary devices were dropped on Radnorshire. They all dropped on open country between Tremain farm in Llanfaredd and Gwenfarch farm at Bettws Disserth. All the bombs burned themselves out without causing any major fires.

CHIEF CONSTABLE'S OFFICE,
LLANDRINDOD WELLS.
31st July 1940.

Telephone P.O. No. 2227.

Dear Sir Charles,

      I enclose fragment of one of the bombs which fell near Gwernaffel on July 1st.

      As this was the first air raid in this County I thought you would like to retain this as a souvenir.

      Yours sincerely,

      A S Michael

Chief Constable of Radnor.

Copy of a letter sent by the Chief Constable of Radnorshire to Sir Charles Venables Llewelyn, then Lord Lieutenant of Radnorshire, together with a piece of the first bomb to fall on the county. (© Radnorshire Museum)

At 10pm on the night of 5 September one high explosive bomb was dropped at Tower Hill, Llanbister. This time the bomb dropped about 50 yards from a smallholding and blew a small number of slates off the roof. Nobody was injured. On 6 September the Luftwaffe flew over again and dropped a 100lb bomb near Cwmdu cottage in Bwlch-y-Sarnau. Four men sitting by a hedge near the cottage heard the whine as the bomb fell and felt the thud as it hit the ground but no explosion came. They immediately informed the local police and joined in the search for the device. It was eventually found well buried in a field of corn stubble and had to be dealt with by the local bomb disposal unit.

That same night over in Yardro, near New Radnor, incendiary bombs were dropped at approximately 1.15am. They landed in a field, causing several small fires that were put out by members of the local civil defence.

On 12 September five bombs were dropped on the Broadheath area of Presteigne. The following night at about 1.30am a single bomb was dropped at Garn Hill, Penguilian Farm, Pantydwr causing a crater 18 feet in diameter. Another bomb, possibly from the same aircraft, landed in open countryside at Gaufron near Nantmel later that night. On 25 September, six large bombs dropped in the region of the junction of the Knighton, Presteigne and Whitton road. Three of the bombs fell on Jenkinallis farm, one on Dyke house farm, one on Bowdler farm and another on Pantyronen farm. On 28 September a small cluster of bombs were dropped in Llaithddu. Some of the bombs fell only about 200 yards from the school, but again no damage was done.

On the night of the 19 October ten high explosive bombs and a stick of incendiaries were dropped on the area that covered Abbey Cwm Hir, Llaithddu, Llanyre and Disserth. Again the Luftwaffe failed to do any damage to Radnorshire.

The highest number of bombs to drop on Radnorshire so far was when around 60 incendiary bombs were dropped on the area around Llaithddu on 2 December. The same aircraft also dropped eight high explosive bombs on Crychell farm; the only damage was to a sheep pen. A further eleven high explosive devices were dropped at Drewern Farm at Glascwm. One of these failed to explode and had to be dealt with by the bomb disposal unit.

At 4am on 5 January 1941, nine high explosive devices were dropped on the Knighton to Llangunllo road, the bombs landing in the vicinity of White Anthony, blocking the road for a length of about 50 yards.

On 1 March 1941 Radnorshire came under attack again. At 9pm a German aircraft appeared over the Elan valley and dropped a number of incendiary bombs near Pencoed House in Cwmdauddwr. The homeowner rushed out as he heard the explosions, to find incendiary bombs burning in his flower beds and on his doorstep. A man of action, he immediately set about beating out the flames and extinguished the fires without injury to himself, but his overcoat was badly burned in the process. The aircraft then flew onwards to Newbridge-on-Wye and released several flares before dropping seven bombs about half a mile south-west of Newbridge police station. The largest crater caused that night was over 30 feet in diameter and 15 feet deep.

At 11.20pm on 11 March, thirteen high explosives were dropped on meadowland and hills around Disserth and Bettws, smashing a plough and damaging a farm gate. On 16 March around a hundred incendiary bombs were dropped in the area of Harley Valley, New Radnor, but all the bombs burned themselves out without causing any real harm.

A party of locals inspecting the bomb crater left at Pantydwr. (© Radnorshire Museum)

At 9.45pm on 3 April a lone German aircraft dropped a number of incendiary bombs and nine bombs at Tynddole near Llanbadarn Fynydd. The same aircraft then flew on and dropped a few more incendiaries and one bomb on Cwmderw Farm in PantyDwr. Although the bomb landed only about 200 yards from the farmhouse no damage was caused. On 8 April at 12pm, nine high explosive bombs and a number of incendiary bombs were dropped on Tynddole Hill, Llananno. Incendiaries were also dropped on Trefoel hill, Llanbadarn Fynydd the same night again with no damage. On 23 April at 1.10am two land mines were dropped on Tregigrin Hill near Dolau. On 7 August an enemy aircraft appeared over New Radnor at about 9.05pm and dropped two large parachute mines on Smatcher Hill just behind New Radnor, causing some damage to the railway station including broken windows. The village school, the police station and around 30 houses all suffered some slight damage as well, and window glass was broken up to one and a half miles away. The largest crater on Smatcher Hill was 46 feet wide and 8 feet deep.

The next incident wasn't until 1 November 1941 when four bombs were dropped very near to Park Farm at Llanbister. They caused damage to farm buildings, windows were broken and the dairy ceiling partly collapsed, but nobody was hurt.

Yardro farm in New Radnor was the last place to be bombed, when three devices fell at 11.40pm on the night of 24 April 1942. It seems that the Luftwaffe gave up on Radnorshire after that.

It has been suggested that none of the above raids was actually a bombing raid in the true sense of the word, but merely lost or damaged aircraft jettisoning their bombs without any clear idea where they were. But whether they were dropped by accident or in anger, there was no lasting damage caused by the Luftwaffe to Radnorshire.

14 Crash-landings during the Second World War

A number of aircraft crash landed in Radnorshire during the Second World War, many of them training flights which got into difficulty, others bombers or fighter aircraft which had strayed off course, usually due to bad weather but sometimes due to radio equipment failure which led to the pilot becoming lost. One was a German aircraft that had first been damaged by anti-aircraft fire and then attacked by a night fighter. Several gliders were also amongst their number, these mainly on training flights from RAF Shobdon in Herefordshire. Following the war a number of RAF jet aircraft came down, as well as a plane being delivered from the Shorts aircraft factory in Northern Ireland to a Royal Naval Fleet Air Arm base in Cornwall, and these are detailed in Chapter 16.

The first aircraft to crash in Radnorshire was also one of the most unusual. The 'Queen Bee' as it was called was basically a De-Havilland Tiger Moth that had been modified in order to allow a 'pilot' to fly her from the ground – the first drone. The aircraft could be used with a conventional undercarriage (wheels) or fitted with floats. The front cockpit was left in its original condition to allow for conventional flying when required, but the rear cockpit was stuffed full of radio equipment. The system basically worked on numbered pulses sent to the aircraft in order to control it, not unlike systems then used in telephone exchanges. The 'pilot' (controller or operator) on the ground would literally dial in a code

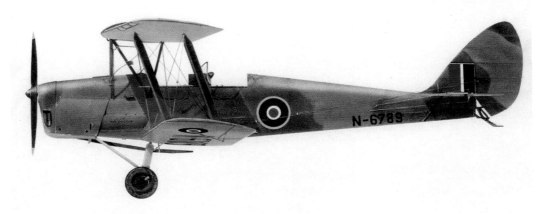

A Queen Bee. (© W. Wallace via author's collection)

which would tell the aircraft which way to fly. Some 400 of these planes saw use before the end of the war, often as targets for anti-aircraft batteries to practise on.

On Sunday 21 November 1940 a Queen Bee belonging to X Flight of No.1 Anti-Aircraft Co-operation Unit, which was based at Aberporth (and which worked with No.1 Heavy Anti-Aircraft practice camp, also based at Aberporth) was hit by gunfire that damaged the control mechanism. The ground controller lost contact with it and the Queen Bee was carried away by the wind and glided serenely over the Elan valley before coming to rest in a bog in the Claerwen valley. The aircraft, which had been in service with the RAF since 1938, was repaired before finally being removed from service after a bad landing at Kidsdale in Dumfries and Galloway on 7 April 1942.

The next aircraft to come down was a much larger beast. On 10 December 1940 Wellington bomber Mk1 serial number L4230, belonging to No.15 Operational Training Unit based at RAF Harwell just north-east of Reading in Berkshire, took off on a routine training flight. It was piloted by Sergeant Earl, and also on board was Squadron Leader Geoffrey Learner, who was probably acting as instructor, while Sergeants Doull (wireless operator), Morley (navigator), Martin (air gunner) and Mullin (air gunner) completed the crew.

The training flight was due to take them from Reading to Aberaeron in Wales. All went smoothly until they got to the mountains of Mid Wales. Mist was covering most of the peaks and the cold damp air was condensing in the engines, causing them to ice up. The aircraft was becoming more and more difficult to control and the crew was considering bailing out, but brief gaps in the clouds showed the pilots that they were far below a height safe enough to do so. A decision was therefore made to try and land the aircraft. Through a gap in the clouds Sgt Earl saw a flattish and obstacle-free mountain ahead of him. Despite having had only 19 hours flying Wellingtons, Sgt Earl calmly flew towards the mountain, reducing speed and pulling up the nose. There was no point in putting the undercarriage down, as that would have made a landing in such conditions next to impossible. So the

A general view of the area where Wellington L4230 came to rest.
(© Author's collection)

crew braced for what was going to be a bumpy ride. Suddenly they felt a jerk that told them they had made land fall. Although they skidded along uncontrollably, the plane was facing uphill, and the combination of the slope and the small tufts and hillocks that would have made an undercarriage landing impossible aided the slowing and eventual stopping of the Wellington. Apart from a few minor cuts and bruises, all the crew were unhurt and thankful to be alive, although the aircraft was a complete write off. The Wellington had come to rest on Great Rhos Mountain overlooking New Radnor.

As the crew pulled themselves out of the wrecked aircraft the lights of New Radnor were just starting to twinkle on. Some of the locals had seen the crash and were starting up the mountain just as the crew were making their way down. The aircraft was fairly accessible by tractor, and the RAF took most of it away, although there are unconfirmed reports that some New Radnor residents helped themselves to various bits of the wreck before the cleanup crew arrived. The parts that were just too awkward to take away were set on fire *in situ* – a common practice to stop the wreckage being mistaken for a newly crashed aircraft at a later date. As the Wellington was constructed of fabric over an aluminium geodetic frame, this was easier than it might sound. Today the only remains on the site are a few lumps of melted alloy in the grass.

For almost eight months Radnorshire was spared any more crash landings, until, on 7 August 1941, Fleet Air Arm pilot Sub Lieutenant H.L. Shanahan took off on a routine training exercise in Fairey Battle T6633 on a cross country solo flight from No.1 Flying Training School based at Netheravon in Wiltshire. He was supposed to fly to RAF Sywell in Northamptonshire but somewhere along the route he got hopelessly lost. A combination of bad weather and inexperience in instrument flying led to him finding himself over Llandrindod Wells. The hilly country below him bore no resemblance to the smooth Northamptonshire terrain he had been expecting, but he decided to put the aircraft down none the less. Precisely where is now unknown – the accident card simply reads 'Llandrindod Wells' – but he ploughed through a hedge, severely damaging the aircraft, although Shanahan himself was uninjured.

The Fairey Battle was a deeply unpopular aircraft with everybody at Netheravon. They had started arriving at the base in September 1939 and were already outdated and poorly maintained. The pupil pilots grumbled that the aircraft was inefficient and the ground

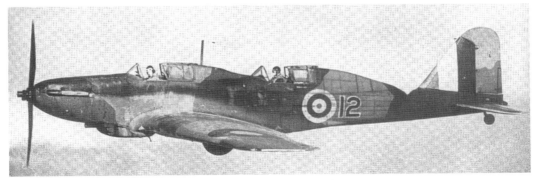

A Fairey Battle (Trainer).
(© Sport & General Ltd via author's collection)

201

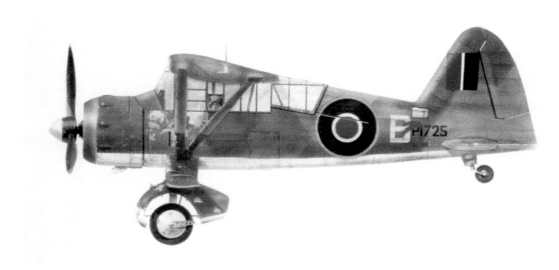

A Westland Lysander MkII. (© W. Wallace via author's collection)

crews despaired at the lack of spares and tools available to maintain them. Shanahan's aircraft had already had extensive repairs after two landing accidents with other pilots in the months prior to his impromptu visit to Llandrindod Wells. In December 1941 T6633 was patched up again and sent off to a RCAF training unit and Netheravon started to get new aircraft.

As the end of October approached Radnorshire was to see a flurry of aircraft tumbling out of the skies. The first was a Westland Lysander being used on a training flight. On 21 October Royal New Zealand Air force (RNZAF) Pilot James Jack Joseph Grevatt, known to his friends as Jim, and his air gunner took off from Old Sarum Airfield in Wiltshire, the home of No.41 Operational Training Unit, in Westland Lysander R2035. Grevatt had gained his private pilot's licence at Auckland in 1939 and was a good pilot, but on this October day his map reading went slightly awry and he was soon lost, and then began to run out of fuel. He therefore took the decision to force-land the aircraft. Having spotted a likely looking spot on Pentre Farm, Rhosgoch he took the aircraft down – it was not so much a landing as a barely controlled crash, for the Lysander was completely written off. The two occupants were only slightly injured but they both suffered minor burns as the aircraft caught fire before they were able to get out.

Grevatt continued flying and joined 239 Squadron based at RAF Gatwick, from where he flew Hurricanes. On 13 March 1942, flying a Hurricane MkIIc serial number BN864, he crashed in the cloud-covered Quantock Hills and was killed.

The next aircraft to come down in Radnorshire, just over ten days later, was to lead to a further two aircraft making unintentional stops. On 3 November 1941 South African pilot Squadron Leader R.G.B. Burns accompanied by his air gunner, Pilot Officer W.R. Smith took off from their base in Wrexham. The base was home to 96 Squadron, who were equipped with Boulton Paul Defiants flying night patrols in defence of Merseyside and the Midlands. At the time of this incident Burns was the squadron's commanding officer.

A Defiant night fighter on display at the RAF Museum at Hendon. (© Author's collection)

This particular flight was a ground control interception exercise. No.96 had just been provided with new radar interception radio sets which consisted of an oscilloscope screen that the pilot would use to detect enemy aircraft; it would also be used to pick up direction-finding beacons. The system was not very popular, not least because switching between the green glowing screen and the dark sky outside the aircraft played havoc with the pilot's night vision. (There is not a single recorded incident in the squadron record books where the system aided the shooting down of an enemy aircraft.) Soon after takeoff the radio equipment failed and Burns, despite being a very capable and competent pilot, reported that they were lost. He tried to raise the homing beacon but to no avail. It was a very dark and cloudy night and Burns flew around the skies of Mid Wales getting more and more lost, the aircraft eventually running seriously low on fuel.

At about 1.40am Burns gave the order to bail out. As they jumped, they had no idea where they might land. P/O Smith hit the ground hard near Newtown in Montgomeryshire and suffered a broken ankle, whilst Squadron Leader Burns landed safely about 4 miles south of Llangurig, also in Montgomeryshire. The aircraft, without crew or eventually fuel, flew on a short distance before crashing into the side of Graig Safn-y-coed near Rhayader.

Meanwhile back at 96 Squadron concern was growing for the long overdue Burns and Smith. Flight Lieutenant V.B. Verity RNZAF (DFC) and Air Gunner Sgt Armstrong took off in the grey morning light to look for their commanding officer's aircraft, it now being assumed that Burns and Smith had crashed as there had been no word from them. The weather was getting worse as they headed roughly along the same route that Burns was supposed to have taken. There was no sign of any wreckage or fire from the first aircraft when suddenly Verity's aircraft began acting up. Black smoke began to pour from the engine, which then burst into flames. For the second time in one day a 96 Squadron pilot gave the order to bail out over Mid Wales. Verity and Armstrong both landed without injury, Armstrong landing not too far from where Smith had landed earlier that night, and the Defiant crashed near Newtown.

The circle marks the location where Defiant T 4008 piloted by Squadron Leader R.G.B. Burns crashed. (© Author's collection)

With two Defiants down (one containing their commanding officer), the squadron made the decision to send out a third. This time Sergeant Alfred Enoch Scott took off, accompanied by a ground crew corporal. It is not clear how this situation came about, especially as the corporal did not know how to man the guns if they had been attacked. When the squadron gremlin struck yet again that day, it also transpired that the corporal hadn't had any parachute training. Not long into their flight, in worsening November weather, Sgt Scott lost contact with the Wrexham homing beacon. His radio was also misbehaving and before long they were also lost. Scott might also have been low on fuel or maybe finding himself in the third 96 Squadron aircraft in trouble that day, he got a little spooked; the official report isn't all that clear. All we know for certain is that Scott became the third 96 Squadron pilot of the day to give the order to bail out. It was then that his passenger announced that he hadn't had any parachute training. Instead of telling the corporal to just jump and hope, Scott prepared to force-land the aircraft.

In the meantime RAF Atcham had obtained a fix on the aircraft and was trying to persuade Scott to fly there instead of Wrexham. Scott had other ideas, however, and successfully put the aircraft down on a farm in Whitchurch, Shropshire without injury to either himself or the corporal. The aircraft was not so lucky. The Defiant was known to have a tricky undercarriage, and landing on a bumpy field was a bit too much for it. The undercarriage collapsed, leading to damage to the propeller and fuselage. Scott had seen action in France in May 1940 and had taken part in the Battle of Britain. He went on to serve with 245 Squadron and was flying a Hurricane on a low level strafing sortie over Dieppe on 19 August 1942 when his aircraft was shot down and he was killed.

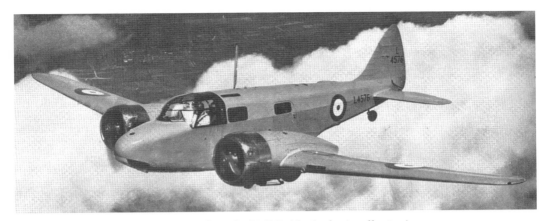

An Airspeed Oxford MkI. (© Author's collection)

Within days the pilot of another aircraft was lost over Mid Wales. On 8 November, Leading Aircraftsman Francis Reynolds was the sole occupant of an Airspeed Oxford serial number V3646 undertaking a cross-country training flight. The Airspeed Oxford was a small three-seater training aircraft, the seating being adjustable according to what training role it was being used for. Having lost his bearings, Reynolds put the aircraft down in a field at Dolyrerw farm near Builth Road, and proceeded to ask the farmer, who had naturally come over to see what the machine was doing in his field, if he knew the way to Oxford. After consulting with the farmer and his map, Reynolds took off again but failed to clear some trees, causing the aeroplane to crash and be completely wrecked, while he sustained severe multiple injuries. Reynolds not only recovered from his injuries but went on to fly again. In 1944 and 1945 he was a ferry pilot with the Air Transport Auxiliary, transferring aircraft between factories and bases, so he would be proficient at flying many different types of aircraft.

Sgt Zenon Slomkowski.
(© M. Matusiak)

After a month's respite, another Westland Lysander pilot got into trouble. On 8 December 1941 a young polish pilot, Sgt Zenon Slomkowski, was piloting a Lysander serial number V9515 on anti-aircraft cooperation duties with No.124 OCTU Royal Artillery based at Llandrindod Wells. With over 700 flying hours to his credit in Poland, Slomkowski fled to England when the Nazis invaded and volunteered his services to the RAF. As he was flying over Llandrindod, the throttle of his aircraft became loose. Unable to control the aircraft he put it down heavily in a field about 1½ miles south-west of the town. The undercarriage collapsed and Slomkowski was seriously injured, although his wireless operator / air gunner, Sergeant Parkes, was unhurt. The subsequent crash report stated that 'this malfunction has occurred twice on this type of aircraft in this unit, a complaint has been forwarded'. A year later on 30 November 1942 Sgt Slomkowski was killed on active service and was buried in Kidlington Cemetery in Oxfordshire. He was 26 years old.

The fields and hills of Radnorshire had a respite for the rest of the winter and early spring, next playing host to an aircraft in April 1942, and this time a German one. On the night of 25 April 1942, German bomber pilot Oberleutnant Gunther Brixius and his crew, Oberfeldwebel Fritz Kreienbrock (navigator), Obergefreiter Paul Kochon (radio operator) and Feldwebel Adolf Leidig (air gunner), left their base on the Evere Airfield in Brussels. The purpose of their mission was to lure British night fighters away from a force of 80 Ju88s that were intending to conduct a bombing raid on the historic town of Bath in Somerset. Prior to this date Bath had escaped any major damage, but that was to change on the weekend of 25 to 27 April 1942, for the Luftwaffe had launched what became known as the Baedeker raids, raids that targeted historic British towns and were named after the Baedeker tourist guides that had been popular before the war. That weekend 417 people were killed and over 1,000 injured, whilst 19,000 buildings were damaged, 218 of them almost totally destroyed. One of the fire fighters who was on duty that night was Harry Patch, a First World War veteran who would become famous decades later as the last surviving soldier to have served in that war.

Brixius and his crew took off from Evere at 11.36pm, apparently the only crew to leave from that airfield, and had been briefed to attack airfields in Wiltshire as a diversionary tactic. The crew were in trouble almost immediately, for their direction-finding equipment was out of order, making it difficult to obtain bearings, and the radio reception was bad. They had only been over England for a short time when the navigator became totally lost. By 12.30 they had not located any Wiltshire airfield and still had their bombs on board. Brixius was flying northward at a height of about 10,000 feet when suddenly they were hit by what they believed to be anti-aircraft fire. The Cardiff heavy anti-aircraft gun site (J16B) located on Flatholm Island was to claim it had shot at a night fighter at about this time, having tracked the aircraft from a range of 42,000 yards and engaged it with six rounds of 4.7in heavy anti-aircraft fire at a height of about 8,000 feet. They further tracked the target through 180 degrees before it lost height and disappeared at an altitude of 6,000 feet at a range of 1,900 yards, crossing the coast somewhere near Chepstow. The wireless operator

Oberleutnant Gunther Brixius.
(© Aircrew Remembrance Society)

Sergeant John Willins (top) and Flying Officer Hugh Wyrill (bottom)

(Paul Kochon) was wounded and a machine gun was put out of action. The aircraft also suffered damage to its starboard engine. Brixius now jettisoned his bombload.

At 10.35pm the same night, Pilot F/O Hugh Wyrill and Radar Operator Sgt John Willins had taken off in a Beaufighter from their RAF base at High Ercall in Shropshire. Initially F/O Wyrill and Sgt Willins were taking part in a training exercise, practising interceptions; soon however the call came from the Honiley ground control interception station that a 'Bogey' (enemy aircraft) was in the area. The Beaufighter obtained a fix on the aircraft, then the flames from the Ju88's exhaust became visible and the Beaufighter reduced speed, closed in and fired a two-second burst at the German aircraft. The Ju88, realising it was under attack, took evasive action and disappeared into the mist, but Willins was able to keep radar contact and followed the aircraft. F/O Wyrill closed in to a range of about 50 yards and fired a four-second burst.

The Ju88's starboard engine was soon on fire and two parachutes were seen leaving the aircraft. Shortly afterwards the Ju88 burst into flames and began to break up in the air. Down below, PC Creed a member of Radnorshire's 22-man police force, was out in his garden having just returned from his rounds in Hundred House. He was used to hearing aircraft in the skies above Radnorshire and almost immediately realised that this aircraft was close, and also that it might be a German aircraft, to judge from the uneven throbbing note of the engines. As he looked up he could see the glowing streaks left by the Ju88's engine fire, followed almost immediately by the sound of cannon fire from the following Beaufighter. PC Creed called to his wife that a 'scrap' was going on. The silhouette of the Beaufighter was clearly defined in the light of the burning Ju88. PC Creed hardly had time to register what he was seeing before the German aircraft crashed into the side of Gwaunceste Hill just above the village. The explosion was heard 20 miles away in Brecon and flames towered up illuminating the terrible scene. PC Creed's house doubled as the local police station and as he told his wife to phone the constabulary headquarters, a neighbour pulled up in a car. Inside were members of the local Home Guard and together they made their way to the crash site. The wreckage was still burning and unused ammunition was exploding in the heat and flying everywhere. They had no way of putting out such a fierce fire and all they could do was watch until the flames died down. There was little that could be done until daylight so PC Creed asked everybody to go home and get some sleep. As he entered his own home he was surprised to see his wife and Zoe Owens, the sister of one of the Home Guard members, attending to two German airmen. Their guns, badges, decorations and small personal belongings were all laid out on PC Creed's kitchen table. Paul Kochon, who had been injured by the anti-aircraft fire, was having his wounds dressed by Zoe. He had managed to parachute out of the aircraft before it crashed and had landed at the isolated Ffynnonav farm and had kicked at the door until he was let in. The farmer had then taken him to PC Creed's house. Exhausted and still in shock, he had fainted when Zoe approached him with a kitchen knife in order to cut his sleeve to dress his wounds. The other airman was Fritz Kreienbrock, the navigator; he too had managed to get out just before the aircraft crashed, and landed on the main road between Builth Wells and Hundred House right in front of a courting couple who were returning from a night out in Builth Wells, frightening the life out of them.

The explosion meanwhile had alerted the Home Guard and police of both Builth and Llandrindod Wells. Sgt Weale of Builth Home Guard had found the remains of a parachute and had swung into action, fanning out his troops to search for the German, cautioning all his men not to present an easy target for the enemy, unaware that the airman were safely in PC Creed's house awaiting the Llandrindod Wells police to come and take them into custody. Paul Kochon was initially taken to the Builth Wells Cottage Hospital to have shell splinters removed from his arm.

The next morning PC Creed went back to survey the scene of the crash, his first duty being to waylay a couple of local souvenir hunters and make them put the items back. Then he set about the grisly task of gathering up the remains of the two airmen who had not been able to bail out. The bodies of pilot Gunther Brixius and air gunner Adolf Leidig were taken into the granary at nearby Llanhailo farm, the nearest available building, to be prepared for burial, initially at Glascwm church, before being reburied many years later with other German war dead at the Deutsch Soldatenfriedhof at Cannock Chase. Both of the airmen had been holders of the Iron Cross.

In the immediate aftermath of the crash, many souvenir hunters went to the site despite PC Creed's efforts, but over the years the site became forgotten. By the 1970s however, many wartime crash sites were being visited by enthusiasts involved in the new field of 'aviation archaeology'. For some this was just an excuse to dig up a bit of Spitfire or German plane, but others took it seriously, forming groups who conducted proper research and treated each site with care and dignity. As a result of the latter group, the Glascwm Ju88 site has been visited many times. Among the things found have been a first aid kit and a flare pistol that were both put on display at RAF St Athan, where one research group were based. On two other separate occasions, rings

Iron Cross 1st Class found on the granary floor at Llanhailo farm.
(© Aircrew Remembrance Society)

were found at the site. One, a three-stoned signet ring, was very badly damaged; the other was a plain gold wedding band. Through an Old Comrades association, Ulrich Brixius, the brother of the pilot, was traced and it was determined that the signet ring was Gunther's and the wedding ring belonged to the air gunner Adolf Leidig; both rings were returned to family members in Germany. The area in which the Ju88 crashed has since been covered in forestry and although it is still accessible with permission, it must be remembered that this is the site of a war grave (it is rarely certain that all human remains have been removed for reburial) and must be treated accordingly.

As for the night fighters, P/O Hugh Wyrill and Sgt John Willins returned safely to base.

On 23 August 1942 Wyrill and Willins shot down a Dornier near Marham in Norfolk. Wyrill was awarded the DFC in October 1942, and at the same time Willins was awarded the DFM. Shortly afterwards 255 Squadron was posted overseas to Algiers. On 20 November 1942 the airfield at Maison Blanche where 255 were stationed was attacked by several Ju87s and 88s. Several fires were started and some of the Beaufighters were damaged. In the chaos of the sudden attack some personnel were trying to move undamaged Beaufighters to safety while others scrambled to take off and intercept the raiders. Wyrill attempted to move aircraft before running towards his Beaufighter in which Willins was already waiting when a bomb went off close by. Wyrill was killed by a bomb fragment and Willins was severely injured. Willins recovered from his wounds and went on to become an instructor in airborne radar, while Wyrill was buried in the Dely Ibrahim War cemetery in Algiers.

Nearly a month after the Ju88 had come down, a second Wellington bomber was to make an unscheduled stop. On 20 May 1942, a Polish crew flying in Wellington bomber N2813 with Sgt P. Bakalarski as pilot and P/O H. Falinski, Sgt Z. Kobiela, Sgt J. Olszewski and P/O B. Boguszewski making up the rest of the crew, had taken off from their base in Bramcote in Warwickshire. The crew was part of No.18 Operational Training Unit, who were flying Wellingtons on night-time training flights. Their route brought them over the hills of Mid Wales. They had left their base just before midnight in increasingly bad weather and although it was now May their high altitude led to one engine icing up and then stopping altogether. The aircraft started to lose height and Sgt Bakalarski gave his crew the order to bail out. The Wellington crashed at 2.50am on high moorland at Esgair pen-y-gareg on the old Rhayader to Aberystwyth Road in the Elan valley; the crew had landed safely further down the valley. In the early hours of the morning Tom Evans of Treheslog farm was

Pilot Officers B. Boguszewski and H. Falinski, crew members of Wellington bomber N2813.
(© M. Matusiak)

awoken by a furious hammering and on opening the door was surprised to see a Polish airman. All the airmen were located safely and the crew went on to operations with 300 Polish Squadron during June 1942. Sergeant Bakalarski was to have anything but a quiet war, as is covered in the Appendix.

Crash landings were happening not just in Radnorshire but in other more remote areas like north Wales, and the haphazard approach to dealing with them led to the death of many airmen who could have been saved with a little organisation. Alarmed by this toll, Flight Lieutenant George Graham, the senior medical officer at RAF Llandwrog near

A Vickers Wellington MkII of 104 Squadron.
This example was lost in 1941 while on a raid to Berlin. (© K. Hazlewood)

General view of the area where Wellington N2813 made its crash landing.
(© Author's collection)

Caernarvon, resolved to change the situation. In early April 1942, Graham used the experience he had gained in places like Switzerland, where he had climbed extensively before the war, along with his medical knowledge, to train a small band of his medical attendants and sick bay orderlies in the skills needed to search for and rescue downed airmen. The minute they were alerted that a crash had happened in their area, Graham's team would set off. Being able to give immediate first aid at a crash site meant the difference between life and death for some airmen. By the end of 1942 Flt/Lt Graham's men had saved the lives of 12 airmen and retrieved the bodies of another 35 so that they could be buried properly. This achievement was rewarded with an MBE for Graham in January 1943. Far more important from Graham's point of view was the fact that the RAF recognised his contribution and began to organise dedicated mountain rescue teams. By the end of 1943, RAF Madley and RAF Shobdon in Herefordshire each had its own mountain rescue team, and these would have attended military aircraft crashes in the Radnorshire area. This was the beginning of today's mountain rescue service.

Meanwhile, early summer turned to high summer in Radnorshire and all was quiet until 22 August 1942, which turned out to be a busy day for unintended landings in the county. Flight Sergeant Idris Berry of 102 Squadron had taken off from his base in Pocklington, Yorkshire in a Halifax bomber MkII (serial number W1238) on a course that was supposed to take him over Reading, Fishguard, the Isle of Man and then back to Pocklington. The crew was on a training flight being instructed in the use of the new 'GEE' radar system. The weather was good and it should have been a routine flight, but on the second leg of their journey one of the port engines started acting up before eventually failing. Idris feathered the engine but the propeller started to windmill, causing considerable drag on that side of the aircraft, and soon the second port engine started to overheat. The Halifax was now beginning to fly around in circles, losing height. Before Idris lost control of it altogether, he decided to try to land. Right below them was the town of Builth Wells and Idris, praying that they wouldn't land on the town, tried to head towards a likely looking landing spot in some fields next to the river about a mile out of town, telling his crew to assume crash positions. Just as they were about to land, the flight engineer Bill Patterson realised that Idris hadn't fastened his safety harness and managed to fix two straps around him before the plane landed, probably saving Idris's life. The Halifax hit the ground hard at Gellicadwgan farm in Llanfaredd and careered across a field, hitting trees and hedges, scattering machine guns, ammunition and bits of aircraft as it went, finally coming to rest with its starboard wing up against a tree and its rear turret hanging over the river. As the aircraft stopped and everything went quiet, Idris realized to his relief that everybody was alive, but they now had

A Handley Page Halifax bomber

The actual Halifax bomber that crash landed at Llanfaredd in August 1942. (© Idris Berry)

to scramble quickly out of the wrecked aircraft for as almost as soon as the Halifax stopped it burst into flames. Help was soon on hand as people came running over the fields. The first to arrive were a couple of small boys who were apprehended by the local constabulary running away from the scene with one the bomber's machine guns and pockets full of ammunition. Soon however Idris and the entire crew of eight were in Builth being given a well earned cuppa and waiting for the cleanup crew to arrive. Idris continued flying and in December 1944 he started his second tour of operations, this time flying Mosquitoes with Canadian F/O Bolender as his navigator. On 2 May 1945 the pair were attacking Kiel when a V2 rocket only just missed them. Idris survived the war.

The afternoon of 22 August was to see a second aircraft come down, just fields away. Sgt Eric William Worswick Feldon of the RAFVR was based at No.5 Glider Training School at Shobdon in Herefordshire from where he had taken off that morning in good weather on a training flight in his Miles Master serial number DL339. The Miles Master was basically a two-seater training aircraft, with the crew sitting one behind the other. Many were adapted to tow gliders. The weather closed in as William crossed into Mid Wales and he soon found himself in thick cloud in a heavy summer rainstorm. He had only been at Shobdon a short time and he was not yet trained in the use of the blind flying instruments. Struggling to avoid the mountains in the bad weather, he suddenly spotted a likely looking spot to land and brought the aircraft down in a field in Llanelwedd (now the site of the Royal Welsh Showground). Feldon was unhurt and the plane was able to be repaired. Feldon continued flying and by July 1943 had graduated to the Mustang and was flying operational sorties over France with 268 Squadron. On 7 March 1944, on his 14th operational sortie on a reconnaissance mission over the French coast, his plane was hit and brought down by anti-aircraft fire near the village of Du Nord. Feldon was killed and buried at the Bayeaux War Cemetery near Calvados.

On 11 September 1942 another Miles Master made an unscheduled stop in Radnorshire. The Pilot was Warrant Officer S. Laskowski of the Polish Air Force, who

A Miles Master. (© Miles Aircraft via T. Bishop)

Warrant Officer S. Laskowski.
(© W. Matusiak)

Sergeant W. Wisniewski.
(© W. Matusiak)

was serving with an anti-aircraft cooperation unit (these units were used to train Royal Artillery anti-aircraft batteries). Also on board was a 16-year-old ATC cadet. Laskowski's engine started to overheat and glycol began to squirt out, covering the windscreen and making it difficult for the pilot to see, so he took the decision to make a forced landing before matters became worse. As he came over Llandrindod Wells he spotted a likely landing place on Dolberthog common at the Ridgebourne, where he put the plane down. Ironically he landed at a time when the district council were trying to get the common turned into an airfield. Although the plane was completely written off and the cadet suffered a minor injury, Laskowski's commanding officer praised his actions. Laskowski was to survive the war.

Just over a month later, on 12 October, another Polish pilot was to land his Miles Master in Radnorshire. As Sgt Wladyslaw Wisniewski, who was based in Cardiff and like Laskowski was engaged in anti-aircraft cooperation duties, crossed into Radnorshire the weather closed in. He had been flying for some time and was obviously lost, for people heard him circling around Painscastle, possibly looking either for a recognizable landmark or a landing place. Suddenly while over Llanbedr hill the engine cut out and people saw Wisniewski's plane nose dive and crash to the ground where it caught fire; the cause of the accident was never discovered. Wisniewski was killed, and he was buried in the cemetery at Ely near Cardiff. Wisniewski had been training to be an aircraft mechanic before the war in Poland and when the Germans invaded he was lucky to escape first to France and then, when France fell, to England. He volunteered for the RAF on 11 September 1941.

December 1942 was to see a third Wellington bomber crash in Radnorshire. On 20 December, Australian pilot Edward Elliott and his crew from No.21 Operational Training Unit had taken off from Moreton-in-the-Marsh for a cross-country training flight. They were flying Wellington serial number R1534 when at approximately 1pm the aircraft developed engine trouble, the starboard engine then exploding making the aircraft very difficult to control. At 1.15 Elliott ordered his crew to bail out whilst he tried to keep the Wellington aloft. The crew all bailed out and landed safely in the vicinity of Penybont. Initially it was Elliott's intention to try to land the aircraft, but having dropped to about 2,000 feet and seen the nature of the terrain below him, he took the decision to also bail out, floating to earth in the hamlet of Nantmel in Radnorshire, where he landed in a tree and was able to watch as his aircraft crashed at Upper Talcoed farm also in Nantmel. Despite this early mishap in his career Elliott would go to win both a Distinguished Flying Cross on 1 April 1944 and an Air Force cross on 14 May 1945, both whilst serving with 104 Squadron with whom he completed 50 operational sorties and flew a total of 1,146 hours and 20 minutes. He returned to Australia at the end of the war.

Early in the Second World War, 350 Lockheed Hudsons, a light bomber, were supplied to the RAF. Some of these aircraft were used by Coastal Command for search and rescue duties and would often carry specially designed lifeboats that could be dropped to downed airmen.

On 21 January 1943 Hudson serial number V9046, belonging to 279 Squadron operating out of St Eval in Cornwall and piloted by Squadron Leader H.G Mossford ('Bertie' to his friends), was sent out to look for a missing Sunderland flying boat which was believed to have crashed somewhere in the Ushant area. He had already turned down two such requests because of an approaching weather front that was beginning to blanket the airfield in cloud and considering that the rescue aircraft would have difficulty landing on return. When a third request came in along with the added 'Can't you have a go though?', Mossford decided to send out two aircraft and to pilot one himself. His decision to attempt the rescue even though the weather was bad may have been coloured by his own experiences. On 6 November 1939 he and a crew of three, then flying out of Wick in northern Scotland, had ditched in the sea in an Anson having run out of fuel. The rescue ship *Quest* had come to their aid, an awkward operation as wind and waves were in danger of sweeping the rescuers on to the rocks and the Anson still had live bombs on board.

It was 5.31pm on a bleak January evening when the two aircraft set off. Both were soon lost in cloud and unbeknown to Mossford the other Hudson turned back and landed almost immediately. Mossford and his crew – Sergeants J.A. Wiseman as navigator and H.C. Macklin as air gunner and the appropriately named Hudson as wireless operator – continued flying to the west to establish a search pattern for the Sunderland. It flew at about 300 feet above the waves in the hope that the Sunderland crew would hear them and send up a flare. They flew around the area for two and a half hours, and having seen nothing, set a return course for base. When Mossford thought he was close to his home

A Lockheed Hudson

base he asked the radio operator for a fix but was told that the wireless was useless and wouldn't transmit. The radar equipment did pick up a signal from a responder beacon near Plymouth and they also picked up a further one near St Austell. Mossford then started to prepare for a landing at St Eval.

To add to their difficulty the altimeter was giving faulty readings due to the variable air pressure. As the airfield was covered in a blanket of cloud, Mossford decided to go around again. They flew out over the Bristol Channel when Mossford realised that they were running out of fuel and only had about 15 minutes of flying time left. He told his crew to don their parachutes and asked the navigator to let him know when the radar showed that they were over the Welsh coast. Mossford then reluctantly gave the order to bail out. This was not a popular command, as the crew could not see through the clouds to where they would be landing. Sgt Wiseman as navigator decided he ought to jump first and show faith in his own navigation; the rest followed and bailed out safely in or around the Swansea area. Squadron Leader Mossford's last act before leaving the aircraft was to set the automatic pilot on the aircraft to make sure it cleared the coastal town below.

At 11pm the Jones family of Maes Gwyn farm, Beguildy was all tucked up in bed when they were awakened by the roar of an aircraft low overhead followed a short while later by a huge explosion and shock waves that shook the farmhouse. The Hudson had crashed into Warren Hill just behind the farm. Mr Jones dressed as quickly as he could and went to help the stricken aircraft. The hill was lit up by the flames from the crash and Mr Jones searched in vain in the widely strewn wreckage for any crewman before returning to his farm to alert the authorities. He had no idea that the crew were all safely in Swansea over 60 miles away.

Winter turned to spring, spring to summer and summer to autumn before the next aircraft descended on Radnorshire. On 9 September 1943 Airspeed Oxford serial number LW743 was being flown on a solo flight by Pilot Officer Frederick Charles Gurr on a night cross-country exercise. He had taken off from No.6 Pilots Advanced Flying Unit based at RAF Little Rissington on the Water in Gloucestershire and at 11.40pm he flew low over Clyro obviously suffering from engine trouble. The weather was closing in and he had been unable to obtain a fix from his homing beacon, so as soon as he was clear of the village he bailed out. The Oxford flew on for a short time before crashing near Maesllwch Castle, disintegrating on impact. It took quite some time to locate P/O Gurr in the dark, but he had landed safely in Gwenffythern Wood just outside Clyro. He continued with the RAF through and beyond the war, eventually relinquishing his RAF commission to join the Royal New Zealand Air Force (RNZAF) on 19 June 1953.

A much more serious crash was to happen just a week later. On 16 September 1943 a B-17 Flying Fortress took off from its base at Knettishall in Suffolk. The aircraft had been named 'Sondra Kay' after the recently born baby daughter of S/Sgt Joshua M. Lewis, one of the air gunners, a daughter yet to be seen by her father. The Sondra Kay was part of 562 Bombardment Squadron and attached to the US 388th Bomb Group. On the night of 16 September she headed for Bordeaux along with 21 other aircraft. They encountered bad weather and only 16 of the aircraft reached their destination. Then the weather closed in completely and unable to find their original target they were diverted north to bomb the submarine pens at La Pallice. This they did successfully and turned for home.

Back over the Channel the weather deteriorated further. The bombers broke formation and each one headed home as best it could. The Sondra Kay flew on, the pilot Lt Henry O. Cox Jr and co-pilot Lt Albert Rubin struggling against the weather while the navigator 2nd Lt Robert B. Leventhal tried to keep them on course and the radio operator T/ Sgt Donald P. Gromis attempted to keep in contact with their base and help fix their position. The remaining members of the crew were T/Sgt Herman J. Ball (engineer and top turret gunner), S/Sgt Francis H. Curry (left waist gunner), S/Sgt Atto V. Kloza (right waist gunner), tail gunner S/Sgt Joshua M. Lewis, ball turret gunner S/Sgt George R. Martin and Bombardier 1st Lt Frank N. Broach Jr.

The Sondra Kay was spotted at 8.37pm crossing the coast of England; by 10pm she was in trouble. A subsequent police report from the Radnorshire constabulary reads as follows:

> Shortly after 10.00pm on the night of 16 September 1943, an American flying fortress attracted the attention of the inhabitants of Rhayader as it flew low over the town, by reason of the fact that its engines were making a noise which seemed to indicate that all was not well with the aircraft. Minutes later the sounds of an explosion were heard and a brilliant flash lit up an area in the Doldowlodd district. It was afterwards found that the fortress had crashed at Upper Cilgee, Doldowlodd, after striking a nearby hill. All ten members of the crew were killed.

Other Fortresses that had been in the original formation with the Sondra Kay also got in difficulty that night, one having an extremely lucky escape. It was eventually able to put down at Shobdon airfield, but ran out of fuel as it taxied along the runway. Another crashed almost as soon as it had crossed the coast, ploughing into high ground at South Molton in Devon. Two crew members were killed. A third B-17, 'Ascend Charlie', crashed into the Black Mountains near Abergavenny, killing the whole crew.

The crew of the Sondra Kay were taken from the wreckage, five of them being buried in the Military Cemetery at Madingley in Cambridge, while the remaining five were returned to the USA for burial by their families.

When the war was over the crash site of the Sondra Kay, like many such sites around Britain, was forgotten by all but a few. Then two members of the now disbanded Powys Aircraft Group visited the site of the crash on 1 March 1987. Phillip Jones and Eddie Reynolds were walking on the area of the crash when they came across a small metal plate.

In Memory of the ten Crew members of the
B17 "Sondra Kay" Fortress aircraft of the 388th BG, USAAF
that crashed at Upper Cilgee Farm, Llanyre,
late on the 16th of September 1943.
after a raid on U Boat Pens at La Pallice, SW France.

Henry O Cox, Pilot   Donald P Gromis
Albert Rubin, Co-Pilot   George R Martin
Robert B Leventhal, Navigator Francis H Curry
Frank N Broach   Otto V Kloza
Herman J Ball   Joshua Lewis

"We will remember them"

Erected by local Friends and Llanyre Community Council
16th September 2003

The commemorative plaque on the Sondra Kay memorial in Llanyre.
(© Author's collection)

Initial thoughts were that it was a piece of aircraft skinning or maybe a work plate. On closer inspection, however, it turned out to be a metal ID plate known as a 'Dog Tag'. The tag gave the name Robert B. Leventhal, army serial number 0-674216, 'T42' which indicated he had a tetanus jab, presumably in 1942, 'AB', his blood group, and the address of his father, Frank W. Leventhal, 1120 Pine Street, St Louis, M.O. As a result of contacting the mayor of St Louis, the tag was eventually returned to Robert's second cousin David Leventhal who in turn passed it on to the Jewish War Veterans Society.

In 2003, sixty years after the tragedy, Mr Dennis Cleaton of Llandrindod Wells arranged for a memorial plaque to the Sondra Kay's crew to be erected alongside the war memorial in Llanyre near to the site of the crash. S/Sgt Lewis's daughter Sondra Kay, after whom the aircraft had been named, came to Wales to attend the service, and to see where the father she had never met had lost his life.

Three of the four next aircraft to come down in Radnorshire were all considerably smaller, being training aircraft, the first a De-Havilland Dominie, a military version of the Dragon Rapide, several of which were based at the No.4 Radio Training School at RAF Madley in Herefordshire.

On 4 November 1943 a Dominie serial number X7442 took off at dusk from Madley on a radio operation training flight. Sgt Pilot Peter Alan Jacobs was at the controls and five RAF cadets were on board. Shortly after take-off Jacobs reported that the weather was deteriorating. Soon he lost his bearings and was having trouble finding his way back to the airfield, so he decided to force-land the aircraft. This he did at Llowes Court near Glasbury-on-Wye, running his plane across a ploughed field and tipping the aircraft up on its nose. Neither Jacobs nor any of the cadets were hurt in the landing.

A De-Havilland Dominie

Jacobs subsequently learnt to fly the Short Stirling. On 29 July 1944 he was on a short cross-country and bombing practice flight when at least one engine stopped and burst into flames, the crew immediately starting to bail out as the aircraft was plunging rapidly to the ground. Four crew members made it to safety but the remaining four, including 21-year-old Peter Jacobs, were killed. The aircraft crashed about 10 miles from Newark-upon-Trent in Nottinghamshire.

The next two training aircraft to come down in Radnorshire were Miles Masters like the pair in August and September 1942. On 7 February 1944, Flying Officer Anthony Brenthall, who was based at No.5 Pilots Advanced Training School at RAF Ternhill in Shropshire, was flying his Miles Master serial number DK799 when it developed engine trouble. Knowing he would not make it back to base, F/O Brenthall decided to land the aircraft and chose a likely looking field at Pantygaragle farm near Beguildy. On landing however the field proved to be not as smooth as he had hoped and the aircraft was badly damaged in the resultant crash, F/O Brenthall managing to escape with only minor injuries. The Miles Master was repaired and flew again, but on 7 April 1944 it was written off in a crash that killed both its occupants. One month after his landing in Radnorshire, on 29 March 1944 Brenthall was killed when he was flying another Miles Master in fog and hit a tree.

The last Miles Master crash in Radnorshire occurred on 20 April 1944. Flying in Miles Master serial number EM287 were the pilot F/Sgt R.L Montgomery from the RCAF and F/Sgt A.R Morris, also a Canadian, operating out of Shobdon with the No.5 Glider Training School. They were taking part in an instrument-flying training exercise when they got hopelessly lost and looked for somewhere to land. As they flew over Springfield near Howey, Montgomery spotted a likely looking landing place but as he put the aircraft down he realized that a ploughed field can be a lot bumpier than it looks from the air. Mercifully he had not attempted to put the undercarriage down and the plane skidded across the top of the soil rather than burying its wheels in the plough lines; both men were uninjured. When they made it back to base Montgomery was severely reprimanded by his commanding officer not only for getting them lost but also for damaging the aircraft.

In the meantime the fourth and final Wellington bomber to crash on Radnorshire had done so on 11 April with a Canadian pilot, F/O David Godwin Chance, at the controls.

That morning Chance and his crew had taken off in Wellington bomber serial number BJ601 from No.22 Operational Training Unit based at RAF Wellesbourne in Warwickshire. They were flying on a cross-country training exercise and initially all went well, but shortly into the trip the aircraft's instruments began registering a steady drop in oil pressure on the port engine. Chance shut off the engine and attempted to feather the propeller, a procedure designed to make a useless engine more manageable. However, the attempt was unsuccessful, the aircraft started to lose height and it became obvious that the crew were going to have to bail out. At approximately 11.35am Chance gave the necessary order, and five members of the crew bailed out over Llanafan in Breconshire while Chance continued to struggle with the aircraft for a few miles more before he too jumped. The Wellington had crossed the border into Radnorshire and crashed into a field of sheep at Wern Breig farm at Ysfa near Doldowodd, killing a ram, five ewes and two lambs as well as injuring a number of other sheep. The farm was quite close to the road and the recovery crews were able to take most if not all of the wreckage away. David Chance went on to have a successful career with the RAF, being awarded the DFC on 15 March 1945, surviving the war and returning to the family farm in Canada.

Mention has already been made of several of the aircraft that had crash-landed in Radnorshire as having taken off from RAF Shobdon in Herefordshire. Not only their aircraft but also a number of their gliders had been crash-landed in the county. The airfield was home to No.5 Glider Training School (GTS), which had been formed in May 1942 at RAF Kidlington just north of Oxford and relocated to RAF Shobdon later that month. By July it was being equipped with new Hotspur Gliders, two of the first batch colliding with each other on landing. After this inauspicious start the school went from strength to strength, albeit that a little over a month later one of the gliders was to crash in Radnorshire. The pilot had flown into a patch of bad visibility and crashed at Farrington farm in Knighton. Neither of its occupants were hurt although the glider was badly damaged.

Gliders continued training over the county for the next few months without incident. However, at 4pm on 13 May 1943 a Hotspur Glider (HH253) that was being towed by a Lysander appeared in the skies over Hundred House. It was very windy and the glider was being buffeted about. The Lysander pilot thought it best to release the glider from its towing gear but the strong wind caused the tow rope to snap back and damage the glider's wing, causing the aircraft to immediately dive towards the ground. On trying to land, the glider hit a tree at Bedw farm and its occupants, Corporals P.H.B. Sullivan and R. Ison, were both badly injured.

On 21 August 1944 two No.5 GTS pilots, F/Sgt G.W. Phillips and Sgt J.W. Munro, were being towed in their Hotspur Glider (HH584) when they encountered some bad weather over Radnorshire. The towing aircraft was having engine trouble, the glider was becoming increasingly difficult to handle in the storm and F/Sgt Phillips, the instructor, took the decision to release the glider from the towing aircraft. Still unable to control the glider, he had to force-land in a field one mile east-north-east of Presteigne. Phillips sustained a cut to his forehead but otherwise both men were unhurt. His commanding officer concluded there was little else he could have done.

On 8 November 1944, Sgt R.G. Brobin of No.5 GTS was being towed in Hotspur Glider serial number HH360 and by the time he reached the point at which his glider was

A Hotspur glider. (© P. Butler)

due to be released there was quite a thick blanket of cloud. The glider did not respond well to the cool damp air and Brobin was forced to land at Moor farm, Presteigne, hitting a hedge with his wing and doing a cartwheel. He sustained minor head injuries from which he made a full recovery.

The four gliders which crashed in Radnorshire were very much the exception to the rule, as No.5 GTS had an excellent record of achievement. Between July 1943 and October 1945, a total of 1,345 glider pilots were trained at Shobdon, along with 291 instructors and 218 tug pilots. In the run up to D-Day, 807 pilots passed through the airfield on refresher courses. It chalked up 96,925 day and night-time glider lifts, a record amongst UK glider training schools, and pilots trained at Shobdon distinguished themselves in every major airborne operation.

Just over six months after D-Day, on 12 December 1944, Halifax bomber serial no LL541 took off from its base at RAF Dishforth in Yorkshire, home of No.1664 Heavy Conversion Unit, for a cross country training flight. It left Dishforth at approximately 10.10am, the weather being a bit cloudy with intermittent rain and light winds, not usually a problem for the heavy bombers. At 1pm another Halifax spotted the aircraft flying at about 18,000ft over Mid Wales, when not all appeared well – it dipped a wing as if to do a corkscrew manoeuvre, then appeared to do a sort of spiral dive from which it righted itself approximately 3,000 feet below its original position. It was then seen to nosedive again and was lost in cloud in the vicinity of the Elan valley. It was next spotted by Mr T.C. Price of the Royal Observer Corps, who reported that the aircraft came out of the clouds in a vertical dive with what appeared to be bits of the aircraft falling off before it crashed into Nant yr Haidd mountain. Three of the crew members had attempted to bail out of the aircraft but it was too low, and all eight crew members were killed.

The entire RCAF crew of Halifax LL541 which crashed in the Elan valley in December 1944.
(© Library & Archives Canada)

The crew had all been Canadian. They were the pilot P/O G.L. Lister, navigator F/O E.H. Brautigam, bomb aimer F/Sgt D. Levine, flight engineers Sgts McMurty and F. Willmek, gunner Sgt J.S. Overland, air gunner Sgt G.G. Goehring and wireless operator/air gunner Sgt J.H. Preece. They were all buried with full military honours in the Chester Blacon cemetery in Cheshire.

Although an RAF investigation team was sent to the crash site and interviewed several witnesses, the exact cause of the crash was never determined. They considered that there might have been a mixture of oxygen starvation to the pilot, causing him to black out and lose control, along with possible structural failure of the aircraft.

The last recorded aircraft to crash in Radnorshire during the Second World War was a glider, but not from Shobdon being a Hamilcar (serial number HH922), a much larger

A MkI Hamilcar glider. (© Phil Butler)

glider than the Hotspur. Sgt R. Tillings and Sgt M. Wright from No.1 Heavy Glider Conversion Unit were being towed by a Halifax bomber and by 11am on 11 January 1945 had reached the vicinity of Llanbister. It was starting to snow and visibility was very poor, a situation further hampered as the intercom between the tug aircraft and the glider was not working. Unable to see properly, Sgt Tillings cast the line off the glider. The Hamilcar attempted a landing at Castle Cwmarron farm, Llanbister road, but as it landed it hit a tree and the wing was broken off. Sgt Tillings was quite badly injured. The official report concluded that the Halifax pilot was to blame for towing the glider into an area of poor weather and that if Sgt Tillings had been wearing his Sutton harness (a type of safety belt) he would have been less seriously injured.

15   After the Second World War

This chapter tells of the careers of some airmen whom we have already met, many of whom remained in the RAF for some years after the end of the Second World war, and also tells the stories of three airmen whose whole service came after the end of that war.

We left Percy Bufton shortly after the end of the First World War, not long after his exploits in bringing tropical fish back to England in a tank he had had specially constructed to fit over his aircraft engine. On being demobbed he had returned to Llandrindod Wells and in 1920 started work for the urban district council as a road surveyor's clerk. The following year he married his sweetheart Eveline Lewis. For some time after their marriage Percy and Eveline lived in Caerhyn in Dyffryn Road with Percy's parents.

On the outbreak of the Second World War Percy offered his services to the RAF and served with the British Expeditionary Force during the phoney war, managing to get out of France two weeks after the evacuation of Dunkirk by hitching a lift on a coal steamer bound for Newport. He was then attached to the British Icelandic Force and became adjutant to 98 Squadron based at Kaladarnes. Also on the island was an RAF photographer who was instrumental in setting up the English version of the Icelandic radio broadcasting service. This was Sergeant Frank Muir, who would gain fame on radio and television in Britain in the post-war years.

Percy spent 13 months in Iceland before returning to England and becoming the camp commander of RAF Gosfield, a No.3 Group Bomber Command station, a post he held until the end of the war. Percy was mentioned in despatches, and although the gazette entry does not specify the reason, it may have been for a sustained period of service.

All the time he was working for the council and serving in the RAF Percy continued his natural history studies and artistic hobbies. He now made his home at Primrose Cottage in Llandegley, where he built a large aviary in the grounds that was soon populated by many exotic birds and colourful finches. There was also a story of Percy ordering some tree frogs by post. They made it to the local railway station but somehow escaped, and sightings of strange frogs peeping into local windows did the rounds for some time until the harsh Welsh winter brought an end to them. Percy became very well known as an authority on native flora and fauna, and was well respected in ornithological circles. He was also no mere amateur sketcher, and as well as holding down his job with the council, he became artist-in-chief at the national weekly magazine *Caged Birds*. As well as keeping a variety of pets at his home (at one time he had two monkeys), he would travel the country acting as an informed judge in many of the county shows. He retired from working for the council on 31 December 1956 and became president of the British Orpington Bantam Association, a breed on which he was something of an authority.

Percy died on 11 July 1961 aged 70, and his wife Eveline died on 9 July 1973 aged 74. They had one daughter, Beryl.

We last met with John Rowland as he was leaving the RAF in December 1944. He was to remain working in the field of flying. With the tide of war turning in the Allies' favour, people were beginning to make tentative plans for the peace. One company that was looking forward to expanding was BOAC, and they struck a deal with the RAF to offer jobs to any tour-expired pilots – that is pilots who were deemed to have done enough flying for their country – who would be employed by BOAC but be on a two year secondment to the RAF. Hopefully by the time that the two years were up (at the latest) the war would be over and peacetime Britain would be ready for a boom in air travel. John was one of those who took up the offer, but in the meantime he was posted to No.1 Lancaster Finishing School, where he would train Halifax crews to fly the Lancaster. Then, on 1 December 1944, the RAF no longer needed him and he headed for Bristol to the headquarters of BOAC, a little sad to be leaving the RAF, now with a DFC and bar as well as a DSO, but excited to be training on the new Dakotas. By January 1945 BOAC had begun weekly flights to Cairo and twice weekly flights to Lagos in Nigeria, as well as to places such as Lisbon and Gibraltar.

After a year with BOAC John began to wonder if this was really what he wanted to do with his life. His mother had always been in the hotel trade and had bought a small hotel in Mid Wales but now wanted someone to run it for her. So 30-year-old John Rowland, DSO, DFC and bar, arrived in Llandrindod Wells to run the Rock Park Hotel in conjunction with his wife. The hotel overlooked the airfield that was the site of the first flights in the town and also the home of the short-lived Llandrindod Wells airport. John displayed

The Rock Park Hotel in the mid to late 1930s. (© Radnorshire Museum)

a few posters from the early days of flight in the hotel bar, but the days of flying from the Ddole were well and truly over.

John ran the hotel for five years, and on leaving he decided that he liked Mid Wales so much that he bought Tan-y-Cefn farm in Rhayader. He also kept laying hens at Dolafallen mushroom farm, and locals well remember the smell as the chicken manure was driven through the streets of Rhayader twice a week between the two farms. John and Jean had two sons, Michael and Philip; they lived at Tan-y-Cefn for 34 years and then John retired to Chester after Jean died.

Paul Webb was last heard of flying missions in support of partisans in Yugoslavia. At the end of the war he was offered a permanent commission in the RAF and in October 1948 he took command of No.612 (County of Aberdeen) Squadron based at RAF Dyce. On a blind date he met Barbara Grace Roberts, who hailed originally from Knighton, and discovered that among the many things they had in common was a shared birthday. The two married in September 1949.

Paul was acting as assistant air advisor in Ottawa, Canada when the RAF undertook the ambitious 'Operation Beechers Brook' in 1952. The RAF had ordered the new Sabre Mk4 jets for use in the cold war; they were to patrol the skies along the 'iron curtain' and be on standby to intercept any hostile jets crossing into allied airspace. The Sabre jets were built and tested in Canada before heading out over the Atlantic. The aircraft were ferried from Cartierville in Canada to Goose Bay then to Labrador. They would then head to Greenland, then Iceland, before arriving in Scotland at RAF Kinloss. Paul had been promoted to wing commander on 1 January 1952, and that December he joined operation Beechers Brook. In the course of the next year the RAF transferred 400 Sabres to the UK.

Air Commodore Paul Webb, CBE, DFC.
(© R. Bright)

Paul spent some time at a radar defence unit in the south of England and then three years at the Air Ministry studying Soviet jets, before acting as air attaché in the embassy in Turkey for four years. This was a key role in NATO's most easterly point and earned him a CBE. On 1 July 1963 he headed back to England, was promoted to group captain and took command of RAF Watton in Norfolk, the home of Signals Command, who were employed in intelligence gathering. Paul also served as air advisor to the British High Commissioner in India and as the British representative on the NATO intelligence committee. In March 1973 he retired from the RAF with the rank of air commodore, and he and Barbara headed to Knighton. Paul had always had a love of the outdoors and spent his retirement shooting and fishing, remaining in Radnorshire. Paul passed away on 10 July 2007 and Barbara on 26 December the same year; the couple had no children.

Richard Powell was last heard of being airlifted home having been rescued from a forced march from his prisoner of war camp close to the end of the war in Europe. After a period of leave in the UK, Dick returned to service, after the war, becoming involved in the RAF's experiments with long distance flying. The English Electric Canberra was chosen for what was to become known as the Aries project, and between 1951 and 1957 this project set many aviation world records. In 1953 the Aries project Canberra performed two record-breaking flights, the first when Canberra WH699 Aries IV flew from London to Capetown on 17 December, the second two days later when Wing Commander Humphrey, aided by Sqd/Ldr D. Bower and Sqd/Ldr Dick Powell (navigator), brought the same aircraft back to London again in record time.

Shortly after the war and before he started work on the Aries project, Dick had resumed his pre-war hobby of playing golf and with some friends would stay at Llandrindod Wells which had a world-class golf course. It was here that he met the lady who would become his wife. Dick and Dorothy M.P. Evans (known to her friends as Maisie) married in 1950. Between September 1954 and April 1956 Dick became the commanding officer of 99 Squadron, based at RAF Lyneham in Wiltshire. In 1957 he was awarded the Air Force Cross (AFC) for his work on the Aries project, then he took a post at the RAF flying college. In 1958 he became officer commanding RAF Idris in Libya. October 1961 saw the now Wing Commander Dick Powell become a staff officer at the Directorate of Quartering (Supplies and Stores) where he remained until 1967, when at the age of 47 he decided to retire from the RAF. Dick and Maisie returned to Llandrindod Wells and renewed their membership of the local golf club.

Sydney Bufton of Pathfinder fame had expressed the wish to remain in the RAF after the war; his wish was granted, and he was posted to Egypt on 7 July 1945 as Air Officer Commanding. At the end of February 1946 Sydney returned to England to complete a course at the Imperial Defence College. He along with a group of selected senior officers studied strategy, international relations and major issues of defence policy.

On the last day of 1946 Sydney was posted to the Central Bomber Establishment at Marham in Norfolk to command its tactics wing. The primary aim of the establishment was to increase the efficiency of bomber crews, aircraft and equipment in all offensive and defensive roles. The role could have been devised especially for Sydney and he embraced his work wholeheartedly.

In 1947 he received another honour as the Queen of the Netherlands made him a Commander (with swords) of the Order of Orange-Nassau.

In December 1948 he was promoted to air commodore on his appointment as assistant chief of staff (RAF) at Headquarters of Air Forces Western Europe in Paris. January 1951 saw him appointed vice-chief of air staff and director of weapons. He was to oversee the planning and development of atomic weapons that were just beginning to be introduced into the RAF.

From August 1952 Sydney was air officer in charge of administration (AOA) at Bomber Command. In January 1953 he was promoted to air vice marshall and on 12 October was posted to Aden as air officer commanding (AOC). The RAF had commanded Aden since 1928 when the British government had discovered that it was easier and cheaper to patrol the area by air. The RAF had provided the bulk of the services in all that time. Sydney's jurisdiction included Kenya, Iran, Iraq and Kuwait.

In October 1955 Sydney was recalled to the UK as senior air staff officer (SASO) at Bomber Command. During this time he had responsibility for the operational side of its two groups, including the new V force. The first V bombers (Vickers Valiants) had just come into service and Britain started testing nuclear weapons at Christmas Island. The next V bomber, the Avro Vulcan, joined 83 Squadron in July 1957. Sydney had already flown in the Vulcan when on 26 March 1956 he and Sir Harry Broadhurst, the air chief marshal and commander in chief of Bomber Command, had been invited on a demonstration flight. Pilot Jimmy Harrison was determined to put the aircraft through her paces now that he had top brass on board and Jimmy asked Sir Harry (a former fighter pilot) if he would like to see a roll. Sir Harry chickened out, citing 'chaps in the back', insinuating that the passengers wouldn't like it. Sydney called out that 'they wouldn't mind', but Sir Harry was not to be persuaded.

On 1 August 1958 Sydney took up the post of assistant chief of the air staff (ACAS) (Intelligence), a post he held for the next three years. On 13 October 1961 he retired from the RAF after 33 years' service.

Sydney soon returned to his old hobby of building radio sets, but this was no schoolboy venture and he quickly came up with a revolutionary new radio construction system. Christened 'Radionic' by its inventor, the new radio was halfway between a fun hobby and a serious educational device. Basically Sydney came up with a radio kit. All the components for making the radio were contained in a smart cardboard box and an instruction leaflet would allow the user to build a fully functioning radio set completely from scratch. Sydney's concise instructions and his use of the barest of components made 'Radionic' simple enough for a child but also allowed for the more serious engineer to develop their skills further. Taking over a factory in Crawley, Sydney oversaw all aspects of the production and was always on hand to answer any queries from customers personally. Radionic won a design centre award and was approved for use in schools and universities. Over 3,000 educational establishments were to have Radionic sets. After eight years of hard and constant work Radionic came to the attention of the Philips Electronics Company. Philips wanted Sydney to sell them the rights to Radionic; eventually Sydney agreed and Radionic became the Philips X30 radio kit. Sydney always slightly regretted the move, as he felt Radionic lost something in the hands of such a big company.

In 1967 Sydney was made the High Sheriff of Radnorshire. Sydney Osborne Bufton died in 1993 at the age of 85.

In March 1944, Sydney's brother Hal, now with the rank of group captain, was given the command of RAF Bourn in Cambridgeshire. August 1945 saw him on the move again, this time to the staff college at Haifa on Malta, for a six month training course. He was next transferred to Air Plan Headquarters in the Middle East for a year. On returning to the UK in April 1947, he required a period of sick leave and it was seven months before he was back on duty, this time at the Air Ministry. He was then posted to RAF Benson for three years, being attached to the flying wing on this reconnaissance station, and settled for a time in Oxfordshire. This was followed by another six month period of officer training at the Joint

Service Staff College in Latimer, Buckinghamshire, before being posted to Washington in the USA. He returned to England in November 1954 and spent two years as deputy director of operations at the Air Ministry. His last overseas posting was a one year stint as senior RAF officer in Bahrain, before returning to England on 28 March 1957. His career ended on a high note when at the beginning of 1960 he became the air aide-de-camp to Queen Elizabeth II.

He eventually retired from the RAF in March 1962, having served for 26 years. He retired with his family to Vancouver in Canada where he died in September 1972 aged just 56.

And then there were the new boys who saw all their service after the end of the Second World War. Raymond Thomas was born to John and Constance Thomas of 4 Railway Terrace, Penybont on 30 April 1928. When Raymond chose to join the Royal Navy is uncertain, but it was possibly as a boy cadet, for just two months after his 18th birthday, on 6 June 1946, he was based at HMS Seruwa, the Royal Naval Air Station that the navy had recently taken over from the RAF at Ratmalana about ten miles from Colombo on the south-west coast of Ceylon (now Sri Lanka). The base was then used as a training and transit camp where Raymond reached the rank of air mechanic second class and was waiting to hear where he was to be posted, when he accidentally drowned in the Lunawa Lagoon. He was buried in the Liveramentu Cemetery in Colombo, the same cemetery in which Peter Ablitt is buried (see page 190).

Wyndham Phillip (Winky) Jones was born in Howey on 29 July 1932 to David Charles and Lillian Jones (née Davies). He attended the council primary school in Oxford Road, Llandrindod Wells, where he gained his lifelong nickname of Winky. Being aged 6 when the Second World War broke out, he spent the entire war in Llandrindod Wells, relatively sheltered from the horrors but seeing the exciting side of service life. There were plenty of soldiers billeted in the town and he would join with the other local boys in watching army exercises in the surrounding countryside, and trying to get sweets and 'gum' out of the Americans who would sometimes come to the town. Wyndham remembers being

Field gun team of the Fleet Air Arm in 1955.
'Winky' Jones is second from the left in the second row from the front. (© Author's collection)

'Winky' Jones as a leading air mechanic (top) and as a naval airman in Malta (bottom). (© Author's collection)

hoisted onto the shoulders of a soldier and being carried around the town on VE Day, the day it was declared that the war in Europe was over.

In 1941 his eldest sister died at the age of 13 and then his mother died just a few months later. He left school at the age of 14 and went to work as junior weighbridge boy at the railway goods yard in the town. Aged 16 and feeling restless, he applied for boy's time in the navy (the period that covered his training up to the age of 18) and was accepted on the understanding that he would join the regular navy on his 18th birthday. By the time of his 17th birthday he was at the naval shore establishment of Royal Arthur in Corsham, Wiltshire, enrolled as boy artificer and apprentice under training to be a naval airman mechanic. Soon he embarked on armament training and thus he was on course to become an armourer with the Fleet Air Arm once his training was completed. From day one Wyndham's conduct and work were marked as good, and he earned a good conduct stripe that was worn on the sleeve of his uniform.

Wyndham's first stop overseas was to HMS Falcon at Hal Far on Malta. HMS Falcon was a 'stone frigate' – a naval base set out and run along the same lines as a ship but on dry land. Young, fit and ready for anything, Wyndham became some-what seduced by the suave uniform and flashy ways of the Americans and for a time considered joining the American Marines; he was quite put out when he discovered that he would have to first become an American citizen. For the first three months of his stay on Malta he was designated an airfield guard. By October 1952 he was involved in live fire exercises, spending over a year as part of the line assessing and range party that spent most of their working day out on the firing range on the island. In January 1954 he was stationed at the armoury on Hal Far; here he would be responsible for the ammunition used by the aircraft. This was during the Korean War, and Malta was a stopping off point for prisoners of war, ships and troops heading to or home from the conflict.

On November 1954 he returned to the UK and was stationed on HMS Goldcrest at Royal Naval Cawdor Barracks near Milford Haven. That was also the year he was picked to become one of the Fleet Air Arm gun crew for the Royal Tournament at Earls Court. Disappointed to be only a reserve for the 1954 team, he formed part of the competing team the following year. In 1956 the Suez Crisis flared up and Wyndham joined the crew of *HMS Eagle*. The aircraft carrier joined *HMS Bulwark* and *HMS Albio*n and the French

HMS Eagle. *(© Author's collection)*

aircraft carriers *Arromanches* and *La Fayette* in Operation Musketeer. All five carriers sailed to the eastern Mediterranean to engage military targets in Egypt. From dawn on 1 November until dusk on 6 November the flotilla of carriers bombarded the Egyptian coast; they completely wiped out the Egyptian Air Force while it was still on the ground and rendered the airfields unserviceable. During the six days the carrier force launched 1,619 sorties, over 600 of which were from *HMS Eagle*. The ship arrived back in the UK just after Christmas and in February 1957 Wyndham was stationed at HMS Daedalus, an accommodation block where men were stationed prior to discharge after their initial term of engagement had ended. Wyndham considered staying on in the navy, but his widowed father was now in failing health and Wyndham took the decision to return home to care for him. Wyndham's commanding officer wrote on his discharge papers that he was 'a hard working rating who has required little supervision and has shown plenty of common sense and initiative. He has always been smartly turned out ...'. He was also known for his sporting prowess, winning several competitions, and there is still a tennis cup bearing his name.

On returning to civvy street he married, had a son and a daughter, and set up a window cleaning business which is still run by his family. He was also a talented entertainer, singing both on his own and with his group the Tritones, and winning amateur competitions as a stand up comedian.

Mike Hines was born in Wolverhampton on 14 March 1933 and was just six months old when his father joined the Radnorshire Constabulary and moved the family to Wales. Initially they lived in Llanbister, where Mike started school, but they soon moved to Llandrindod Wells, where Mike continued his education at the County School.

Like 'Winky' Jones, Mike was just 6 years old when the Second World War broke out. Although the town was quite sheltered from many effects of the war, young Mike experienced the pill boxes and the barricades, the excitement as the town filled up with uniformed young men, watching the manoeuvres and even seeing the odd aeroplane flying overhead. His real taste of war came during the summer holidays when he would go and visit his grandmother in Wolverhampton, where they would spend the nights in an Anderson shelter listening to the thumps and bangs as the bombs fell. In the morning Mike would join the local boys as they hunted for shrapnel in the craters. He would also get to talk to his RAF ground gunner uncle who would regale him with exciting tales, one of which included his shooting the tail off a German Dornier. His uncle was invalided out of the RAF early in the war but would spend time making models for his nephew.

All this left Mike hankering to join the Royal Air Force and he got a lucky break at the age of 16. Most grammar school boys were expected to go on to higher education, but Mike failed part of the necessary exams. The headmaster called him into the office to ask what he thought he was going to do now. Mike immediately piped up that he would like to do an apprenticeship in the Royal Air Force. The headmaster was so pleased with this answer that he rushed to get the enrolment forms. Two weeks later Mike was called back to the headmaster's office to find out that he was about to be enrolled in the Royal Navy. Mike politely declined and waited a few more weeks for the correct forms to arrive. Mike soon found himself at RAF Hornchurch for selection. Two weeks later, on 22 September 1949, Mike was heading to No.1 School of Technical Training at RAF Halton, which was still run on much the same lines as it had been when Jack Hanne had attended in 1930. The boys were given 'school' lessons as well as instruction in their trade and, as in Jack's time, they were encouraged in hobbies and sport. There was even a little flying, first in an Anson and then in a Tiger Moth, which was Mike's favourite. Mike did exceptionally well at Halton and at the end of the course was chosen to receive the Colours from the Queen on behalf of the training school.

Mike was still keen on taking up a technical trade in the RAF, but after he had passed out of Halton he was awarded a cadetship to Cranwell and whilst there was offered the chance of a 12-hour flying aptitude trial at RAF Digby. Mike jumped at the chance and went solo within the prescribed 12 hours and couldn't wait to get back to Cranwell to continue his training. After 2½ years training on Chipmunks and Bristol Balliols, Mike was ready to graduate. He passed with flying colours and took the Sword of Honour for best all round cadet.

His first posting after Cranwell was to RAF Worksop, where he learnt to fly the Meteor jet, and from where he headed to RAF Bassingbourne for a course of instruction on the Canberra. On 23 April 1956 he was posted to 12 Squadron, and in October and November saw action when he made three bombing sorties over Egypt during the Suez crisis. He married in 1957, then the following July was posted to RAF Waddington, where he completed a Vulcan bomber co-pilot's course. In January 1960 he followed this up with a pilot/captain's course. In 1962 Mike (who had by this time reached the rank of squadron leader), his wife and their two children headed for Australia, where he joined a group of RAF pilots flying the V force bombers (Victor, Valiant and Vulcan). Mike described this as his happiest flying time. He returned to the UK by sea in 1964 and for the next few years was mostly occupied with RAF administration, though he did do a refresher course on the Jet Provost. In 1971 he was posted to RAF Scampton, where he became commander of 617 (Dambusters) Squadron. Thinking he was settled for a while, Mike and his wife bought a house in Scampton. However in 1973 he was off again, this time to Germany, where he worked in a multinational tactical air force HQ alongside German, Dutch and Belgian officers. Three years later he was in the defence sales department in London being (as he put it) told what to do by a bunch of civil servants. By 1984, although now a wing commander, Mike had had enough of the air force and applied for voluntary retirement. He finally left in October of that year, having spent 35 years in the RAF. On retirement he and his wife set up an antiques restoration business in the village of Scampton.

Of Welsh parentage, Elwyn David Bell was born on 11 December 1941 in Cape Town, where his mother was evacuated during the war from Cyprus, where his father was working. He and his sisters Janetta and Rosemary grew up in Malawi and Southern Rhodesia (now Zimbabwe). Elwyn took his private pilot's licence while in Rhodesia and took Rosemary up for a flight. He gained a BA at the University of Rhodesia and Nyasaland (as Malawi then was), married and then came to Britain where he joined the RAF. Elwyn became a pilot officer on 6 October 1962 and although he could already fly he had to start his training from scratch just like any other recruit. He graduated in April 1965 as a qualified RAF pilot and on 6 October became a flight lieutenant. In late 1965 and early 1966 he attended a basic helicopter flying course at RAF Ternhill.

RAF Linton on Ouse. The presentation of a cup to Flying Officer Elwyn Bell whilst he was stationed at RAF Linton on Ouse circa 1970.
(© R. Williams)

Shortly afterwards, Elwyn joined 110 Squadron. This was the same squadron that Jack Hanne from Llandrindod Wells was flying with when he became the first airman from Radnorshire to be killed in the Second World War. The squadron now flew Westland Whirlwind helicopters. December 1962 had seen the Brunei revolt and British forces had been deployed in considerable numbers to help quash Indonesian-sponsored aggression in Borneo and Malaya. Five helicopter squadrons were eventually sent to bases in the Far East and Elwyn and 110 Squadron were based in Singapore, spending a month at a time in Borneo. Shortly after Elwyn arrived the troubles started to subside, and it was decided to send some of the squadrons home, but No.110 were tasked with helping the Malaysian government, who had now retaken responsibility for internal security, and they were moved from Singapore to Labuan. They were also involved in transporting troops to and from remote jungle locations.

The base was basic and the jungle environment harsh, and Elwyn and his friend Colin Cummings set about thinking of ways to make things just a little more comfortable. Somebody had mentioned that a fridge that belonged to the squadron had been left behind when No.110 had moved from Bario c.1966. As luck would have it, a mission was planned for the very next weekend that would involve Elwyn and his co-pilot flying to a jungle landing zone to pick up a patrol of Gurkhas and take them to Bario. The first part was simple enough, but on arrival at Bario the camp was a little chaotic – part of the camp had already been dismantled and moved on to the next post and it soon became obvious that the fridge had been one of the first items taken. After a bit of detective work it was discovered that the fridge was probably sitting on the airfield at Brunei, which was a sort of halfway house where equipment was stored before being re-allocated to the next camp. A quick calculation revealed that Brunei could technically be considered on the way home and that the helicopter had enough fuel for the journey. On arrival at Brunei Elwyn's co-pilot John Hockin jumped out and made enquiries as to the whereabouts of the 'store'. On being told it was way over the other side of the airfield, John hopped back in and Elwyn flew the helicopter across the base. As they touched down beside a gated compound they could see the fridge sitting on the concrete. There was a large contingent of Gurkha guards so Elwyn, John and Colin all gesticulated and shouted in bad Gurkhali trying to get them to understand that they had to remove the fridge. To their amazement the gates suddenly opened and a group of Gurkha soldiers carried the fridge out through the gates and loaded it into the back of their helicopter. They hopped back in themselves, flew across Brunei bay and marched the fridge triumphantly into their base. They waited for some angry missive to reach them from a disgruntled quartermaster, but didn't hear a thing about it.

Shortly after that Elwyn returned to Singapore and Colin Cummings was sent to Hong Kong. When Elwyn returned to England he attended the central flying school, where he became a qualified RAF flying instructor, flying the Jet Provost aircraft. On 2 March 1971 he was flying a Jet Provost over Yorkshire with his pupil, Pilot Officer Bruce Blackett. As they neared Turnham Hall at Selby in North Yorkshire the plane collided with a Royal Navy Sea Prince aircraft from Church Fenton piloted by Cdr David Dunbar-Dempsey. All three men were killed.

The accident report listed a catalogue of errors. The aircraft were on a collision course; Elwyn was flying the Provost into the sun and David was in the left hand seat of the Sea Prince which had restricted visibility. All three men failed to see each other in time to take any evasive action or use their ejector seats. It was concluded that there were mitigating circumstances on both sides.

Shortly before his death Elwyn's parents had returned to Wales, where they had settled in Llanbister at the Old Vicarage, and Elwyn was laid to rest in the churchyard of St Cynllo's church close to their home. He left a wife and three young children. He is commemorated on the armed forces memorial at the National Arboretum.

16   Further Crash-landings in Radnorshire

On 21 December 1945, over six months after the end of hostilities in Europe, a Miles Martinet took off from Aberporth on the west coast of Wales, bound for Castle Bromwich in the West Midlands. On board were 27-year-old Flying Officer Morris Davies and 40-year-old Flight Lieutenant George Horace Hammond. When the Martinet was long overdue and there had been no radio message or other indication that it had landed elsewhere, the decision was made to send out a search party, and four Spitfires from Aberporth were sent out to look for the missing aircraft.

The weather had been reasonable when Davies had set off, but by the time the search was launched the weather had closed in and the four Spitfires returned to base with nothing to report. The next day three more Spitfires went to look for the aircraft but again nothing was found. The weather hampered searches over the next few days, although there was some hope when one search aircraft spotted some wreckage on Plynlimon, but this turned out to be the wreckage of a Lockheed Lightning that had crashed some time before. All through Christmas and the New Year there was no sign of the aircraft. The last recorded official search for the missing airmen was carried out by 595 Squadron on 2 January 1946. For most of the time that the RAF had been searching, the mountain tops had been covered in cloud, and now there was a blanket of snow on the ground which further hampered the search.

A Miles Martinet. (© T. Bishop)

Cwm Bach gully, the final resting place of the Martinet (left) and the crumpled remains of the aircraft's Bristol Mercury 30 engine (right). (© Author's collection)

On 2 February 1946, a month after the last official search, Richard Watkins of Dolau farm, near the village of Dolau, found the wrecked aircraft on the western side of Great Rhos very close to the head of Cwm Bwch. The crash was just over three miles south of the direct route from Aberporth to Castle Bromwich. The aircraft had been badly damaged by fire and the bodies of both airmen were still inside.

An inquest was held at Llandrindod Wells where the bodies were formally identified. F/O Davies had kept his RAF identity card in a cigarette case he always carried and although it was badly charred his number was still visible. No explanation for the crash was put forward; the coroner did however note that there had been very few days that winter when the tops of the mountains had not been obscured by clouds.

With the ending of the Second World War and a huge reduction in the size of the RAF and of the USAAF based in Britain, coupled with the associated reduction in training flights, it is not surprising that crash landings became less frequent, and it was not until the summer of 1963 that another military aircraft came down in the county. On 2 August that year, civilian ferry pilot Mr H. Proudlove was making a delivery flight in a Fairey Gannet. The journey was to take him from the Shorts aircraft factory in Belfast to the Royal Naval Air Service station at Culdrose near Helston, on the Lizard in Cornwall. It was now common practice for civilian pilots to deliver military aircraft as there was no longer a Ferry Command branch of the RAF.

The Fairey Gannet T.5 serial number XG887 left Belfast at 9.35am and within five minutes radio contact was lost, something which at this point worried nobody at either the factory or the base. Mr Proudlove may have had no reason to use the radio and may have been unaware of the situation; he was not well versed in flying the Gannet on instruments and had been told to fly by Visual Flying Rules (VFR). This literally meant that he was relying on good visibility at all times. His route was to take him first to the air base at Yeovilton, as this was his alternative landing ground if Culdrose was fog-bound when

A Fairey Gannet

he arrived. The Gannet turned landwards over the north Wales coast and headed down towards Mid Wales. At approximately 10.40am the Gannet was seen in the vicinity of Michaelchurch-on-Arrow, witnesses testifying that the aircraft was flying at about 500 feet and trailing black smoke; fuel had started leaking from an internal pipe and was dripping on to the hot exhaust. Mr Proudlove may well have been startled by the drop in the fuel gauge and without a radio to guide him he may have been looking for somewhere to land before he ran out of fuel. Several witnesses saw the Gannet veer off course and described both smoke and flames issuing from the plane. Close to the source of the fuel leak was a fire extinguisher, but this exploded as the heat and flames built up. The aircraft started to disintegrate almost immediately, the wreckage being spread over an area of three miles. Unsurprisingly Mr Proudlove was killed.

Mid Wales was to become an area for the jets of both the Fleet Air Arm and RAF to practise low flying and even for the occasional mock bombing exercise. Given the amount of low flying that has been practised in Radnorshire, aircraft crashes are mercifully rare, but they do still happen.

A Hawker Hunter. (© www.mapaircraftphotos.com)

On 3 March 1969 Sub Lieutenant Hugh Mansel-Smith of the Fleet Air Arm took off from his base at RAF Brawdy, Pembrokeshire, the home of 738 Squadron. He was flying a Hawker Hunter jet aircraft, serial number XE680, while taking part in a simulated raid on a target near the town of Rhayader. As he reached the target area he found it was entirely covered in mist and low cloud, overshot the target and was seen flying low over the town. Locals commented that he almost hit the top of the church tower. As he tried again to reach his target, the clouds parted slightly and he realised that he was heading straight for a mountainside. Seeing that he would be unable to pull the aircraft to a safe height he took the decision to eject, but the aircraft was far too low and he did not have time to separate from his ejector seat or deploy his parachute. He was killed the instant his seat hit the ground. The Hawker Hunter crashed into the montainside above the A44.

The next aircraft to get into difficulties over Radnorshire was a Hawker Siddeley Buccaneer. This two-seater jet, serial number XW525, was being flown by Flight Lieutenant Summers with Fl/Lt P.J.R. Hall as his navigator; both men were from 208 Squadron. They took off from their base in Honington in Suffolk on the morning of 4 April 1977, their mission to 'bomb' the Claerwen dam in the Elan valley. The weather was clear and they reached their target without a hitch. With the help of his navigator, Fl/Lt Summers lined up perfectly on the dam for his 'bombing' run, but then things took a dangerous turn, for Summers and Hall were not the only aircraft to be flying over the dams that day. Seemingly out of nowhere two Hawker Hunter jets appeared flying straight towards them. Fl/Lt Summers took immediate evasive action, but he yanked the aircraft so violently in a bid to avoid a collision that the airframe was unable to withstand the pressure and the aircraft's tail fell off. Luckily, both Summers and Hall were able to eject safely, and they and the remains of the Buccaneer landed in the reservoir behind the Claerwen dam. The Buccaneer was subsequently found to suffer from metal fatigue in the tail area, and after a routine inspection of all the aircraft many of the RAF's Buccaneers were grounded.

Nearly forty years after the end of the Second World War, three nations that had once fought each other in the skies above Europe were about to unite in the skies above Radnorshire. After two years of negotiations the Tri Tornado Training Establishment was formed. The TTTE, as it would become known, was based at RAF Cottesmore, not far from Peterborough in East Anglia. On 1 July 1980 the establishment's Tornados started to

A Hawker Siddeley Buccaneer. (© www.mapaircraftphotos.com)

A Panavia Tornado. (© www.mapaircraftphotos.com)

arrive, and Cottesmore would soon play host to Tornados of the RAF, the Luftwaffe and the Italian Air Force. All three would train and fly together. Germany provided 23 Tornados, the UK 19 and Italy 6. All aircraft kept their original country's livery with an added TTTE logo on the tail. The training aimed to mix crews and aircraft, which meant that RAF and Luftwaffe airmen, for example, could well be flying an Italian Tornado. No weapons were handled at Cottesmore, as it was purely a flying training establishment. All maintenance was done by RAF ground crew. The base commander with the honorary title of chief instructor was rotated between the three countries.

A TTTE Tornado flown by West German Pilot O/Lt Peter Kasner with RAF Squadron Leader John Towl as navigator took off from Cottesmore on 16 June 1986. They were involved in a very low-flying exercise known as a ground-following sortie, the area chosen for the exercise being the Elan valley. O/Lt Kasner would have been detailed to fly as low as he felt able, following every bump and bend of the hills and valleys. As the aircraft flew over the Claerwen valley Kasner and Towl must have realised they were far too low. Kasner took evasive action, tipping the Tornado over onto one wing, to try and avoid hitting the approaching mountain. Sqd Leader John Towl, realising they were not going to make it, ejected. The angle of the aircraft and the close proximity to the ground meant that his ejector seat flung him straight into the side of the hill and he was killed. O/Lt Kasner and the Tornado crashed into the hillside; he too was killed.

The three nations later decided to follow their own training patterns and the TTTE was disbanded on 24 February 1999.

Just over a year after the Tornado accident, on 24 June 1987, Fl/Lt Ian Hill of No.226 Operational Conversion Unit took off from his base at RAF Chivenor in Devon. In company with two other Jaguar aircraft, he was taking part in an ultra low level flying exercise. Hill was a very experienced pilot and one of the RAF's foremost instructors on the Jaguar; he also used to fly the Jaguar at RAF flying displays. Exactly what happened to his aircraft is not yet a matter of public record, but just before 11am he flew very low over the village of Aberedw, at least two eye witnesses subsequently recounting how the aircraft appeared to have debris dropping from it. It appeared that the pilot was attempting to

A Sepecat Jaguar. (© www.mapaircraftphotos.com)

steer the aircraft away from the village, which he managed as the plane crashed just outside Aberedw in a field on Pantau farm. The owner, Mr John Davies, was in the field spraying nettles as the aircraft crashed next to him, and he ran for his life as the resultant fireball sent bits of Jaguar flying over his head.

Fl/Lt Hill was killed. His wife, with the help of the Davies family, erected a cairn on the spot, while the villagers of Aberedw arranged a collection and had a plaque fixed to the wall in the local churchyard, remembering Fl/Lt Ian Hill and his heroic struggle to keep their village safe.

Flight Lieutenant Ian Hill is the last military pilot to have been killed in Radnorshire.

Epilogue

The story told here began and ended with planes crash-landing in Radnorshire, the recent crashes having rather more dire consequences than those early haphazard landings. The ponderous stick and string propeller driven machines had been swept aside and sleek all metal jet fighters now sped across the skies of Radnorshire. Vivian Hewitt had appeared alongside the river smoking a cigarette just minutes after his plane went down, the new age jets were not so forgiving. But it was not just the aircraft that had changed so dramatically.

Flight, once the privilege of the rich, was soon to become within easy reach of almost everybody. Before and during the First World War pilots were an elite band of rich or possibly mad young men who took to the skies with a devil-may-care attitude. They were idolised and admired but always somehow different, and the majority of the population were more than content to keep their feet on the ground. By the 1930s, however, these restless men who had never really got used to civilian life after their time with the air force were using their skills not only to thrill the crowds as they took to the skies with what became known as 'flying circuses', but also – by offering joy rides – were giving the ordinary man or woman or even child in the street a chance to fly for just a few shillings. The likes of Robert Kronfeld and his Super Drone glider were promoting flight as a cheap way to travel about the country. Llandrindod Wells had an air taxi service and pleasure flights operating from its small airfield on the edge of the town.

It would be hard now to calculate exactly what effect the flying displays had on the generation of young men who were about to step up to the mark and offer their services to the RAF as the world was plunged into yet another war. Most of the flying circus pilots had seen action in France during the First World War and had lived to tell the tale and there is an echo of those early dare-devil pilots in the fighter pilots who served in the RAF during the Second World War. Also as bomber aircraft became far larger and more complicated they needed more than just a pilot and observer to operate them. Young men from Radnorshire who may have initially headed to the RAF with the hope of becoming pilots now found themselves flying as wireless operators, air gunners, flight engineers or navigators in crews that consisted of four if they were in a Hampden, or seven for a Lancaster or even ten men for a Sunderland flying boat, a plane that could spend so long airborne it was often necessary to take along extra crew members. The book has shown how men from a sleepy forgotten corner of Wales headed to the USA and Canada for training and then served in all theatres of the war. It has featured not only the men whose lives were tragically cut short by enemy action or accidents but also the men who never made it through training before tragedy struck. These men stand side by side with the decorated heroes, the men who served not just in the war but made the RAF their lives, and also beside the men who in their own words had a pretty easy war which they will always remember as the time of their lives. Chapters have also covered events at home, noting the bombs that the Luftwaffe dropped on Radnorshire, 'raids' that still cause controversy as people are divided into those who consider that the Elan valley dams which fed the industrial towns of the Midlands were the target and others who consider that the bombs were jettisoned by lost or damaged aircraft trying to get to safety.

As the war ended, Radnorshire lads still joined the RAF and the Fleet Air Arm, but the numbers were greatly reduced. No.579 Air Training Corps is still thriving in Llandrindod Wells and now has girls as well as boys attending its twice weekly meetings. Once the jet age was reached, Radnorshire acted as a low fly zone, and screaming jets sped through its valleys in terrain-hugging flying exercises. This brought tragedy to the county as some of those jets crashed. As the new century dawned and aircraft became ever faster and more sophisticated, Radnorshire has got just a little bit left behind. True, we still see the RAF practising in the skies above the county, and contrails from holiday flights criss-cross the skies daily, but in many ways Radnorshire is once more removed from aviation. There are no landing strips in the county, the nearest aero club, over the border in Herefordshire, offers pleasure flights to those who can afford it while those who can't look wistfully up and try and guess what plane is flying overhead. Occasionally hot air balloons still drift over but they are not from any headline grabbing air race, but usually a family marking a special birthday. Gliders ride the thermals from Shobdon, not now filled with men training for daring raids on the enemy, just enthusiasts enjoying their weekend hobby, flying quietly over the countryside maybe looking for a promising field to land in that isn't too bumpy and not too far away from help.

Gustav Hamel landed here in 1912, the proud owner of Royal Aero Club Certificate no.64. It is now estimated that seven out of ten adults in Britain have been up in an aeroplane. Many of them would never have had the chance if it hadn't been for the men who passed through or hailed from Radnorshire and who by skill daring or courage made the world and aviation what it is today.

Appendix   The later exploits of Sergeant Bakalarski

On 26 July 1942, Sgt P. Bakalarski as pilot and P/O H. Falinski, Sgt Z. Kobiela, Sgt J. Olszewski and P/O B. Boguszewski, the same crew that had bailed out over Radnorshire on 20 May 1942, took off to bomb Hamburg. On the return flight they were attacked three times by an Me110 night fighter All the crew were wounded except Bakalarski and all the aircraft instruments were rendered unserviceable. Coupled with severe fuel leakages, this made it impossible to get the aircraft back to England and Bakalarski set course for Sweden but had to make a forced landing on a beach somewhere north of the Elbe estuary. The aircraft came down very close to a German anti-aircraft post and within minutes German soldiers arrived bringing medical aid, but P/O Boguszewski died as he was being taken out of the aircraft.

Sgt Bakalarski was then separated from the rest of the crew, whom he did not see again, and was eventually taken to Frankfurt, where he was interrogated for 4½ days in solitary confinement before being sent to Stalag VIIIB (Lamsdorf), where he arrived on 7 August. On 7 September he attempted to escape with a navigator from the RCAF, but after three days and two nights they were recaptured near the Polish border close to Gogolin and sent back to Lamsdorf. During November the German guards carried out reprisals for the escape attempts, and for the next three months Bakalarski was kept tied up with string. In January 1943 the guards changed the string to chains and he remained shackled until March, when he and other POWs who had suffered the same punishment were unchained and transferred to another compound.

Here Bakalarski changed identities with another POW, a Palestinian private named Moritz Leder, and under his changed name he was able to volunteer to go out on a working party, being sent to Tarnowitz, but he was strictly guarded all the time and was unable to attempt an escape. He then asked to be allowed to work in a coal mine and was sent to the Dachsgrubein (Jaworzno), where he worked with another Polish airman, Sgt Withold Raginis. It was here that he made contact with Polish civilians who were working in the mine and were part of an organization which could help him escape. On 9 June 1943 he cut the wire at the camp where he was confined at night and at 1am on 10 June, when the night shift was returning from work and there was a great deal of movement in camp, he got out through the gap in the wire. It seems that the Germans had some news of the attempt, for the Gestapo were waiting where he was to rendezvous with a member of the organization near some railway sidings. As Bakalarski and the Pole met, the German soldiers opened fire with machine guns and the Pole was killed. Bakalarski threw himself on the ground and lay still until a goods train came along on an adjacent siding, and under cover of the noise of the train he managed to get to the railway. After falling three or four times in his attempt to board the train, he got into the last wagon and travelled about 30km to Szczakowa. He then walked towards Olkusz.

He was, however, rounded up by a battalion of the SS who were searching for Polish patriots. As he was in civilian clothes he was taken for a civilian, a pretence which he kept up in the hope of being sent to Germany, where he thought escape would be easier. However his true identity (as a Palestinian private) was discovered and he was sent back to Jaworzno, where he was sentenced to two months in jail.

While he was serving his sentence he was able to renew his contact with the Polish organization. On completion of his sentence, he went to work in the Leopoldsrube, another coalmine in Jaworzno. Here he worked on the night shift – the shifts were changed every fortnight – and on 10 July, his last day on night shift, he escaped from the mine. With the help of the Polish organization he was moved to several locations until on 18 August he met up with Sgt Withold Raginis who had been at liberty since escaping on 10 August. By 15 September they had reached Luneville (Meurthe-et-Moselle) in France. Here they approached a local gendarme for help (not always a wise move for not all gendarmes would help an escaped prisoner), and his first act was to put them in the cells of the local police station. Raginis's parents lived in the French town of Montlucon and he begged the gendarme to contact them. Two days later a telegram came back confirming Raginis's identity and the gendarme decided that he would help the pair on their way. They were taken 'under arrest' (so no questions would be asked if they were stopped by any Germans) to Nancy, where an organization was based that helped allied airmen escape from the Continent.

They were moved around from private houses to hotels and even factories and kept hidden while their identity was checked and new clothes and false papers could be obtained for them. It took until 20 October for the two airmen to be fitted out with new clothes, shoes, identity cards and work permits. Both Bakalarski and Raginis were good German speakers and this greatly helped the fiction that they were part of a work party. The organization was hoping to get them to Andorra and from there back to the UK. On 24 October Raginis and Bakalarski were joined by Geoff Williamson, a British airman who was also hoping to escape and could also speak fluent German as he had lived in the country before the war, and Sgt S.J.V. Philo.

The four were guided from the village of Urs and spent the night in a cave. At 6am on the morning of 26 October another guide met them who was to take them over the mountains via a mule path and into Andorra. The guide set off at a brisk pace, it was starting to rain heavily and it was bitterly cold. The four ex-POWs had endured over a year of bad food in German prison camps and were all in appalling physical condition. The guide had hoped they would be in Andorra by about 2pm that afternoon, but at midday they stopped for a rest. The rain had turned to snow, and Williamson was suffering severe pain in his legs and was falling behind the others. As Williamson slowed the party up, the guide lost his temper and suggested that he be left behind, but the others wouldn't hear of this and started to drag Williamson along between them. By 4pm in the blizzard and failing light the guide suggested that he and Raginis should go ahead and he would point out the way for the others to follow. Bakalarski was also now beginning to suffer pains in his legs. Raginis got lost in the darkness and unbeknownst had headed back into France when he saw a small hut in the grey light of dawn and was thinking of knocking on the door when he saw two German soldiers come out. Raginis turned around and walked for about two hours in the other direction before he came across a small group of Spanish and French road menders who took him to their hut where he recovered over the next few days. Raginis was eventually to make it back to England on 29/30 November. In the meantime Bakalarski, Williamson and Philo waited in the dark, but Williamson was getting weaker and died at 6pm that first night. Philo and Bakalarski waited for the dawn and then headed down the mountain. Philo was suffering from frostbite in his feet and hands, for in a semi-delirious state he had taken off his shoes and was walking in his socks. Bakalarski had dry socks in his pack and massaged some life back into Philo's feet, and the next day they set off again. On 27 October, two days and a night after they had set off, they reached a cottage that they were sure was on the Andorra side of the mountain, and here they were taken in and given warm milk and some food and allowed to sleep in the hay loft.

They were handed on to Spanish border guards who made a play of putting them on a bus, then in the middle of Barcelona the guard got off the bus and they were told by the bus driver to go to a certain hotel where a British representative was waiting for them. Bakalarski was given a room in the hotel and Philo was taken to hospital. Their next stop was Gibraltar and by 16 November they had both made it home. Both Bakalarski and Raginis were awarded the Distinguished Conduct Medal for their efforts to escape. Philo was mentioned in dispatches but he did not live to see the end of the war; he was flying with 196 Squadron on a Special Operations Executive drop when his plane was shot down. Bakalarski remained in England after the war, but was killed in a road accident on 18 November 1966.

Notes

Chapter 3

1. The full story of Gilbert's three attempts can be read in *Observer* by A.J. (Jack) Insall published by William Kimber in 1970.

Chapter 5

1. The role of the Observer Corps did not stop after the end of the Second World War. Although the corps was briefly stood down on 12 May 1945 it was back on duty before the end of the year. In 1947 it held the first of a series of small scale exercises in southern England. It was the beginning of the Cold War, and the ROC were now trained to handle a new threat. With the jet age, the RAF had far less to gain from the spotting role the ROC had been designed to do, but with the nuclear threat there was a greater need for the organisation to play a civil defence role. ROC posts around the country were expected to plot the progress of nuclear fall-out and to assist the army with evacuation in the event of a nuclear war. In order for them to be effective in this role many of the ROC posts were rebuilt underground. The 1990s saw even more advances in technology and by 1995 the decision was made to close down the remaining ROC stations. On 8 December 1995 the ROC standard was laid up in the Rotunda at Cranwell. There it remains on display with other stood down regimental standards for possible reactivation in times of need. The ROC headquarters at Bentley Priory was closed on 31 March 1996.

2. On 15 July 1944 a rally was held of Air Training Corps units from mid Wales. Nine flights took part, including 2142 Flight from Llanwrytd Wells that was made up of Czechoslovak cadets who were the sons of refugees. Other flights there that day, were 938 Welshpool, 1277 Llanidloes, 1540 Brecon, 1569 Builth Wells, 1907 Newtown and 1952 Hay-on-Wye, and 1822 Presteigne-Knighton. Initially cadets travelled from Presteigne to join 579, but by July 1941 Pilot Officer W.J. Owen had taken over the Presteigne flight and they no longer needed to travel to undertake training. In 1942 a separate flight was formed at Knighton under the command of Pilot Officer Edwards. By 1944 these two flights were united as the 1822 Presteigne-Knighton Flight under the command of W.J. Owen who had now reached the rank of flying officer. 579 still meets in Llandrindod Wells.

Chapter 6

1. Wolfgang Falck wrote his memoirs in the book *FalkenJahre Erinnerungen* published by Dr Kurt Braatz. He was interviewed for the 1997 documentary on BBC2 'The Nazis: A warning from history' and is featured in the last episode.

Chapter 8

1. Unfortunately we have not been able to trace anyone who knew the young Ronald Beaumont. We have however had the opportunity to talk to Sgt R.I. Hudson (known as Allen) who served as a mid-upper gunner with Beaumont during the Second World War. Allen and Beaumont had met while training and would become operational together as part of the same crew.

2. It wasn't just in Europe that the MRES worked; they followed the paths of downed airmen from the Arctic Circle to the jungles of Burma, often uncovering harrowing details and even war crimes. Not only did they have to locate the site of the grave; many of the airmen were exhumed and reburied, leading in some cases to advances in forensic science. The airmen were often reburied in official war cemeteries although families were given the options of having their loved one brought home. Wherever the remains were interred the families were also given choice of headstone from a series of specially produced ministry designs, and could add personal inscriptions. The graves were then reregistered and can be found on the Commonwealth War Graves site. The MRES carried out its work well into the 1950s and countless families were able to grieve knowing where their loved ones had been laid to rest.

Sources

Archives
From the National Archives the following have been used:
Air 27 – Operational Record Books for RAF squadrons
Air 29 – Operational Record Books for miscellaneous RAF units
Air 76 – British Royal Flying Corps/Royal Air Force officers service records 1912-20
Air 79 – British Royal Air Force Airmen 1918-39 and Royal Naval Air Service ratings who transferred to the RAF after April 1918.
ADM 188 – Admiralty Records for Royal Naval Ratings
ADM 171– British Military Gallantry Medals
W0339 British Army Service records 1914-1922 (for those men who transferred from army units)
Air Ministry form 280 Record of Service for J.H. Hanne
Air Ministry form 1406 Record of Service for Anthony & Beaumont
Air Ministry form 543 Record of Service for W.C. Evans
Air Ministry form 543A Record of Service for Cyril Williams
Air Ministry form 1180: Accident Crash Cards
Air Ministry form 78, various aircraft movement cards
MI9/SPG   TNA form W0208-3307 Escape and evasion report for Harry Emlyn Bufton.
TNA form W0208-1570 (Poland) Escape and evasion report for P. Bakalarski

Books
Bowyer, Chas, *Sunderland at War*, Ian Allen (1976)
Chorley, W.R., *RAF Bomber Command losses 1939-45*, Midland Counties Publications (9 Vols, various dates
Clutton Brook, Oliver, *Footprints in the sands of time; RAF Bomber command POW in Germany 1939-1945*, Grub Street (2009)
Cobham, Alan, *My Flight to the Cape and Back*, A&C Black (1926)
Australia and back, A&C Black (1927)
Twenty thousand miles in a flying boat, Harrap (1931)
A time to Fly, Shepheard-Walwyn (1978)
Copemen, Geoff D., *Bomber squadrons at War*, Sutton Publishing (1997)

Cornwell, Peter D. *The Battle of France then and now,* after the battle (2007)

Docherty, Tom, *Dinghy Drop 279 Squadron RAF 1941-46*, Pen and Sword (2007)

Franks, Nick and Carol, *The Distinguished flying Cross and how it was won 1918-1995*, Savannah (2 vols) (1998)

Furse, Anthony, *Wilfrid Freeman, The genius behind allied survival and air supremacy 1939-45*, Spellmount Ltd (1999)

Goss, Chris, *It's Suicide bit it's fun; the story of 102 (Ceylon) Squadron*, Crecy Books (1995)

Hadaway, Stuart *Missing Believed Killed; casualty policy and the Missing Research and Recovery Unit*, Pen and Sword (2012)

Halley, James A., *The Squadrons of the Royal Air Force and the commonwealth 1918-1998*, An Air Britain Publication (1988)

Henshaw, Trevor, *The Sky their battlefield air fighting and the complete list of allied Air casualties from enemy action in the first world war, British commonwealth and United states air service 1914-1918*, Grub Street (1995)

Hobson, Chris (ed), *Airmen who died in the Great War 1914-1918 roll of honour*, Spink and son (1995)

Hywel, William, *The Modest Millionaire*, Gwasg Gee (1973)

Insall, A.J., *Observer*, William Kimber (1970)

Kinsey, Gordon, *Seaplanes*, Terence Dalton Ltd (1978)

McCudden, James, VC, *Five years in the Royal Flying Corps*, Portway (nd)

McCarron, Donal, *Letters from an Early Bird*, Pen and Sword (2006)

Melinksy, Hugh, *Forming the Pathfinders the career of Air vice Marshall Sydney Bufton*, The History Press (2010)

Merrick, Kenneth A., *Flights into Forgotten Special Duties Operations in WW2*, Wiedenfeld Military (1989)

Middlebrook, Martin, and Chris Everitt, *The Bomber Command War Diaries*, Viking (1985)

Musgrove, Gordon, *Pathfinder Force a history of 8 group*, Macdonald and Janes (1976)

Rowland, John, *Return Flights in war and peace the flying memories of Squadron Leader John Rowland DSO DFC and Bar*, Pen and Sword (2010)

Sarker, Dilip, *Through Peril to the Stars; RAF Fighter Pilots Who Failed to return 1939-45*, Ramrod Publications (1993)

Scott, C.W.A., *Scott's Book*, Hodder and Stoughton (1934)

Sturtivant, Ray, John Hamlin and James Halley, *Royal Air Force flying training and support units*, An Air Britain Publication (1997)

Thomas, Mick, *RAF top gun; the story of Teddy Donaldson*, Pen and Sword (2008)

Wakefield, Kenneth, *The First Pathfinders*, William Kimber (1981)

Warner, Graham, *The Bristol Blenheim a complete history*, Crecy Publishing (2002)

Wynn, Kenneth G., *Men of the battle of Britain; a biographical dictionary of the few*, The Battle of Britain Memorial Trust (2015)

Index of Radnorshire Places

General Index
(including RAF Bases)

Index of Personal Names